Inside
The League

Inside
The League

THE SHOCKING EXPOSÉ OF HOW
TERRORISTS, NAZIS,
AND LATIN AMERICAN DEATH SQUADS
HAVE INFILTRATED THE WORLD
ANTI-COMMUNIST
LEAGUE

Scott Anderson
Jon Lee Anderson

Dodd, Mead & Company   New York

To our father
John William Anderson

Published by Dodd, Mead & Company, Inc.
79 Madison Avenue, New York, N.Y. 10016

Distributed in Canada by
McClelland and Stewart Limited, Toronto

Manufactured in the United States of America

Designed by Tom Mellers

First Edition

1 2 3 4 5 6 7 8 9 10

Library of Congress Cataloging-in-Publication Data

Anderson, Scott.
Inside the League.

Includes index.
1. World Anti-Communist League. 2. Anti-communist
movements. I. Anderson, Jon Lee. II. Title.
HX11.W653A53 1986   324'.1   85-27587
ISBN 0-396-08517-2

CONTENTS

IN CONSIDERING THE WORLD ANTI-COMMU-NIST LEAGUE YOU HAVE ENTERED A WORLD OF IDEOLOGICAL FANATICISM, RACIALISM, IGNO-RANCE AND FEAR WHICH IS ALMOST BEYOND THE COMPREHENSION OF THE AVERAGE AMER-ICAN. . . . YOUR SUBJECT MATTER IS A COLLEC-TION OF ORIENTAL FASCISTS, MILITARISTS, RIGHT WING TERRORISTS WHO PUT BOMBS IN CIVILIAN AIRCRAFT, DEATH SQUADS, ASSASSINS, CRIMINALS AND MANY PEOPLE WHO ARE AS MUCH OPPOSED TO DEMOCRACY AS THEY ARE COMMUNISM. YOU ARE IN SOME DANGER YOURSELF.

*—Letter to the authors
from a former League member*

This book is about specific people and organizations that have belonged to the World Anti-Communist League. It may be presumed that all members of the League share a strong anti-communist sentiment, but it doesn't necessarily follow that they share a common strategy in acting upon this sentiment. Not all League members are Nazis or death squad leaders; some are respectable, influential conservatives in their respective nations. They will no doubt be dismayed to find themselves discussed in conjunction with outright thugs, terrorists, and criminals. Nevertheless, it is a situation of their own choosing.

No League member can claim ignorance of the dark side of the World Anti-Communist League: in the past decade, investigators, newspapers, even League members themselves have publicly exposed some of its seamier aspects. Although it seems inconceivable to us that the bona fide conservatives involved in the League do not know about the unsavory background of some of their fellow members, without evidence to the contrary we must give them the benefit of the doubt and ascribe their association with the League to naïveté rather than to an orientation shared with their infamous associates. If nothing else, perhaps this book will cause mainstream conservatives to be more selective about who they choose to ally themselves with in the future.

In *Inside the League*, we discuss organizations on six continents with histories dating in some cases to the 1920s or before. In the interest of brevity and readability, we have avoided elaborating on some issues that are subjects of debate in some circles (such as exactly when an organization was founded, what other organization it grew out of, and so on) and that can only serve to further complicate an already complex subject. In the same vein, one organization is often known under a variety of names (the Iron Guard, the Legionary Movement, Miscarea Legionaria, Garde de Fer, the Legion of the Archangel Michael) or is spelled in a number of ways (Ustasha, Ustashi, Ustascha, Ustase). In these cases, we have chosen the name and spelling in most common usage while leaving the other spellings in place in cited sources. In addition to this, many Asian names can be transliterated in different ways. Wherever possible, we have written their names as they seem to prefer, with the result that their last names occasionally appear before their first names.

This book cannot presume to be a definitive work on the international alliances of the extreme right or on the history of unconventional warfare. We have examined the World Anti-Communist League and placed special focus on it because it is the one organization in which representatives of virtually every right-wing extremist movement that has practiced unconventional warfare are to be found. The League is the one constant in this netherworld; whether looking at Croatian terrorists, Norwegian neo-Nazis, Japanese war criminals, or American ultra-rightists, you will find them here.

If this book gives comfort or rhetorical ammunition to the far left, it is unintentional. This book is not an attack on any respectable conservative political movement. To the contrary, much of our most important information came from conservative individuals and organizations who were appalled by the inclusion of what they view as fascist elements under the mantle of anti-communism. It should be unnecessary to state that the average conservative has as much in common with a man like Roberto D'Aubuisson or an organization like the Mexican Tecos as the average liberal does with Carlos the Jackal or the Italian Red Brigade.

To expose the World Anti-Communist League is not to be "soft on communism." If anything, such an endeavor should assist the anti-communist cause, since the worst aspect of the League is that it maligns legitimate organizations and libels a legitimate political cause.

Few would argue that Romania, for instance, languishes under a rigid communist dictatorship or that Romanians deserve to be freed from this repression. With that said, many may question whether this cause is best represented by men who, earlier in life, skinned alive five-year-old children.

PREFACE

The knock on the door of room 604 of the Hotel Istmania came late at night, two days after one of the authors had conducted the "Lobo" interview. When the author answered it, he was confronted by three young men wearing windbreakers; the pistols concealed in their pockets were aimed at his stomach.

"Good evening," their leader said, flashing a badge and pushing past, "I'm from Interpol. I have orders to check the status of foreigners in Honduras."

The other two secret police guarded the door as the leader rummaged through the author's papers and clothes.

"So how is your wife?" he asked.

"Fine."

"She's not sick?"

"No."

The Honduran officer straightened up and grinned. "Are you sure?"

When he heard the knock, the author had placed the notebook containing the details of the "Lobo" interview underneath some newspapers; now the interrogator crossed to the desk, leafed through the newspapers, and found the notebook. Inexplicably, he didn't open it.

"Are you planning to leave Honduras tomorrow?" he asked casually.

The agent walked back to his two comrades, then turned. "You write until very late at night, don't you? Maybe it is not the best thing to do."

When they were gone, the author retrieved the "Lobo" notes. Placing a call to Washington, D.C., he read them into a tape recorder, then tore them into little pieces and flushed them down the toilet. By the morning, there was no evidence in Honduras that the interview had taken place.

Several days later, Lieutenant Yanez, chief of the Homicide Division of the National Investigations Administration (DNI), housed directly across from the Hotel Istmania, admitted he had sent the agents to room 604. "I saw light and heard noise. If I had known it was you, I wouldn't have bothered."

A week later, a guest at the Hotel Istmania disappeared. The body of Professor Salvador Diaz del Valle was found in the trunk of his car the next day, his head full of bullets. The DNI denied complicity. The author left the country. The story of "Lobo" could be told.

The coauthor's visit to Tegucigalpa, capital of the Central American nation of Honduras, was in March 1983. It was at a time when the Reagan Administration had begun to pour military and economic aid into the country, portraying it as a bulwark of democratic stability in contrast to the bloody chaos that afflicted the rest of the region. When questioned about the appropriations of money and materiel, the joint military exercises in the Honduran countryside, and the horde of military advisers who had inundated Tegucigalpa and taken up all the best hotel rooms, the Administration had only to point to Honduras's three neighbors—to the leftist Sandinista regime in Nicaragua, to the vicious civil war in El Salvador, and to the festering guerrilla war in Guatemala—to drive home the need to keep Honduras peaceful and safe.

But there was something else occurring in Honduras. Just as in Guatemala and El Salvador, people were disappearing. Rumors were circulating that death squads, sanctioned by the government, had been established. It was a story that had not been widely reported and one that both the Honduran and American governments were denying.

"The so-called 'disappeared ones,'" General Gustavo Alvarez Martínez, chief of staff of the Honduran army, had said, "are probably off in Cuba or Nicaragua training in terrorism to subvert the Fatherland."

The author had gone to Tegucigalpa to find out the real story. An agent in DNI's political division had admitted the existence of Honduran death squads and had promised to arrange an interview with one of their leaders.

"But it can take time," "Jorge" had cautioned. "I'll have to assure him that you are okay, and we'll have to arrange a safe meeting place."

In the following weeks, the planning for the clandestine interview seemed hopelessly bogged down. The contact had trouble locating the death squad leader; when he did, the man was suspicious. Then there were the matters of confidentiality and of arranging the time and place for the meeting. What ensued was a volley of cryptic messages left at hotel reception desks and promises of positive developments "soon."

One evening, the author had arranged to meet "Jorge" in the coffee shop of the Hotel Istmania. When "Jorge" arrived, he was accompanied by a thin, fair-haired Honduran doctor in his late twenties, still dressed in his hospital "whites." The doctor sat in the seat across from the author and gave a thin, nervous grin. It was "Lobo," a doctor at the National Hospital in Tegucigalpa by day, a secret member of the Anti-Communist Combat Army (ELA) at night. It was the first acknowledgment by a participant that death squads existed in Honduras.

"It was formed in 1979 by eighty-five of us," the doctor explained, "mainly graduate students in the law, pharmacology, psychology, engineering, and medical faculties at the National University. We wanted to do the things the police couldn't legally do."

Since its inception, the ELA had grown to between three and four hundred members. Their actions ranged from disrupting gatherings of leftist university students, to sending anonymous warnings to the political opposition, to murder.

"First we investigate and follow a suspect. Then we either kidnap him or leave an anonymous warning.

"If the suspect heeds our warning," "Lobo" continued, "we leave him alone after confirming his rehabilitation. If he doesn't reform, we machine-gun him. We've eliminated sixteen people so far, mostly labor unionists and university professors, all confirmed Marxists."

The doctor then offered a tour of the ELA's clandestine cemetery. "We'll arrange it; I'll have to clear it with the others."

"Lobo" became more extroverted and, losing some of his caution, bragged about the ELA's international connections. He began with a general discussion of the "talents" and track records of other Central American death squads. "The Guatemalan one is very efficient," "Lobo" said. "That's ESA, the Secret Anti-Communist Army. In El Salvador, it's the Maximiliano Hernández Martínez Brigade [named for a Salvadoran dictator of the 1930s]. He knew what to do; he killed every Commie he caught."

"What of La Mano Blanca?" the coauthor asked, referring to The White Hand, the death squad label that appeared repeatedly in Central America.

The doctor smiled. "We are all La Mano Blanca. We work together. We're in contact with groups in other countries, Guatemala and [El] Salvador. I attended a big conference in Argentina. Everyone was there."

"Who do you mean, everyone?"

"Leaders of all the groups, from Central America, South America, Mexico. Everyone."

The story that emerged over the next hour with the doctor was incredible. Not only did the ELA have connections with the military and security forces of Honduras (as the intermediary role of the secret police agent clearly attested) and with a political front group for protection and cover, but it had links to other death squads throughout the continent. The name of one organization, however, came up repeatedly in the conversation: "Our movements are coordinated out of Mexico. That's where CAL is located."

CAL, it turned out, was the acronym for the Latin American Anti-Communist Confederation. An intelligence informant in Mexico confirmed its existence and described it as a neo-Nazi splinter group formed after World War II.

"CAL is also called The White Hand, The White Force, and The White Brigade," the source explained. "It got its name because it has the backing of powerful people who erase all evidence surrounding a murder."

CAL was a confederation of anti-communist movements in countries throughout South and Central America, but the Mexican delegation had long been in control of its direction and activities. We then looked in two directions at once, both at the composition of the Mexican chapter of CAL and at CAL's external links.

We discovered that the Mexican chapter of CAL was called the

Mexican Anti-Communist Federation (FEMACO) a~~n~~
power base and the home of its leaders were in the cit~~y~~
lajara, more specifically at the Autonomous University of
jara. The school was controlled by a secret society called The
(Owls). The Tecos, virulent anti-communists and anti-Semites,
control over many of the students and staff; they forced loyalt~~y~~
pledges and operated their own spy network on the campus. Professor Raimundo Guerrero taught at the university; Guerrero was also
head of FEMACO and the chairman of CAL. We now had tangible
clues that some of the death squads of Latin America operated in
loose coordination through a central body—the Latin American Anti-
Communist Confederation.

That proved to be just the beginning. The confederation, in turn,
belonged to an even larger international organization. CAL was the
Latin American affiliate of an organization called the World Anti-
Communist League (WACL).

The World Anti-Communist League was founded in 1966 in
South Korea; it held its first conference in 1967. Its stated goals were
ambitious:

> What Does The WACL Seek To Accomplish?
> First: Through all forms of mass media and personal contacts, to
> urge all freedom loving peoples of the world to defeat and frustrate
> communist aggression and subversive activities.
> Second: To aid liberation movements of captive nations under
> communist rule.
> Third: To develop political and psychological warfare methods to
> expose and counteract communism.
> Fourth: To promote the exchange of cultural and informational
> material among freedom loving peoples to neutralize communist strat-
> egy and tactics.
> Fifth: To train anti-communist leaders to build a better world im-
> bued with freedom and to overcome the communist menace.[1]

Its chief organizers were the Taiwanese and South Korean governments and an organization called the Anti-Bolshevik Bloc of Nations
(ABN). Since that time, it has grown to have chapters in over ninety
countries on six continents, and even a cursory glance at its membership reveals some alarming facts. There among the names of
American congressmen and senators, Catholic archbishops, and Brit-

e Nazi collaborators, fugitive Europe-
squad leaders from Central America.
inquiry. One traveled throughout
overing the international links of the
ther searched for its benefactors and
Europe. In the process, they inter-
d exiles, government officials, and
ue is the story of that two-year in-

had collaborated with the Nazis in
countrymen and who had escaped
retribution to continue their activities in the United States. They
learned how European and Latin terrorists shared information, weapons, and credit for assassinations, and how the official Argentine
government death squad advised like-minded groups in El Salvador
on the most effective means of liquidating their opposition. Most of
all, they uncovered the international fraternity of the practitioners of
unconventional war, old and new.

As defined by a League member who advocates its use, unconventional warfare includes, "in addition to terrorism, subversion and guerrilla warfare, such covert and non-military activities as sabotage,
economic warfare, support to resistance groups, black and gray psychological operations, disinformation activities, and political warfare."[2]

Certainly the Nazi forces of World War II and the rightist death
squads of El Salvador and Guatemala today are among this century's
most accomplished practitioners of this unconventional warfare, and
even a casual observer will be struck by the similarity among the
ideologies, tactics, and policies of, for example, the Croatian Ustasha
of the 1940s and those of the Guatemalan MLN or of the Salvadoran
ARENA in the 1980s.

But this is a historical comparison that many historians, political
scientists, and military theoreticians have already noted. What has
not been as well publicized is that the Salvadoran rightist killing
peasants today learned his methods from the Nazis and their collaborators in Europe, and that he didn't receive this knowledge through
the reading of books but through careful tutoring.[3]

This international transfer of the fine art of unconventional warfare was made through the one organization to which all the necessary groups belonged—the World Anti-Communist League.

ACKNOWLEDGMENTS AND DISACKNOWLEDGMENTS

In the process of investigating the World Anti-Communist League, hundreds of individuals from some thirty countries on six continents shared information with us. Many of them did so at immense personal risk. If their names were revealed, they could reasonably expect to be embarrassed, denounced, deported from their present safe havens, lose their jobs, or be murdered. A very special thanks must go to these courageous men and woman, some of whom literally trusted us with their lives.

Another great debt is owed to the many conservative individuals, including former League members, who agreed to be interviewed. These men and women, who revealed much of the League's inner workings, were motivated not by personal or political gain but by disgust at those who, under the League banner, called themselves fellow "anti-communists." They, too, have asked for anonymity.

While we cannot begin to list all those who assisted us and agreed to have their names used, chief among them are Dale Van Atta, a reporter for columnist Jack Anderson, who helped in the original investigation of the Mexican Tecos, and Russ Bellant, an investigative reporter who generously shared his information on Nazi war criminals in the United States and Europe. Sincere thanks are also due to Jack Anderson, Larry Birnes, Charles Bonnay, Fred Clarkson, Ferox Microsystems, Leonel Gomez, Pharris Harvey, Tom Hutton, J. T. Johnson, Harry Kelly, Allen Klots, John Loftus, Anne Marie O'Connor, and Jean Marie Simon. A special debt is owed to Juana

Arias de Anderson and Barrie Kessler, who tolerated and encouraged us, and to our mother, Joy Anderson, who nurtured our desire for writing.

At the same time, there were those who had the ability and the self-interest to assist us in this work but who failed to do so. The Anti-Defamation League of B'nai B'rith, which had at first denounced the anti-Semitic elements in the Latin American Anti-Communist Confederation, inexplicably declined to furnish us with their material. The irony of receiving information from a contrite Nazi collaborator on the activities of Nazi war criminals, while failing to receive the same cooperation from the most important Jewish organization in the United States, was just one of many encountered while researching this book.

The biggest disacknowledgment, however, must be reserved for the U. S. government. Many articles have been written about how the present Administration has gutted the Freedom of Information Act, and we do not intend to add to them here save through furnishing one further example. According to correspondence received by the authors, the FBI has a 107-page file on the World Anti-Communist League. Under a Freedom of Information Act request, they furnished forty-three pages. Of these forty-three pages, less than three pages of FBI-originating text remained, the rest having been censored and blacked out. One might wonder what interest the U. S. government has in protecting an organization so inimical to American goals and values.

Inside
The League

I

ONE

We maintain that the freedom-loving peoples must work in close cooperation to overcome the evil force of communism and strengthen their unity to expand the sphere of freedom.

Preamble to the WACL Charter

THE EVENING CROWDS on Calle Atocha on January 23, 1977, had already thinned by nine-thirty. Tourists, who never frequented that middle-class shopping street in the heart of Madrid, were inside the cafés in Plaza Mayor or strolling along the ornate Gran Via. By ten o'clock, the *Madrileños* had joined them; Calle Atocha was virtually deserted. At ten-fifteen, no one noticed the two young men in long coats on the corner.

José Fernandez Cerra casually gazed up and down the four-lane street. The movie at Cine Consulado hadn't let out yet, but he noted with satisfaction that the shops—the little place at number 42 that sold watches, the Icartua stationery store, the photo kiosk—were all closed. Only the lights of the El Globo bar showed activity, but even there the waiters were mopping the floors. Just beyond El Globo was the stairway leading down to the Metro station and, in the little triangle of grass and sidewalks and park benches that were the Plaza San Martin, the large illuminated clock said it was ten-twenty. José gazed at the building before him: number 55 Calle Atocha.

It was a dreary five-story building. The ground floor was occupied by a branch of the Banco Hispano Americano, dark and shuttered at this hour. The second floor was of the same drab concrete, the large windows giving onto small balconies enclosed by wrought-iron grills. The top three floors were of brick, alternating red and white, giving it a reticulated effect. Most of the rooms were dark, with shutters pulled tight, but not the apartment José was watching. On the third floor, light shone through the slats and voices were heard. José walked to the entrance and Carlos Garcia Julia followed.

The green front doors were open, and the two men ignored the intercom system. They had expected the doors to be locked—after all, 1977 was a violent time in Spain. Their luck held as they crossed the foyer and started up the stairs, passing the small window of the sleeping watchman's room. They walked softly up the creaking wooden stairs, keeping close to the wall where the boards had a firmer foundation. The stairs wound their way around an open elevator. Its ropes and pulleys looked ancient, but it wasn't for safety reasons that José and Carlos had opted to walk.

They reached the second floor, passed the closed door of a *pension,* and continued up into the darkness. They stood outside the oak door on the third floor and waited for their eyes to adjust to the weak light, the sole illumination coming from the glow of the dirty skylight one floor above. Carlos stuck his hands into his coat pockets as José rang the buzzer.

The eight men and one woman in the room fell silent at the sound of the buzzer. The lawyers—some communists, some merely liberal, all active in labor law—were having a reunion of sorts, and their number was complete; they had no idea who could be arriving at this late hour. Maria Dolores Gonzalez Ruis rose from her chair and left the smoke-filled front room.

As soon as the bolt was lifted, José and Carlos burst through the door. Maria Dolores fell silent upon seeing the pistol aimed at her head. Following their hushed orders, she led the two intruders into the conference room.

"Get against the wall!" José shouted at the stunned men.

"What's going on?" one of the lawyers demanded as they stood against the white wall. "What do you want?"

Neither Carlos nor José answered.

With the eight men and Maria Dolores facing the wall, Carlos took the safety off his gun. José turned to him and nodded. Carlos started at the left, José at the right, each working toward the center, as they carefully put a bullet into the back or head of each of the nine occupants of apartment three.

As the bodies fell, the intruders reloaded and fired into the heap. The room became thick with gunpowder. The screams of shock turned into moans of pain and the deep wheeze of the dying. Carlos and José calmly put away their guns, stepped out onto the staircase into the chaos of half-dressed residents awakened by the gunfire, descended to the street, and disappeared.

Jozo Damjanovic was a man driven by one consuming passion, and he had carried it with him from Europe to South America: to find officials of the Yugoslavian government and kill them.

A fanatical Croatian nationalist, Damjanovic had dedicated his life to a deadly war against the Tito regime, which had incorporated his homeland into the Socialist Federal Republic of Yugoslavia. Damjanovic had been one of a group of terrorists who had stormed the Yugoslav Embassy in Stockholm in 1971 and killed two diplomats. After a brief stint in a Swedish jail, other Croatian terrorists had hijacked a plane and won their freedom. Damjanovic and his cohorts had then gone underground to Spain, eluding Interpol and various European police agencies for three months. In July 1973, they had found their savior in the form of General Alfredo Stroessner, the dictator of the South American country of Paraguay.

Stroessner was in West Germany visiting his ancestral home of Hof when contact with him was made by the Croatian fugitives. They were on the run, the Paraguayan strongman was told, and needed a safe asylum. Stroessner, a longtime guardian of Nazis and right-wing terrorists, readily agreed. Damjanovic and eight others were given safe passage to Paraguay, where they were put to work training Stroessner's secret police and personal bodyguard squad.

That had been three years ago, and the Croatians chafed under their isolation from the front lines of their war with Yugoslavia. As international fugitives, however, they could not risk returning to Europe. In 1976, they decided to strike in the only avenue open to them—locally. The new Yugoslavian ambassador to Paraguay seemed an appropriate target, one whose assassination would put the hated Titoists on notice that the Croatians had not disappeared.

This was the reason why Jozo Damjanovic was waiting on a streetcorner in Asunción, the capital of Paraguay, on June 15, 1976.

Seeing the black limousine making its way through the traffic, he removed his pistol from its holster, tucked it under his arm, and waited.

Carlos Abdala, the new Uruguayan ambassador to Paraguay, looked out the window of his limousine at the main shopping street of the capital. He was getting used to Paraguay, though Asunción had none of the excitement or cosmopolitan flavor of Montevideo, the capital of his homeland. It was really more of an overgrown cow town; its few tall buildings and fancy shops gave way to slums and shantytowns and then to the great flat expanse of pampas that made up most of Paraguay.

Still, it was a safe assignment. There was virtually no crime in Paraguay, except for that which was sanctioned by the government of Alfredo Stroessner. Paraguay was the smuggling and black-market hub of South America, but there was no murder or rape or anti-state activities to speak of. As his limousine pulled to the curb and the chauffeur jumped out to open the door, the ambassador really had nothing to fear as far as his personal security was concerned.

Which is why Carlos Abdala, stepping from the car, was probably more surprised than frightened by the burly young man who stepped toward him with an upraised pistol.

"Freedom for Croatia!" Jozo Damjanovic shouted before firing the bullet that ended the life of Ambassador Abdala.

Bernardo Leighton and his wife, Ana, stepped from the taxi on Via Aurelia in Rome and, gathering up their shopping bags, walked toward the entrance of their apartment building. They didn't see the young man who had awaited their return and who now fell into step behind them.

It was October 6, 1975. Bernardo Leighton was sixty-six years old and an exile from his native Chile. A cofounder of the Chilean Christian Democratic Party and leader of its most liberal branch, he had fled his homeland two years earlier after the bloody coup that overthrew the elected leftist government of Salvador Allende. During his exile in Rome, he stayed active in his opposition to the right-wing military government of General Augusto Pinochet. Because he maintained contact with liberal political forces within Chile and was a respected voice in the international brotherhood of Christian Democrats, Leighton worried the Chilean government, and some months earlier they had decided to silence him.

Getting rid of the politician presented a logistical problem. Although it was an international pariah after the savagery of the 1973 coup, the Pinochet government had been slowly achieving, if not respect, at least recognition, in other capitals, and it just would not do for it to be known that this government was in the habit of murdering its opposition in other countries. The assassination of Leighton was therefore to be a contract job.

The young man with the handlebar moustache three feet behind the Christian Democrat pulled out a 9-mm Beretta, pointed it at the politician's head, and pulled the trigger. Bernardo Leighton pitched face forward on the sidewalk. Ana stared in shock at her fallen husband until she too was shot in the back. The gunman hesitated for a moment, debating whether to administer the coup de grâce with a couple of close-range shots to their heads; deciding they were already dead or dying, he turned and fled.

Bernardo survived his massive head wound and recovered; Ana was partially paralyzed and remains in a wheelchair. Their attacker was not immediately identified, and no arrest was made. Four days later, the Cuban Nationalist Movement, a right-wing Cuban exile group in New Jersey, took credit for the shootings; they imparted details that the Italian police said only the assailant could have known. Why a group of anti-communist Cubans in the United States would want to kill a liberal Chilean in Italy was a question that wouldn't be answered for some time.

In March 1979, Manuel Colom Argueta, leader of Guatemala's United Revolutionary Front (FUR) political party, gave an interview in which he frankly described the political scene in his country. Although it was reformist, despite its name the FUR was hardly revolutionary. From a wealthy landowner family, Manuel Colom was a liberal democrat who sought to push his policies—land reform, dissolution of the oligarchy, curbing of human-rights abuses—through participation in whatever semblance of democracy existed in Guatemala. Just a few days before the interview, Colom's party had received the government permission necessary to campaign in the upcoming elections. Shortly thereafter, he received a call from a friend of his in the ultra-right party, the National Liberation Movement (MLN).

"Quit, Manuel," the man told him; "if you don't, they're going to finish you."

But Manuel Colom had been battling the Guatemalan institutions of fraudulent elections, death squads, and political assassinations for too long to stop then. Even the threat from the MLN, which was blamed for organizing the nation's death squads and for carrying out a two-decade campaign of terror, did not dissuade him.

"Mario Sandoval Alarcón," he said in the interview, referring to the head of the MLN, "is a buffoon straight out of the middle ages. The army uses him a lot, but he also knows how to use the army. . . . He knows how to blackmail the army. . . . He wants to polarize the political struggle, to make himself and his movement indispensable as 'bastions against communism.' "[1]

At eight o'clock on March 22, Manuel Colom left his home in Zone 15 in Guatemala City and headed for his office downtown. He had been taking different routes from his home to the office for safety reasons, but he apparently didn't notice the helicopter that followed him that morning.

He worked in his office until about ten-fifteen, when, glancing out at the normally busy Calle 5, he noticed that the street was virtually deserted. It was a familiar sight in Guatemala, this prelude to an assassination, and Manuel reacted quickly. Getting on the phone, he called his political contacts in Guatemala's various political parties.

"Who is it for?" he asked each of them.

No one knew or would tell until he reached his contact in the MLN.

"It's for you, Manuel."

Colom descended to the alley and climbed behind the wheel of a car while his bodyguards piled into another. They raced out the building's back entrance and managed to speed past one roadblock before the bodyguards' car careened and crashed, riddled with machine-gun fire.

Alone, Manuel raced through the city and reached the airport road. On the straight stretch, though, he looked back to see motorcycles gaining on him. One of them, carrying two men, caught up and came abreast. The passenger drew out a machine pistol, aimed it at the head of the FUR leader, and squeezed the trigger. Manuel Colom was dead, one more of the thousands of Guatemalans to fall victim to the right-wing death squads and political assassins in 1979.

When the U. S. ambassador to Paraguay, Robert White, walked into the auditorium housing the thirteenth annual conference of the World Anti-Communist League in Asuncíon, Paraguay, on April 24, 1979, he was not warmly received. The ambassador, who several years later would achieve fame and notoriety for his outspoken opposition to American policies in El Salvador, was an unexpected visitor to the conference, and when the participants caught sight of him, the proceedings came to a virtual halt.

What Robert White had intruded upon was a meeting of the leaders of conservative movements from around the world. Government ministers were present, as were religious leaders and notable conservatives from the United States. It was, by outward appearances, a polite gathering of anti-communists, dedicated to fighting totalitarianism and communist expansion from around the world. But it was in fact another meeting of the organization that unites and gives a common front to the most brutal and deadly extremists to be found anywhere.

Among those attending was Blas Piñar, the leader of the Spanish political party, Fuerza Nueva. Two members of his organization had gunned down the nine lawyers on Calle Atocha in 1977. Nearby was the aging, mustachioed Giorgio Almirante, leader of Italy's fascist MSI party; it was Pierlugi Concutelli, a member of the youth wing of the MSI, and not Cuban exiles, who had shot Bernardo Leighton and his wife on the streets of Rome four years before. Mario Sandoval Alarcón, the head of Guatemala's MLN, the political party responsible for institutionalizing the death squads that had killed Manuel Colom, was a distinguished main speaker. And somewhere around the conference hall, seeing to the safety of conference chairman President Alfredo Stroessner, was Jozo Damjanovic, the assassin of Carlos Abdala.

TWO

A good Ustashi is one who can use a knife to cut a child
from the womb of its mother.

Ante Pavelic
Croatian Fuhrer

ON A SEARINGLY COLD December day, one of the authors turned
into the driveway of a nondescript tract house in the Philadelphia
suburb of Chester. A short, elderly man in an overcoat waited for
him on the front step, stamping his shoes against the concrete to
fight the cold. It was Janos; after months of phone calls and letters,
he had finally agreed to the interview.

The eighty-year-old emigré ushered the author into the living room
of his modest home. "Perhaps we should have postponed our meeting," Janos said, sinking onto the uncomfortable couch. "With these
winds, I was worried about you."

The wall behind Janos was studded with two dozen framed photographs, medallions, ribbons, and plaques. They ranged from cita-
tions from the deposed king of his native country to letters of
appreciation from the Republican Party of New York for his selfless
dedication. There was even one from Chiang Kai-shek, the late generalissimo of Taiwan. The bright ribbons and shiny metal did not,
however, alter the general dreariness of the room, the house, or the
neighborhood.

The interview lasted nearly five hours, during which Janos's wife
produced a steady stream of sandwiches, coffee, and biscuits. Every

time this doting, plain woman in her late sixties entered the room, Janos stopped talking, turned to her, and smiled, love showing in his sparkling eyes.

The author asked Janos about other emigrés.

"Chirila Ciuntu? Very strong. Big, powerful arms. Short. Doesn't speak English very much."

Yaroslav Stetsko?

"Stetsko." Janos sat back, cocked his head, and looked imperious. "Aloof. Not arrogant, but aloof. He always has this look about him. He always looks . . . angry."

And Stejpan Hefer?

"Ah, Stejpan!" the old man cried, leaping to his feet. He puffed out his chest, put his hands on his hips, and strutted about the small room. "This is how Stejpan walked. And when he spoke, he always shouted and waved his hands. Very intense, very emotional."

When the author was leaving, Janos resumed his vigil on the doorstep, waving and watching after the car until it disappeared from sight.

There was no way one could dislike Janos. His solicitude and warmth, the teenage adoration he showed toward his wife, all gave one a feeling of affection for the old man.

Which was disquieting, because Janos was a Nazi war criminal. The friends he had caricatured in his Chester living room were also war criminals.

While there is no evidence that Janos ever directly participated in atrocities, his three friends certainly had. Each had played key roles in three different genocide programs, in Romania, in the Ukraine, and in Croatia, that had exterminated at least two million people.

The common bond of all four men was membership in the World Anti-Communist League.

The League was founded in 1966 as a public relations arm for the governments of Taiwan and South Korea. It has since grown to be something far more important: an instrument for the practice of unconventional warfare—assassinations, death squads, sabotage—throughout the world.

There is nothing new about the World Anti-Communist League. Its stated purpose, to form a unified front against communism, was first expostulated in Hitler's anti-Comintern policy. Likewise, the means it has chosen to fight communism—unconventional warfare, counterterror, political warfare, it goes by a variety of names—were first employed by the Nazis.

While the employment of unconventional warfare is certainly not solely the domain of the ultra-right, as the pogroms in Stalinist Russia and Khmer Rouge Cambodia make clear, it was the Nazis and their collaborators who "best" employed it with such hideous efficiency.

The World Anti-Communist League hasn't merely borrowed these concepts or tactics from the Nazis; it has incorporated the Nazis themselves as well. Many of the major figures behind the creation and promotion of the League are men who first practiced their brand of warfare in the streets, ghettos, and concentration camps of World War II Europe.

The deserted gas chambers, ovens, and mass graves of Treblinka and Auschwitz are not the only relics of the Nazis' and their collaborators' impact on civilization. There are living relics scattered in every corner of the globe. Even before the dust had settled on Hitler's shattered Third Reich, many of those responsible were escaping to work for the formation of a Fourth Reich. From their havens, they have nurtured their cause and kept it alive, they have recruited younger generations, and they have formed networks for safety and strength, bonds that remain to this day.

When most people think of Nazis, two images are evoked: aging war criminals, the Josef Mengeles and Klaus Barbies living in frightened obscurity somewhere in South America, or else of disenchanted youths who, in brown shirts and jackboots, vandalize synagogues and march through city streets. But there is a third type of Nazi, who is far more powerful, public, and dangerous than the other two: these are the Croatians, Slovaks, Ukrainians, Latvians who carried out the German-dictated massacres, who never faced a Nuremberg, and who joined the World Anti-Communist League.

The participation of these Eastern Europeans in the Holocaust remains one of the least-told stories in modern history. The reason this is so is simple: many if them were recruited by American and British intelligence, brought into the United States and Canada, allowed to rise to prominent positions in their emigré communities, and ultimately to revise history.

Today, their rhetoric is different; they no longer talk very much about the "Communist, Jewish, Freemason conspiracy," for now they have allies who need them to be more discreet than that. In 1986, as in 1936, they hide behind the buzzwords *anti-Bolshevism* and *anti-communism* to further their goals and to forge links with others.

Through the World Anti-Communist League, the Ukrainian nationalists who assisted the Nazis in their invasion of the Soviet Union, the Ustashi of Croatia who murdered nearly a million Serbs, the Romanian Legionnaires who slaughtered over four hundred Jews in one day in 1941—all have made contact with their younger Latin, European, and Asian counterparts. Through their front groups and their involvement in American politics, the Nazi collaborators have blended in and become respectable.

Chirila Ciuntu. Yaroslav Stetsko. Stejpan Hefer. Three men from three different countries without, at first glance, a lot in common.

Chirila Ciuntu, his close-cropped black hair now graying, is a refugee from Romania who has labored for over thirty years in the steel mills of Canada. A regular churchgoer to the Romanian Orthodox Church in Detroit, the retired Ciuntu now spends his days in a high-rise apartment building in Windsor, Canada.

Escaping the repression of the Stalinist regime in the Soviet Union, the stooped and bespectacled Ukrainian Yaroslav Stetsko formed and continues to head an organization of Eastern European exiles called the Anti-Bolshevik Bloc of Nations (ABN). Now residing in Munich, West Germany, Stetsko has long been active in urging American and Western European governments to take a firmer stand against the Kremlin. In 1983, he met with President Ronald Reagan at the White House.

Stejpan Hefer, a Croatian lawyer who fled his homeland in 1945, resided in Argentina until his death in 1973. Although he was a fiery orator in the cause of Croatian independence, his short stature, angry gestures, and slightly crossed eyes were sources of some amusement for his listeners. In his capacity as president of the Croatian Liberation Movement, he established ties with many American conservatives and made frequent trips to the United States.

From different places and with different causes, these three men are, nevertheless, united by certain similarities. All were Nazi collaborators before and during World War II. All were accused of war crimes. All escaped the judgment of history. All built respectable new lives and carried on their efforts for international fascism through front groups, intelligence agencies, and churches. All joined the World Anti-Communist League.

Today in the United States, Canada, South America, and Western Europe there exists an elusive network known as the Legion of the Archangel Michael. Also called the Iron Guard, the Legion is composed of Romanian emigrés and their children. Calling themselves Legionnaires or Guardists, they have regular gatherings and maintain contact through certain parishes of the Romanian Orthodox Church. But the Legion is not primarily a fraternal or religious organization; it is, foremost, a cult of death.

Today the Legion is run from a well-guarded building in Madrid by a droopy-eyed, elderly man named Horia Sima. One of its chief lieutenants in North America is Chirila Ciuntu.

As Legion spokesman in the Detroit-Windsor area, which has the greatest concentration of Romanian exiles in North America, Ciuntu holds a position of great power in the Iron Guard, which also explains his prominence in the World Anti-Communist League. In 1981, he was in the Romanian delegation to the fourteenth annual League conference held in Taiwan. He has also attended League conferences in Washington and Luxembourg. He planned to attend the 1984 conference in San Diego but was ill.

Others might try to hide their involvement in an infamous organization, but not Ciuntu. A Detroit reporter who met with him in 1980 described his home:

> The walls of the small flat are festooned with flags and tapestries. The Romanian national flag—red, yellow and blue—flies atop his television set. But *his* flag has, stitched at its center, three horizontal and three vertical intersecting lines—the symbol of the Iron Guard. The same symbol appears on wall tapestries and small embroidered doilies. . . . Books, many with the Iron Guard cross on their bindings, are everywhere. A green military-style shirt hangs from the back of a chair.[1]

Although he is obviously proud of his position within the Legion, Ciuntu is also sensitive to criticism of it. "Most of the stories about the Legion, with a few exceptions, are a complete distortion of truth and realities," Ciuntu wrote one of the authors in 1985. "The Britannic and American people have permanently been deceived by those who wrote about the movement and did not have the courage of objectivity to re-establish the truth."[2]

The Legion is still built around the idol worship of Corneliu Codreanu, who, in 1927, literally galloped out of obscurity on a white stallion, clutching a revolver in one hand and a crucifix in the other. He was the *capitanul* (captain) of the Legion of the Archangel Michael and was dedicated to purging Romania of Jews, foreigners, communists, and Freemasons. "Before we aspire to take helm of the country's rule," he wrote, "we must mold a different type of Romania totally cleansed of today's vices and defects."[3]

Handsome and articulate, Codreanu urged authoritarian nationalism to implement this spiritual renaissance and purification, and his followers, among them Chirila Ciuntu, steeped themselves in the eerie mysticism of his brand of fascist Catholicism. Clad in green shirts and wearing silver crucifixes, the Legionnaires took blood oaths to their comrades and their *capitanul*. Each vowed to commit any act necessary, including murder, to avenge the death of any Legion member.

> With a smile on our lips
> We look death in the eye
> For we are the death team
> That must win or die.[4]

One who incurred the wrath of "the death team" was Mihail Stelescu, a Legionary leader who had become disillusioned and split with Codreanu. Ten Legionnaires, chosen by lot for the honor of silencing him, caught Stelescu in July 1936, as he recovered in a Bucharest hospital from an appendectomy. He was shot 120 times and mutilated with a hatchet; then, according to an official account, the killers "danced around the pieces of flesh, prayed, kissed each other and cried with joy."

When Codreanu was assassinated for his intrigues by King Carol in 1938, leadership passed to his lieutenants who fled to the safety of Nazi Germany. Among them were Horia Sima and Viorel Trifa, the latter the head of the Legion's youth wing. Later, as an Archbishop in the United States, it was Trifa who would be most responsible for resurrecting the Legion in North America.

Those who remained in Romania, including the young Chirila

Ciuntu, went further underground and waited. They formed secret cells, or "nests." Each nest consisted of thirteen members, who paid dues to propagate the "faith." According to one Guardist, now living in the United States, "the Movement spent the money obtained through the nest system exclusively for the necessities of battle."[5]

In hiding, all remembered their blood oath to avenge Codreanu and, ten months later, they did. As the limousine carrying the Prime Minister of Romania entered a plaza in central Bucharest, it was riddled with machine-gun fire from a Guardist hit squad.

The Germans used the Legionnaires as a trump card to control Romania. In May 1940, Nazis forced a detente between King Carol and the exiled Guardists. Carol abdicated in September 1940; he made a mad dash for the border, chased by Iron Guardists intent on killing him. He himself eluded the Legion of the Archangel, but most of his entourage were caught and thrown in prison.

The government of Romania was now in the hands of two men, Iron Guard leader Horia Sima (who had returned from Germany with Trifa) and non-Guardist General Yon Antonescu. The alliance was an uneasy one, for each man was vying for the favor of the Nazis. Iron Guard officials were placed in key government posts, and Guard commissars were appointed to see to the "Romanizing" (purging of Jews) of industry and commerce. Twenty-six-year-old Viorel Trifa, who blamed the "kikes" for all the ills of the nation, was named president of the National Union of Christian Romanian Students. As the Legion of the Archangel gained power within the bureaucracy, the plan for a complete take-over took shape. As was the Guard's custom, that plan was executed in blood.

At 11:45 on the night of November 26, 1940, a gang of Legionnaires entered the prison where King Carol's government ministers were being held. They dragged the men, sixty-four in all, from the cells, shouted "For the Guard!" and chopped them to pieces with axes, picks, and shovels. The butchery signaled a holy call to arms; the followers of the Archangel answered the cry. During the next three days, they tortured to death more than three hundred victims throughout Romania. Typical was the case of Nicolae Iorga, a pre-eminent Romanian historian and former prime minister. On the night of November 27, a squad of Legionnaires raided his home. The

Guardists ripped his long white beard from his face and castrated him before stabbing and beating him to death.*

The carnage of late November did not immediately result in the revolution that many had expected, but it was the prelude to one. The final spark came seven weeks later when, during a power struggle between Antonescu and Sima, the Guard was called into action. "In Germany, national socialism . . . is preached by old foxhole fighters," Trifa, the student union leader, exhorted on the evening of January 20, "is borne in the hearts of the German people and is carried to triumph by German youth. Besides this huge battle for national socialism which leads to unmasking and fighting Judaism, if Adolf Hitler had done nothing else, he would still have risen to the highest peaks of history for opening the way."[6]

On January 21, 1941, throughout Romania the Iron Guard took to the streets, roaming for loyalist soldiers, Antonescu supporters, and especially Jews. Shortly after three in the afternoon in Bucharest, three hundred Guardists, wearing the Legion's distinctive green shirt and silver crucifix and shouting "Death to Freemasons and Kikes!" turned onto Calea Victoriei and moved toward the Prefecture, the main police station. With them was Chirila Ciuntu.

The small army charged through the doors of the Prefecture, seizing the building in the name of the revolution. Within minutes they had taken the weapons from the loyalist policemen, disposed of those who refused to participate, mounted machine guns on the fourth-floor balconies, and covered the avenues of approach. With this secure base, they then dealt with their victims in the basement.

Constantin Antonovici, a Romanian Christian, survived his internment in the Prefecture and now lives in seclusion in the United States. Opposed to the Iron Guard's anti-Semitism and violence, on January 21 he had been on a Bucharest street urging people to ignore the Guard's call to murder. He was spotted by Guardists, beaten, and dragged along to the Prefecture. He was in the basement when Trifa entered.

When they [Trifa and his aides] arrived at the first cell, I heard them order the guards to open it. Immediately, I heard a few pistol shots being fired and cries from the people being killed. I had not reached

*Traian Boeru, the leader of the Iron Guard squad that murdered Iorga, was never brought to justice and, as of 1981, was living in West Germany.

the end of the corridor before I heard more begging and shots in the next cell. My guards said, "They will kill all the Jews who are in these cells."[7]

Ciuntu was also in the Prefecture at the time but denies any involvement: "I didn't kill anyone. . . . I didn't see anything, just a few people running around the streets. . . . I don't know what was going on in the basement. It was a big building. I don't know anything."[8]

With the capture of the Prefecture, the members of the Legion of the Archangel had achieved one goal, but they had still others. In the next thirty-six hours, they razed eight synagogues, destroyed the Jewish ghetto in Bucharest, and murdered over four hundred Romanians with gasoline, axes, knives, meathooks, and shovels.

"A mob of several hundred attacked the Sephardic Temple," American correspondent Leigh White reported at the time, "smashing its windows with stones and battering down its doors with lengths of timber. All its objects of ritual—prayer books, shawls, Talmuds, Torahs, altar benches and tapestries—were carried outside and piled in a heap which was soaked with gasoline and set afire. A number of Jewish pedestrians were herded together and forced to dance in a circle around the bonfire. When they dropped in exhaustion they were doused with gasoline and burned alive."

Jewish prisoners were taken by the Iron Guard to the municipal slaughterhouse. "There," White wrote, "in a fiendish parody of kosher methods of butchering, they hung many of the Jews on meat hooks and slit their throats; others they forced to kneel at chopping blocks while they [Iron Guardists] beheaded them with cleavers."[9]

One of those who observed the scene was the American envoy to Romania, Franklin Mott Gunther. In his report to Washington, he recounted seeing about "sixty Jewish corpses on the hooks used for carcasses, all skinned. The quantity of blood about [indicated] that they had been skinned alive."

By the twenty-third, the rebellion, which had failed to receive the support of the Germans, had been put down. In the streets of the capital and other Romanian cities and in the Bucharest slaughterhouse were the mutilated remains of the Legion's victims. "In the morgue, bodies were so cut up that they no longer resembled anything human. In the municipal slaughterhouse a witness saw a girl of five hanging by her feet like a calf, her entire body smeared with blood."[10]

The massacre did not mean the end of the Legion. The German SS commander in Romania, Otto von Bolschwing,* hid the top Legion leaders and spirited them across the border into Germany in SS uniforms. Among them were Horia Sima and Viorel Trifa; they were shortly joined by many more. There they were placed under "protective custody," in which they received the same privileges as German officers.

In a letter to one of the authors, Chirila Ciuntu admitted as much, giving the lie to Guardist claims that they had been interred in concentration camps. "They [were] offered a strange political asylum, because they were sent to special camps to work for German industry . . . It was a political game. The presence of the Legionnaires in Germany represented, in Hitler's mind, a permanent threat to Antonescu's government; in this way Hitler kept a tight hand over Antonescu's rule."[11]

Ciuntu, one of several thousand Iron Guardists who surrendered after the abortive coup, didn't share the benign fate of his superiors at first. Although the Guard's atrocities in Romania demanded punishment, the Romanian government knew that the German authorities wouldn't allow a wholesale crackdown or dissolution of the Legion, a realization amply reinforced by the SS's role in whisking the leaders out of Bucharest.

Given the narrow confines within which the Antonescu government found itself, it decided to pursue only the most flagrant criminals among the remaining Guardists and even then to make sanitized charges against them.

Among the hundred-odd men charged with insurrection and rebellion was Chirila Ciuntu. He was found guilty of rebellion and sentenced to five years in prison and three years of interdiction (loss of civil rights). It was one of the more severe sentences passed by the Martial Court of Bucharest, but Ciuntu would never serve it. "The Nazis offered Legionnaires protection," he explained to *Windsor*

---

*Otto von Bolschwing was never brought to justice for his role in harboring the Iron Guardists or for his other war crimes; after the war, he worked for the American army Counter-Intelligence Corps, emigrated to the United States in 1961, and remained a free man until his death in 1982.

Star reporter Lynda Powless. "I left in a German jeep with two SS officers; they took me to Bulgaria."[12]

Once in Germany, the Romanian fascists were housed in an SS "home," and photographs of the period show them relaxing in the sunshine. Viorel Trifa, the future archbishop in the United States, took the waters in a spa in Bavaria and beseeched an SS commandant for a special diet to nurse his ulcers. In their wartime exile, the Iron Guard continued to be ardent suitors for Nazi favor.

"Your Excellency," Iron Guard leader Sima wrote to Himmler in 1944, "has surely heard that His Excellency Foreign Minister von Ribbentrop has authorized the formation of the topmost Romanian commandos of the Romanian national forces. Along with this body, a future Romanian army is to be prepared under my supervision. My wish is that out of the ranks of the best, Legionnaires will join the accomplished Waffen-SS in which they will, I am convinced, not only receive the best technical military training but, above all, the best political world view."

Ciuntu was among the "ranks of the best"; in 1944 he joined a contingent of Iron Guardists who were fighting the Soviets on the Eastern Front. Sima remained in Germany, awaiting approval from the German high command to return to Romania and finish the job the Legion had begun in 1941.

It was not to be. In August 1944, a new Romanian government signed an armistice with the Allies and declared war on Germany. The Germans responded by launching a massive air strike against Bucharest and racing the Legion leaders to Vienna in preparation for infiltrating them into Romania. Within a week, however, the Soviet army entered Romania, and the remnants of the Iron Guard fled to safety before the onslaught. Sima declared a government-in-exile in Vienna, a shadow government that did not disband until nine days after the death of Hitler in his bunker.

Yaroslav Stetsko is chairman of the Anti-Bolshevik Bloc of Nations (ABN) and a major leader of the World Anti-Communist League. He was involved with the League even before its official founding in 1966. In journeys to Taiwan in 1956, 1957, 1961, and 1964, and at many Asian People's Anti-Communist League conferences (the precursor to the World League), Stetsko pursued his long interest in Taiwan and its generalissimo, Chiang Kai-shek. Stetsko found a reflection of his own beliefs in the ferocious anti-communist stance of the Taiwanese government and in its willingness to combat communism by any means necessary. In 1958, he took part in the preparatory conference of the World Anti-Communist League in Mexico City and was one of those most responsible for its ultimate creation. In 1970, he was elected to the executive board, the League's elite governing body.

Today, Stetsko maintains his respectability and authority in anti-communist circles throughout the world. Those introducing him at receptions or forums describe him as a patriot and a freedom fighter as well as a "survivor of Nazi concentration camps." He has conferred with prominent conservatives, among them heads of state and American congressmen and senators.

Stetsko has covered his tracks well. According to his official biography, during World War II he fought against both the Soviets and the Germans in his struggle for Ukrainian independence. Thrown into the Nazi concentration camp at Sachsenhausen, so the account goes, "he was subjected there to continuous and inhuman torture which was to have a permanent effect later upon his physical condition."

It is an interesting claim by one of the most important Nazi collaborators alive today.

In 1938, Stetsko's physical appearance was deceiving. It was hard to imagine that this son of a priest, with his thinning hair, sparse goatee, and round spectacles, was capable of anything at all malicious, let alone murder. But there were clues in the face: the thin lips were fixed in a permanent bitter sneer, and the eyes, cold and angry, glared out from behind the glasses with charismatic rage. Even in prison, there was no softening of the hatred, no weakness in the resolve to attack again; perhaps this was why the Nazis showed a special benevolence toward Yaroslav Stetsko.

By the time the Nazis took notice of him, Stetsko had spent nearly two years in a Polish prison for his role in the murders of Polish government officials. As a leader of the Galician* branch of the Organization of Ukrainian Nationalists (OUN), Stetsko's disdain for parliamentary rule and his proven willingness to liquidate its proponents were qualities the Germans were looking for.

*Present-day southeastern Poland and western Ukraine S.S.R.

The Nazis saw the Ukrainians as potentially important allies. Their ideology—fanatical racism against ethnic Poles and Russians, and virulent hatred of Jews—meshed perfectly with the Germans'. In the late 1930s, they had grand plans for the Ukrainian nationalists, and they organized them in earnest while planning the invasion of Poland. The Germans even bandied about the idea of setting up a nominally independent Ukrainian government in Galicia under OUN control; this would depend on whether the Ukrainians could "produce an uprising which would aim at the annihilation of the Jews and Poles."[13]

By 1938, the Nazis had compelling reasons to save Stetsko from penal obscurity. The previous year, a Soviet agent had slipped a bomb into the coat pocket of the pre-eminent pro-German Ukrainian leader and killed him. Since then, the OUN had lost much of its direction. Two opposing camps had formed: the cautious old guard, and the young radicals like Stetsko, bold and ready for war. Once plucked from jail, Stetsko became a driving force behind the creation of a new Organization of Ukrainian Nationalists, the OUN/B, led by Stefan Bandera. Bandera chose Stetsko to be his second-in-command, forming an alliance that would last nineteen years. (Bandera would be assassinated on a Munich street by a KGB agent in 1959; Stetsko would go on to meet the president of the United States.)

While the Germans had hoped to use Stetsko to unify the OUN, throughout the war they would support both major Ukrainian camps. The dirty work, however, would be OUN/B's chief domain.

While preparations were under way for Operation Barbarossa, the invasion of the Soviet Union, the Nazis organized their Ukrainian helpers into regiments. One regiment, the Nightingales, which consisted mainly of Bandera-Stetsko followers, would be in the vanguard of the German invasion of the Ukraine wearing Wehrmacht uniforms. The Nightingales' mission was to carry out sabotage and to engage the Red Army in rearguard skirmishes and guerrilla warfare.[14] The OUN/B also formed a secret police, the Sluzhba Bezpeky, which would see to the purging of Jews, ethnic Russians, and Communist Party members for their Nazi allies; they would accomplish this mission with terrible skill. Its chief was Mykola (Nicholas) Lebed, who, according to even a sympathetic writer, John Armstrong, "was to acquire for himself and his organization an unenviable reputation for ruthlessness."[15] Lebed was named third in command of OUN/B, behind Bandera and Stetsko. He would be responsible for the murder of thousands of Germany's enemies in the Ukraine and of scores more in the displaced persons camps in Western Europe after the war. He lives today in New York City.

When the Germans invaded the Soviet Union in June 1941, they were greeted by the people as liberators from the horrible repression of the Stalin regime. They struck deep into the heart of the Soviet empire as the Red Army fell back in disarray; tens of thousands deserted or surrendered. By June 30, 1941, advance units of the Wehrmacht had reached the city of Lvov. With them were the Ukrainian Nightingales, led by a German officer, Theodore Oberlander, and Yaroslav Stetsko.

Stetsko immediately organized a "congress" in a small meeting-room. From the podium, he announced the creation of the Ukraini-an State, and named himself premier. Whether Stetsko thought he had tacit approval from the Nazis for the independence declaration or whether he was attempting to present them with a fait accompli is open to debate. But certainly the news, broadcast out of Lvov by Stetsko over the radio station, did not have the desired effect on his allies: The Germans were outraged, but, not wanting to alienate their Ukrainian surrogate soldiers, they vacillated. In the confusion, Stetsko scrambled for approval, crowing his obedience to the Nazis:

> The Ukrainian State will closely cooperate with great National So-cialist Germany which under the leadership of Adolf Hitler will create a New Order in Europe and throughout the world. The Ukrainian army will fight together with the allied German army for the New Order in the world.[16]

The shaky alliance held long enough for the average Ukrainian peasant to realize that the liberating Nazis and the OUN were just as brutal as the Red Army had been. The pogroms, code-named "Action Petlura," began within hours of Stetsko's arrival in Lvov. Jews, intellectuals, greater Russians, Communist Party officials—any-one suspected of opposing the "New Order"—were rounded up and executed in these joint operations of the Nazis and the Ukrainian nationalists.

"The Galician capital of Lvov," wrote historian Raul Hilberg, "was the scene of a mass seizure by local inhabitants. In 'reprisal' for the deportation of Ukrainians by the Soviets, 1000 members of the Jewish intelligentsia were driven together and handed over to the security police."[17]

This roundup took place on July 2, 1941, two days after Stetsko had arrived in Lvov and assumed the premiership of the Ukraine. During the period in which Stetsko was in Lvov and, by his own claim, in charge of the city, an estimated seven thousand residents, mostly Jews, were murdered. Tens of thousands more were exterminated in the surrounding countryside by marauding OUN/B units. In the following four years, the entire Jewish population of Lvov—about one hundred thousand—and more than a million Jews in greater Ukraine would be annihilated by the Nazis and their coworkers, the Ukrainian auxiliary police.

> Moving with speed, the Einsatzgruppe (German mobile killing units) organized a network of local Ukrainian militias, making them partly self-financing by drawing upon Jewish money to pay their salaries. The Ukrainians were used principally for dirty work—thus Einstatzcommando 4a went so far as to confine itself to the shooting of adults while commanding its Ukrainian helpers to shoot children.[18]

Stetsko would not be a witness to these later activities of his followers. On July 9 he, Bandera, and their immediate aides were placed under "honorary arrest" by the Germans because of the independence proclamation and sent to Berlin. After refusing to rescind the proclamation, they were placed in Sachsenhausen prison.

Bandera and Stetsko were now quarantined in Germany, but this did not mean that the Germans had lost faith in the Ukrainians, or vice versa. The OUN/B continued to do the German's bidding at the same time as they fought for Ukrainian independence. While attacking units of the Red Army, the OUN/B also launched frequent purges of other partisan groups whom they suspected of communist or Russian sympathies.[19] For most of the rest of the war, their chief field commander was Mykola Lebed, who in turn carried out orders from Bandera and Stetsko. At least once, in 1943, Stetsko went to Poland to confer with Lebed; this was at a time when, according to his own account, he was languishing in a Nazi concentration camp.

Having proved themselves trustworthy Nazi allies, many Bandera-Stetsko followers were later recruited to assist in the transfer of

Jews from the ghettos to the concentration camps or to serve as guards in the camps themselves.

> The Ukrainians were involved in the fate of Polish Jewry as perpetrators. The SS and Police employed Ukrainian units in ghetto-clearing operations, not only in the Galician district but also in such places as the Warsaw ghetto and the Lublin ghetto. The Ukrainians have never been considered pro-Jewish.[20]

As the war turned against the Germans, they increasingly relied on their nationalist allies. By 1944, Ukrainian assistance was desperately needed to harass the advancing Soviets and try to slow their advance. To this end, the Ukrainian Insurgent Army (UPA) was formed, and Stetsko, Bandera, and other leaders were released from their confinement-to-quarters in Germany to lead the struggle. Toward the end of the war, when it was clear that the "Thousand Year Reich" was finished, some Ukrainian elements also began sniping at the retreating Germans; this allowed Stetsko later to claim that the UPA fought the Nazis as well as the Soviets, an assertion that continues to serve him well.

Stejpan Hefer was a short, bespectacled man, one who didn't attract much notice at World Anti-Communist League conferences—until he took the podium. Then his fiery oratory, the harsh, rapid-fire succession of his words, the wild gestures of his hands, the strong timbre of his voice, all served to energize—and amuse—the crowd.

Until his death in 1973, Hefer was an important and frequent visitor to the United States. As the world leader of the Croatian Liberation Movement (known by its Croatian acronym, HOP), he oversaw a network that spanned the globe. From his headquarters in Buenos Aires, Hefer established Central Boards of Croatian Societies designed to coordinate the activities of HOP chapters in Europe, Australia, and the United States. Those activities were directed against the Yugoslav government of Josip Broz "Tito."

This campaign operated by rallying Croatian emigré groups, by building support within their communities and churches, by holding anti-Yugoslav rallies, and by joining organizations such as the World Anti-Communist League. On another level, the work was less benign: through hijackings, assassinations, bombings, and sabotage of civilian aircraft, the Croatians waged a war of terror.

Hefer did not always enjoy so much power as he wielded in the HOP and in the World Anti-Communist League. In the spring of 1941, he had played a subservient role to another Croatian, Ante Pavelic.

The two men had had much in common. Both had been lawyers, both were middle-aged Roman Catholics, both had been members of parliament, and both were officials of a terrorist group called Ustasha (roughly translated "to rise" or "to awaken"). Both men participated in the genocide of their countrymen, in murders carried out with sadism that would shock even their Nazi allies. Ante Pavelic, as *poglavnik* (Führer) of the nation of Croatia, and Stejpan Hefer, as governor-general of Baranja County, assured their places in history atop the mutilated bodies of nearly a million victims. (After the war, the similarity of their lives would continue, for both would escape to Argentina to resurrect their movement in exile.)

The nation of Yugoslavia in the 1920s was an amalgam of six republics, with four main languages, a half-dozen distinct ethnic groups, and three religions. In the complex maze of Balkan politics of the time, this made the country unusually easy prey: Yugoslavia's neighbors could always find one group or another to work toward the dissolution of the nation. A favorite such group were the ultranationalistic Croatians.

Croatia, a large area in northern Yugoslavia, has never been a region of either distinct borders or homogeneous people. At the outset of World War II, Croatia had a population of about three million Catholic Croatians, nearly two million Serbs (most belonging to the Orthodox faith), a million Moslems, and about fifty thousand Jews. Nationalistic Croatian zealots were pounding home a doctrine of racism and historical revisionism to appeal to the suspicions and prejudices of the people and gain support. The extremists had a solution for the dilemma of the melting-pot nature of Croatia: the removal of non-Catholic, non-Croatian citizens either by deportation or liquidation. Ante Pavelic and his Ustasha movement were the voice for these fanatics.

In order to make Croatia racially and religiously pure, it was, of course, first necessary to destroy the Yugoslav state, and to this end Pavelic could depend on the help of foreigners. By 1929, when the government of King Alexander clamped down on the Croatian nationalists, Pavelic had his external contacts well in place. He simply led his Ustashi into training camps in Italy and Hungary; from these bases, they kept up a steady terror campaign against the Yugoslav government, which culminated in the assassination of King Alexander in Marseille in 1934, a killing that Pavelic personally supervised.

The Ustashi emulated Adolf Hitler and Benito Mussolini, cloaking themselves in the physical trappings of fascism and adopting the upraised arm salute and the goose-step march. Under Italian supervision, wearing the black uniforms of the Italian fascist militia, the Croatians prepared for guerrilla operations and the "liberation" of their homeland.

That opportunity came in March 1941, when the Yugoslav people rebelled after the government signed an accord with Hitler.

"It is especially important," Hitler demanded as the Germans prepared to invade, "that the blow against Yugoslavia be carried out with inexorable severity."

A Ustasha unit entered Zagreb, the Croatian capital, with the German army on April 10 and declared the independent nation of Croatia in the name of Ante Pavelic. Decamping from Mussolini's Italy, Pavelic and his followers, carrying Italian rifles, arrived in Zagreb. A thug and a sadist, Pavelic was not about to show himself to be an unreliable ally of the Nazis and immediately set about purifying the new Croatian nation. The new governor-general of the Veliki Zupan (county) of Baranja, Stejpan Hefer, would prove himself to be the model of a fascist bureaucrat, so endearing himself to the *poglavnik* that their partnership would last until 1959. Hefer zealously put the Ustasha creed to practice in Baranja.

> The principles of the Ustashi were officially declared to be "the actual needs of the Croatian people." In theory, this meant "the virtues of ancient heroism and courage." . . . In practice, it meant that the slaughter of Serbs and the deportation of Jews to the Nazi SS was official state policy, carried out by vigilante bands of Croatian terror squads who traveled the hills and valleys in search of families.[21]

The Ustashi did not dispatch their victims with the clinical efficiency of their German masters. Rather, they derived pleasure from torturing before killing. Most of their victims were not shot but were strangled, drowned, burned, or stabbed to death. Serbs were herded into Orthodox churches by Ustashi who then barred the doors and torched the timbers. One captured photograph shows Ustashi smiling for the camera before a table displaying the body of a Serbian businessman whom they had castrated, disemboweled, carved with knives, and burned beyond recognition.

"The massacres began in earnest at the end of June [1941]," wrote Fitzroy Maclean, Britain's military liaison to the anti-Ustasha partisans, "and continued throughout the summer, growing in scope and intensity until in August the terror reached its height. The whole of Bosnia ran with blood. Bands of Ustase roamed the countryside with knives, bludgeons and machine guns, slaughtering Serbian men, women and little children, desecrating Serbian churches, murdering Serbian priests, laying waste Serbian villages, torturing, raping, burning, drowning. Killing became a cult, an obsession."[22]

The Ustashi competed among themselves on how many of "the enemy" they could kill. In order to impress the *poglavnik*—Pavelic—and be promoted or singled out for "heroism," the bands would pose with their victims before cameras. Captured photographs—they are too grisly to reproduce—show Ustashi beheading a Serb with an axe, driving a saw through the neck of another, carrying a head through the streets of Zagreb. In all of them, the Ustashi are smiling and crowding themselves into the picture, as if to prove they had a role in the atrocity. "Some Ustase collected the eyes of Serbs they had killed, sending them, when they had enough, to the Poglavnik for his inspection or proudly displaying them and other human organs in the cafes of Zagreb."[23]

Eventually, the obscenities that the Ustashi reveled in committing were too much even for some of the Germans and the Catholic clergy who had initially backed them.[24] The Nazis went so far as to intervene and disband one Ustasha regiment in 1942 in reaction to the atrocities it had perpetrated. Italian troops stationed in the coastal areas Mussolini had annexed hid Jews and Serbs and refused entry to Ustasha bands, declaring that to do otherwise was "incompatible with the honor of the Italian Army."

But as governor-general of Baranja County, Hefer was able to fulfill his duty. "In this capacity he issued orders for the mass deportation of the Serbian and Jewish population of the area concerned particularly in the Podrevska Slatina district. These people were taken by Ustashi men to different concentration camps and partly driven out into Serbia. Most of those held in camps perished. . . . In the Slatina district alone 35 Serbian families were so depossessed. Besides these there were driven from their homes all Jewish families and they were sent to many camps; any further traces of them disappeared in the Auschwitz butchery."[25]

Although it could be said that Hefer had an easier time than other Ustasha governor-generals since the terrain of Baranja County is flat and agricultural and hence afforded few hiding places for the hunted Serbs and Jews, he was promoted in 1944 to minister of food for his exemplary record and transferred to Zagreb. He remained there until the government collapsed before the advancing Soviets in 1945. Then he joined Pavelic in the Ustasha exodus to Austria, where both would slip away and keep the fires of Ustasha burning in exile.

THREE

Our organization was never a study group, and it will never
be one. ABN is an organization of fighters in the first place.
Into it should come only people of courage, men dedicated to
the liberation of their countries, and ready for sacrifice. We
have no time and no room for orators. ABN is for action.

> Dr. C. J. Untaru,
> ABN official,
> London, 1968

THE IRON GUARD, OUN, and Ustasha movements did not ex-
pire in the ashes of the Third Reich. The refugee relief offices of the
Vatican Church provided them with new passports and false iden-
tities and protected them until they could be secreted out of Rome.
American and British intelligence agencies recruited hundreds of them
to work in their propaganda and spying missions directed at Soviet-
controlled Eastern Europe, then smuggled them out through "rat
lines" in Trieste and Genoa.[1]

In contrast to many of the German Nazis who escaped, the Romanian, Ukrainian, and Croatian fascists did not "disappear" to end
their days quietly. In exile in South America, Western Europe, Canada, and the United States, they rebuilt their networks and kept alive
their ideology, their hatred of the Jews, and their cries for a New
Order. They formed front organizations with benign-sounding names
and attended international forums where they orated on the necessity
of combating communism. They rose to positions of prominence

within emigré communities and in political groups in their adopted countries. In the United States, they became Republican and Democratic Party officials, attended receptions in the White House, and met with presidents, vice-presidents, congressmen, and senators. United under the banner of the Anti-Bolshevik Bloc of Nations, they helped found the World Anti-Communist League.

After the war, the Legionnaires of the Archangel Michael melted away, concealing their identity in the chaos of postwar Europe. Most of those who were trapped in Romania by the approaching Soviet army or who were repatriated after the war were executed by the new communist regime. Some escaped to South America. Others remained in displaced persons (DP) camps in Western Europe until they were processed and deemed innocent of war crimes and fascist involvement; they were then allowed to emigrate to countries where they had relatives or sponsors. A large number of them came to Canada and the United States, often under the aegis of the Romanian Orthodox Church.

Horia Sima, the man most responsible for the massacres of 1940 and 1941, slipped across the Austrian border into Germany in May 1945.

> In October 1945, we came out of hiding, thinking that we were the only survivors. We thought that the other Legionnaires had been captured by the Allies and handed over to the Soviets, as had happened to other groups of refugees. We discovered that they were not only free but that they had regrouped and organized committees to help the refugees in all the occupied zones.
>
> This exception was granted to the Iron Guard because we had been subjected to German concentration camps. It is true that we formed a government in Vienna and that we fought on the German side to the end. However, the Allies took into consideration the fact that we had no authority over any territory, that we had not participated in the declaration of war and that we had not committed any crimes against humanity.[2]

The Iron Guard leader eventually landed in an Italian DP camp, where he avoided detection by assuming the name "Crivat" until he was able to secure his escape. Taking on yet another identity, he entered France before finally fleeing to Spain, where he lives today.

By his own account, Chirila Ciuntu's escape was not as dramatic.

At the end of the war, he worked for a farmer in Germany, then as a painter in France, until sailing to Argentina. There he found two benefactors, a doctor "who had a good friend at the Canadian Embassy" and a priest in the Romanian Orthodox Church in Canada. Under their patronage, Ciuntu emigrated to Canada. Still wanted in Romania for war crimes, he went to work in the steel mills and slipped into the emigré community of Windsor. It ended his flight, but not his mission, for in North America he was reunited with Viorel Trifa.

Trifa, who had exhorted the Legionnaires to war against "the kikes" in the name of National Socialism, escaped to Italy in 1945. There he taught at a missionary college for five years before emigrating to the United States. In 1952, he was named bishop of the Romanian Orthodox Episcopate of America. Three years later, he led the opening prayer for the United States Senate, the invitation extended by Vice-President Richard Nixon.

By then, Trifa was using the Romanian Orthodox Church to keep the Iron Guard movement alive in parishes throughout the United States and Canada. Under the auspices of the World Church Service, according to a 1972 official Church publication, "the Episcopate inaugurated a program of theological training in this country and of recruiting parish priests from among Romanian Orthodox priests who left Romania after World War II due to the communist takeover in Romania. Most of the priests who took refuge in Europe or on the American continent were given a chance to serve under the jurisdiction of the Episcopate."

Those recruited were often not priests but Iron Guard killers. At least seventeen of the forty-six priests listed in the publication have been linked to the Iron Guard by Holocaust researchers. By the 1970s, those that had skinned children alive in 1941 could be found throughout the United States and Canada on pulpits, clad this time not in green shirts but in priests' robes. Churches regularly held masses in memory of fallen Legionnaires, altars were adorned with Legion flags, and the fascist salute was exchanged.

As the spiritual leader, Trifa oversaw a complex and multifaceted fascist network in the United States. The Iron Guard was resurrected not only through the Church but also through various front groups, newspapers, and periodicals.[3]

Ultimately, Trifa's past caught up with him. Almost solely due to the efforts of Dr. Charles Kremer, a Romanian Jew whose family had been annihilated by the Iron Guard, Trifa was stripped of his citizenship after years of court cases and was deported to Portugal in 1984. Even then, his "spiritual children" did not abandon him.

> Your Eminence,
> When you came:
> We were few; but with your help we are now many. . . .
> We were divided; you leave us united. . . .
> We were weak in our faith; you made us strong. . . .
> We were unaware of our heritage; now we are proud of our origin.[4]

The political arm of the Iron Guard is still directed by Horia Sima in Madrid. Over the years, he has published several books, which carefully avoid discussion of Legionary atrocities or blame them on *agents provocateurs*. Not wishing to dwell on the past, Sima's Iron Guard has joined the global anti-communist movement and has achieved legitimacy through its international affiliations, including the World Anti-Communist League.[5]

Chirila Ciuntu, a Romanian delegate to World Anti-Communist League conferences, remains an active Guardist. According to Howard Blum in his book *Wanted!*, Ciuntu is "the most important figure in the resurrection of the Iron Guard in America. As treasurer of the American legionnaires, he collects the contributions from the American nests and personally delivers these monies to Sima in Spain. . . . 'What do I do in Spain? I buy books, anti-Communist books. We find that Jews are Communists. We find that everywhere we live the Jews are trouble.' "[6] Through this husky retired steelworker, the Legionnaires of "Captain" Codreanu, the assassins of at least three Romanian prime ministers, the killers of at least a thousand of their countrymen, the men who urged "Romanization" through the eradication of Jews and Freemasons, have formed a liaison with their compatriots around the world.

With the collapse of Nazi Germany, hundreds of thousands of Ukrainians found themselves in displaced persons camps at the end of the war. Among them were thousands of Nazi collaborators, including Stetsko and his followers. Although the camps were searched for possible war criminals, the Ukrainians had little to fear, for one of their last missions before fleeing the Soviet onslaught had been to gather up every stamp, seal, and letterhead that might prove helpful in exile. In safehouses, they forged passports, produced bogus seminary records, and even made up fake Nazi hit lists of Ukrainians slated for execution for anti-fascist activities. Those on the lists, of course, were the Ukrainians who had been steadfastly loyal to their German masters. With such documents in hand, the collaborators simply headed west into the displaced persons camps administered by the British or the Americans.

In the camps, the Bandera-Stetsko Ukrainians, with their secret police still intact, continued the pogroms that they had initiated in the Ukraine. Rival nationalists, Jews, even fellow collaborators—anyone who had evidence or firsthand knowledge of the genocide in the Ukraine and who could not be counted on to keep silent—were murdered. As a result of these purges, the OUN emerged as the "voice" of Ukrainian emigrés.[7]

Most importantly, the Bandera-Stetsko forces were aided by their British and American captors, who recruited hundreds to conduct espionage activities against the Soviet Union. An American reporter who toured the camps in 1948 discovered that the Counter-Intelligence Corps "concerns itself almost wholly with anti-Soviet intelligence. This work has led it into liaison activity with the present Nazi underground, so its interest in apprehending former allies of the Third Reich has dwindled."[8]

Harry Rositzke, a former high-ranking CIA official, refers to this policy in oblique fashion in his book, *The CIA's Secret Operations*:

> Agent candidates were recruited from displaced persons camps in Germany, from among recent Soviet military defectors in Europe, Turkey, Iran and South Korea, and through the auspices of various emigre groups. Military defectors and men sponsored by an emigre group were carefully interrogated and assessed by their prospective case officers. Our spotters in the DP camps helped interview recent refugees and brought likely candidates to our notice.

What Mr. Rositzke did not know, or is not admitting, is that among these candidates were a good many Nazi collaborators and men wanted for war crimes. The emigré groups he refers to were usually ones like the OUN. The American officials involved with the OUN recruitment program revised the group's history, stating that they had "fought bitterly against the Germans." It is a claim embraced today by Stetsko but contested by most experts.[9] Among them is John Loftus, author of *The Belarus Secret,* who spent two years as an investigator for the Nazi-hunting Office of Special Investigations in the Justice Department:

> This [revision] was a complete fabrication. The secret internal files of the OUN clearly show how most of its members worked for the Gestapo or SS as policemen, executioners, partisan hunters and municipal officials. The OUN contribution to the German war effort was significant, including the raising of volunteers for several SS divisions.[10]

With such prominent benefactors, many Eastern European Nazi collaborators not only ensured that their war crimes would go unpunished, but were also able to reorganize. With American government funds, the OUN formed a regional anti-communist federation, the Anti-Bolshevik Bloc of Nations (ABN), which, according to a former high ABN official, also received funding from Great Britain and "substantial" assistance from the postwar West German government.

Much has been written about different Nazi networks—ODESSA, Kamaraden-werk, etc.—that were created after the war to enable war criminals to escape and work in exile toward the formation of a Fourth Reich. No other organization, however, approaches the scope, depth, or influence of the Anti-Bolshevik Bloc of Nations. Since its inception, it has grown to become the largest and most important umbrella for Nazi collaborators in the world. The organizer and chairman of this "ex-Nazi International" is none other than Yaroslav Stetsko.

Though still largely controlled by the Ukrainians under Stetsko, the ABN now has chapters from other Soviet republics as well and from all of the Eastern European countries under Soviet control. A prime criterion for membership appears to be fealty to the cause of National Socialism; ABN officers constitute a virtual *Who's Who* of those responsible for the massacre of millions of civilians in the bloodiest war in history.

After Stetsko, the most important official of the Bloc in the 1940s was the chairman of its council of nations, Alfred Berzins. Described by Stetsko as "also a former prisoner of Nazi concentration camps," Berzins was in reality a Latvian who volunteered to serve in a Nazi-sponsored police battalion responsible for the roundup and extermination of his nation's Jews and Communist Party members. In February 1942, he joined the Latvian SS and was awarded the German Iron Cross, First Grade. In exile, he was secretary of the Central Committee of the Dangavas Vanagi ("Danaga Hawks"), an organization composed of the Latvian SS officers and government ministers who oversaw the Final Solution in their country. Until his death, he lived under his own name in Hampton Roads, Virginia.

As chairman of the ABN Central Committee in the 1950s—a position he continues to hold—Stetsko overcame nationalistic differences and embraced fascists from all regions. Today, Byelorussian, Hungarian, Bulgarian, Romanian, and Croatian Nazi collaborators, to name but a few, are all represented in the ABN. The Croatian delegation is made up of Ustashi from the Croatian Liberation Movement of Pavelic and Hefer. The Bulgarian chapter is the Bulgarian National Front Inc., the front group for the fascist Bulgarian Legionnaries of World War II. The Romanian delegation is composed of Iron Guardists.

The bloc has not even taken the basic step of drawing some of its officers from younger, untainted members. On a 1980 list of its central committee members, the overall leaders of its various activities, at least seven of the eleven listed are accused of being war criminals.

Through its headquarters in Munich and its main branch in New York, the ABN has gone a long way toward promoting a version of modern history that bears no resemblance to fact. All mentions of the various members' services to the Nazis have been purged in favor of laudatory passages about the great sacrifices they endured in their struggle for world freedom and independence.

Despite its origins and membership, the ABN does not meet in secret covens in mountain hideaways. It is an extremely visible international network that publishes magazines, holds demonstrations, and lobbies elected officials in the United States and Western Europe. It has branches in England, the Netherlands, Belgium, Canada, Spain, Italy, and Argentina. It created the European Freedom Council, whose Western European members consist of prominent conservatives, as well as the requisite Nazi collaborators. Chapters of American Friends of the ABN have been established in cities throughout the United States, including Detroit, Chicago, Los Angeles, Cleveland, and

Miami. Its officers meet with congressmen and senators to solicit support, and both Democratic and Republican officials have been honored guests at its functions. Serving on its honorary committees have been high-ranking former military officers, including General Daniel O. Graham (former director of the Defense Intelligence Agency), General Bruce Holloway (former commander in chief of the Strategic Air Command), and General Sir Walter Walker (former British commander in chief of Allied Forces–North).

An examination of one ABN chapter's activities in one year alone illustrates the degree of access to elected officials that they have attained. In September 1981, the Chicago chapter of American Friends of the ABN elected new officers. Among those elected were John Kosiak, a Byelorussian Nazi collaborator; Romanian Iron Guardist Alexander Ronnett; Anton Bonifacic, a former official in the Croatian Ustasha foreign ministry; and George Paprikoff, who had belonged to the pro-Nazi Bulgarian Legionary movement. The following month, they accompanied the visiting Yaroslav Stetsko as he addressed a joint session of the Illinois state congress and had a private audience with Governor Jim Thompson. In June 1982, several members went to Washington, where "they were briefed by CIA and FBI officials, Secretary of the Department of Interior James Watt, Chairman of the Board of Governors of the Federal Reserve System, and Secretary of the Department of Commerce Malcolm Baldridge, as well as have had [sic] an opportunity to privately converse with Senators Charles H. Percy and Alan J. Dixon and Congressman Henry J. Hyde."[11]

Today, in Ronald Reagan, the ABN has found the closest thing ever to a White House ally. On July 13, 1983, Yaroslav Stetsko, a man who went to prison for participating in the murder of Polish officials, who once proclaimed his devotion to the Nazis, whose followers assisted in the slaughter of Jews in the Ukraine, sat in the center of the front row of a reception hall to hear Reagan announce, "Your dream is our dream. Your hope is our hope." Afterward, he shook the president's hand and posed for photographs.

"Whatever we may think of Reagan," Roman Zwaryz, an ABN official, told a reporter in 1984, "the Captive Nations Week ceremonies during the Reagan Administration have been at least an indicator of a basic, fundamental shift in American foreign policy and it has led to certain tactical changes that have benefited us. For the first time in twenty, twenty-five years, we are being consulted as to the content of [Radio Liberty] broadcasts being sent into the Ukraine. Prior to the Reagan Presidency, no one in the foreign policy elite in the U.S. saw it even necessary to contact us."

The effect of those consultations could be seen in 1985; at the beginning of Reagan's second term in office, congressional investigators found that Radio Liberty and Radio Free Europe were broadcasting "unacceptable material . . . characterized as anti-Semitic, anti-Catholic or even anti-Western" into the Soviet bloc. Among the offending broadcasts was "a positive description of the Nazi unit Galizien [Galician SS], which was responsible for allowing Ukrainians to murder thousands of Jews in Lvov."[12]

> From the forests of Zhytomyr to Washington DC, from the journal, *Our Front* in 1940 to the White House, from the OUN Manifesto of 1940, the political basis of the ABN, to this year's grand commemoration of the ABN's fortieth anniversary, to the raising of the ABN emblem in the hallowed halls of Congress, in this citadel of freedom . . . the road has been hard and difficult. . . . We were able to traverse the hard and bitter road from the forests of Zhytomyr to the White House only with your continuous support!—ABN Central Committee, 1983[13]

Perhaps no other European fascist group escaped quite as intact as the Croatian Ustasha. Although thousands of lesser officials and soldiers were captured by either the Soviet army or Tito's partisans (and almost always summarily executed), virtually the entire leadership escaped.

Responsible for the slaughter of a million of their countrymen, the Ustashi were able to elude justice through a combination of Allied incompetence, Vatican complicity, the chaos of postwar Europe, the mutual suspicions of the United States and the Soviet Union, the generous assistance of the Argentine and Spanish governments, and the solidarity of Croatian emigrés in every part of the world.

Thousands of Ustashi retreated with the German troops in May 1945 and attempted to surrender to British forces at the Austrian border.[14] When the British refused them entry, the Ustashi improvised. Ante Pavelic clipped his recognizable bushy eyebrows, donned a beard, and, with an Argentine passport, slipped into Austria under the name "Ramirez." He hid in the Convent of St. Gilgin until picked up by British occupation forces. He was released and surfaced two years later in Italy dressed as a priest and secreted in another convent. It is believed that from there, with a new Argentine passport under the name "Pablo Aranyos," he sailed to Buenos Aires in 1948.

Stejpan Hefer also escaped into Austria. He was there on August 19, 1946, when the Yugoslav government filed documents asking for his return to Yugoslavia to stand trial for war crimes. The American and British authorities were apparently unable to locate the former governor-general among those in the displaced persons camps, for he surfaced a year later in Italy. From there he sailed to join his *poglavnik* in Argentina.

Hefer was helped out of Europe by the most important Croatian escape route, which operated out of the Instituto di Santa Jeronimus (Institute of St. Jerome) at 132 Tomaselli Street in Rome. This Catholic foundation, run by Fathers Draganovic and Levasic, facilitated the escape of thousands of Ustashi to South America.

"The organization [St. Jerome]," U.S. State Department agent Vincent La Vista reported in 1947, "provides free food, board and eventually clothing to its members. It would appear that necessary sums come from Vatican circles, who had previously actively supported this organization in 1923–1941. Membership of Ustascha and Catholic religion are compulsory for help and assistance in leaving Italy."[15]

The Institute provided passports for fugitive Ustashi through two sympathetic officials in the foreigner's police branch of the Italian government. Once the passports were signed by the Italian officials, Father Levasic would deliver them to the Argentine consulate, where immigration permits were quickly issued. Shipping space was then arranged for the next available space on a ship bound for Argentina. In Buenos Aires, the refugees could receive assistance from a group of exiled Croatian Catholic monks. In this way, as many as five hundred Ustashi a month were able to slip away.[16]

Besides whatever aid they may have received from sympathetic priests or fellow fascists, the Ustashi were also greatly assisted in their escape by the simple fact that no one was really looking for them. In 1948, the undersecretary of state for foreign affairs of Great Britain announced that, in spite of the fact that Yugoslavia had petitioned for the extradition of eighteen hundred Ustashi to stand trial for war crimes, the British government would assist in the cases of only nineteen, "who rendered such signal service to the enemy that it would be difficult if not impossible for us to justify a refusal to consider surrendering them."

Among those select nineteen was Pavelic, whom the British had previously captured and released. As for the others who were wanted for war crimes, including Stejpan Hefer, "we propose to take no further action and we will not now accept any fresh requests for surrender. We feel that it is time for this matter to be brought to an end."[17]

Portraying themselves as victims of communist persecution whose only "crimes" were to be Croatian patriots, the Ustashi quickly set up front groups in their exile communities. In 1956, Pavelic founded the Croatian Liberation Movement (HOP), with its headquarters and its supreme council in Buenos Aires. Stejpan Hefer, the loyal hench-man, was named to the supreme council.

In exile, Hefer made no attempt to hide his allegiance to the Us-tasha cause or his bitterness at the United States and Great Britain for having failed to accept the Croatians as allies: "The great Western powers preferred to fight against the idea of nationalism because of their own selfish reasons. . . . The Western democratic powers also accepted the propaganda of Tito and the Yugoslav Communists and proclaimed Croatian nationalism and Croatian revolutionary struggle for freedom . . . under the leadership of the Croatian USTASHA Movement as *nazi-fascism*."[18]

After rival Croatians attempted to assassinate Pavelic the follow-ing year, the *poglavnik* sought refuge in Spain. He lived quietly and reclusively in Madrid until his death from natural causes in December 1959. He is buried in a secret cemetery outside Madrid.

On Pavelic's death, the leadership of the HOP passed to Stejpan Hefer. Other factions appeared, each claiming to be the true inheritor of the Ustasha creed; some were more than willing to display their adherence to Pavelic's teachings by acts of terror. One, the Croatian Revolutionary Brotherhood, a hit squad formed in Australia in 1961, is composed mainly of second-generation Croatians who have main-tained close ties with the old Ustasha network.

The brotherhood has been responsible for much of the "secret war" waged against the Yugoslavian government during the past fifteen years, including the bombing of a Yugoslav passenger plane in 1972 that killed twenty-seven people and the 1976 hijacking of a TWA plane in New York that resulted in the death of a New York City policeman. And, like their older compatriots, the new generation of Ustasha has shown itself to be willing to rely on the help of sympathetic third parties.

Two Croatian terrorists, assisted by five conspirators on the outside, entered the Yugoslav Embassy in Stockholm in April 1971. Their target was Vladimir Rolovic, the Yugoslav ambassador and the man who two years earlier had given the Australian government a report on Croatian terrorist activities originating there. For exposing their operations, Rolovic's punishment was death. After binding and taunting the ambassador, the Croatians killed him, instantly becoming *causes célèbres* in Croatian emigré circles around the world.

In reaction to their subsequent life sentences, three other Croatians hijacked a Swedish plane in September 1972, demanding the release of their seven comrades. The Swedes released them and all except one, who refused to leave the Swedish prison, were then given asylum in Spain. They contacted the vacationing Paraguayan president, General Alfredo Stroessner, in West Germany in 1973.

Stroessner, moved by their plight, agreed to take them in; seasoned "anti-communist freedom fighters" were hard to come by. The Paraguayan president immediately put them to work training his country's army and police. One, Jozo Damjanovic, would later kill the Uruguayan ambassador to Paraguay (mistaking him for the new Yugoslav ambassador), while another, Miro Baresic, would be discovered serving as a bodyguard at the Paraguayan Embassy in Washington and be deported back to Sweden.

The leader of the Croatian killers was Dinko Sakic of the Ustashi. Sakic is wanted both for his World War II war crimes as a concentration camp commandant and for his role as Pavelic's chief of cabinet. He is accused by the Yugoslav government of coordinating much of the anti-Yugoslav reign of terror in the 1970s. In 1979, he attended the World Anti-Communist League conference in Paraguay.

The Ustashi and their progeny have sought to keep themselves in fighting form for the day when they will "liberate" Croatia. Croatians were recruited as mercenaries by Rafael Trujillo in 1959 for help in putting down the rebellion against his savage rule of the Dominican Republic. In the 1960s, Croatian mercenaries fought in the Congo, and Croatian exiles in Australia reportedly offered that

42

government a thousand men to help out in the Vietnam war. In 1972, in a mission dubbed Operation Phoenix, twenty Croatian nationalists slipped into Yugoslavia on a combat mission, only to be wiped out by the Yugoslavian army.

The Ustashi continue to have a great deal of strength within Croatian emigré communities throughout the world, including in the United States. They now portray themselves as "democrats," "in harmony with the American tradition of freedom and independence." But such Croatian newspapers as *Danica* and *Nasa Nada,* the latter the official newspaper of the Croatian Catholic Union of the United States, continue to pay reverence to their fallen *poglavnik* and his Ustasha cause.[19]

The Ustashi have managed to get their voices and demands heard not only through acts of terrorism but also through the forum of international organizations like the World Anti-Communist League. After the death of Hefer in 1973, his place as head of the Croatian chapter of the League was taken by Anton Bonifacic, another former Ustasha official, living in Chicago. As president of the fallen Pavelic's Croatian Liberation Movement, Bonifacic now represents Croatia at League conferences, giving speeches and passing resolutions on the continuing struggle for the independent state of Croatia, liberally rewriting history in doing so.

> Whereas . . . the Croatian Nation was subjected to the unprecedented genocide in which massacre about one million of Croatians were slaughtered by Communists or Serbs, who were opposed to the Croatian self-determination and national independence;
> Therefore, the 11th. conference of the WACL resolves . . . to declare that the Socialist Federal Republic of Yugoslavia, this artificial creation of Versailles et [sic] Yalta, should be substituted by free, independent and democratic states.[20]

Interestingly, Taiwan, the chief sponsor of the WACL, is one of only two nations in the world to recognize the Croatian Liberation Movement as a legitimate government-in-exile.

The extent to which the Ustashi have been able to influence world opinion and portray reports of their past crimes as nothing more than communist propaganda is perhaps best illustrated by the machinations over April 10, 1941.

April 10, 1941, was the day the Germans invaded Yugoslavia and established the Ustasha regime. Today, among both the old Ustashi and the new, April 10 is known as Croatian Independence Day; to Yugoslavians, especially Serbs and Jews, it is remembered as the day their Holocaust began. During his tenure as governor of California, Ronald Reagan passed a resolution recognizing the date as Independent Croatia Day as a favor to his Croatian constituents. He later rescinded the proclamation and apologized to the Yugoslav government when informed of the true significance of April 10.

A simple, if embarrassing, mistake; but others haven't picked up the cue. In a pamphlet put out by the National Republican Heritage Groups Council, a branch of the Republican Party, entitled "1984 Guide to Nationality Observances," there is this heading under April 10:

> *Croatian Independence Day*
> The Independent State of Croatia was declared by unanimous proclamation in 1941 thus ending an enforced union with Royalist Yugoslavia in which Croatian independence was subverted and threatened. Lack of Western support and Axis occupation forced the new state into an unfortunate association with the Axis powers.

The Ustasha historical revisionists could not have said it any better.

We have examined the history of three Nazi collaborators who belonged to the World Anti-Communist League. We did not have to cull membership lists or examine the backgrounds of all League members to find them; they were chosen virtually at random to serve as examples. They are not the three "bad apples" of the League; they are, in fact, in the company of many other war criminals, some of whom committed even worse crimes.

A frequent attendee of League conferences was a silver-haired elderly man named Dimitri Kasmowich. Kasmowich returned from exile to his native Byelorussia with the invading Germans in 1941. Designated police chief of Smolensk, he purged the area of Jews, partisans, and Communist Party members, destroying entire towns and villages to clear the path for the Nazis. As the war began turning against Germany, Kasmowich was sent to an SS commando training center in Germany; he returned to Byelorussia to lead a unit of Byelorussian Nazis of the Abwehr-sponsored "special intelligence operations" section in guerrilla warfare behind the Red Army front lines.

Escaping to Switzerland, Kasmowich later surfaced as a refugee rations officer for the United Nations Relief and Rehabilitation Agency (UNRRA) in France. In a displaced persons camp, he was recruited by British Intelligence and smuggled to England, where he lived under the name "Zarechny." Returning to Germany in the 1950s, he organized Byelorussian Nazi collaborators for the U.S. State Department's Office of Policy Coordination while working as an accountant for the U.S. Army. The result, the Byelorussian Liberation Movement, was designed to gather information and carry out intelligence missions for the Americans. Due to this high status within the Byelorussian emigré community, Kasmowich headed the Liberation Movement delegations to World Anti-Communist League conferences from 1966 until the late 1970s.

Today, the Byelorussian Liberation Movement is still the official Byelorussian League chapter. Leadership has passed on to John Kosiak; he too meets the requirements of a war criminal. Appointed an engineer in Byelorussia by the SS, Kosiak used slave labor to repair war-damaged factories, and he constructed the Jewish ghetto of Minsk. He lives in Chicago and has been active in Republican Party politics.

Theodore Oberlander, the German commander of the Ukrainian Nightingales, has continued his partnership with Yaroslav Stetsko through the World Anti-Communist League. A staunch Nazi, Oberlander joined the Nazi Party in 1933 and was made an honorary officer of the Nazi SD (Gestapo) in 1936. The Ukrainians accused of carrying out many of the purges in the Lvov area in June 1941 were under his command.

After the war, Oberlander became a member of the Bundestag, controversial for his habit of carrying a loaded gun onto the assembly floor. He served as West German minister of refugee affairs until 1960, when details of his wartime role became known and he was forced to resign. A year later, German prosecutors dropped the charges against him, citing "lack of evidence," and stating that they had heard testimony from at least 150 Soviet citizens attesting to his innocence. What was not said was that most of these character witnesses were Ukrainian Nazi collaborators and members of the OUN/B in exile.

In other words, Oberlander was cleared largely on the testimony of men who had served under his wartime command. Oberlander's special relationship with Stetsko—each knowing intimate details of the crimes of the other—continues today; Oberlander is a high officer of the ABN's European Freedom Council and leads German delegations to World Anti-Communist League conferences.

The presence of Nazi collaborators in the League, both individuals and entire organizations, is staggering.

St. C. de Berkelaar, who heads an organization in the Netherlands called Sint Martinsfonds, attended the 1978 League conference in Washington, D.C. Sint Martinsfonds is a brotherhood of three to four hundred former Dutch SS officers.

Ake Lindsten, chairman of the Swedish National League, headed the Swedish delegation to the League conference of 1979. Lindsten was a member of a Nazi youth group in his native country during World War II and has been censored by the Swedish government for his group's racist proclamations.

The Slovak World Congress, the Slovakian chapter of the League, is composed of Nazi collaborators and their progeny. They are represented in the League by Josef Mikus, who was an ambassador for the Nazi-puppet Slovak government in World War II.

The Latvian chapter of the League is controlled by the Danagaus Vanagi ("Danaga Hawks"). Operating out of Münster, West Germany, and publishing a newspaper in Canada, the Hawks are a band of Latvian leaders who assisted the Nazis in exterminating the Jews of their Baltic homeland.

If one wants to find Nazi collaborators, it is only necessary to examine the European chapters of the World Anti-Communist League.

With the creation of the World Anti-Communist League, there came into existence a worldwide network of fascism. Today, League conventions afford the opportunity for the old-guard war criminals to meet with, advise, and support the new-guard fascists. Thus today a man like Chirila Ciuntu, who helped slaughter "Communist-Jews" forty-five years ago, can sit down in the same room with an Italian fascist who killed "Reds" ten years ago and with a Salvadoran who is killing "subversives" now.

FOUR

The Taiwanese really insist on this "war of organizations."
If an infantry battalion isn't adequate to combat guerrillas,
let us design an organization that works.

> Roberto D'Aubuisson,
> death squad leader in
> El Salvador, 1983

*I*N THE 1960s, five Asians made major contributions to creating
and promoting a movement that would spread to nearly one hundred
nations on six continents. One was a ruthless dictator who had seen
his vast domain reduced to a tiny island through corruption and a
series of military blunders. Another was a former communist who
had saved his own life by turning in hundreds of his comrades for
execution. Two were gangsters; the fifth was an evangelist who
planned to take over the world through the doctrine of "Heavenly
Deception." They weren't what one would call a sterling assortment
of characters; four of the five had spent time in prison, two for war
crimes, one for anti-state activities, another on a morals charge. Yet
if it weren't for the collective efforts of Chiang Kai-shek, Park Chung
Hee, Ryoichi Sasakawa, Yoshio Kodama, and the Reverend Sun
Myung Moon, there probably would not be a World Anti-Communist League today.

The organization that Stetsko's Anti-Bolshevik Bloc of Nations
joined forces with in 1966 was dedicated to stemming the communist tide in Asia: the Asian People's Anti-Communist League

(APACL). Formed in 1954, the Asian League was dedicated to uniting conservatives from all over the continent to battle the "Red hordes" that threatened them all. When the ABN, the APACL, and other groups merged in 1966 to form the World Anti-Communist League, it did not mean the end of the Asian People's Anti-Communist League, but its stature was reduced to regional affiliate of the larger organization.

Although the Asian League was hailed in 1954 as a private formation of concerned citizens, parliamentarians, and clergy, it was actually a creation of South Korean intelligence agents and the Chinese government-in-exile of Generalissimo Chiang Kai-shek. In many respects, South Korea and Taiwan appeared to be natural allies. Chiang's Nationalists were isolated on the tiny island of Taiwan, or Formosa, and Korea was devastated and impoverished after the Korean War; both nations were desperately seeking anti-communist allies throughout the world. An organization in which conservative leaders from the United States and Europe could meet with their Asian counterparts seemed a good avenue for this.

Chiang Kai-shek had waged a bloody and cruel twenty-year war in China against the Mandarin warlords, the occupying Japanese, and the communists led by Mao Tse-tung. Chiang's rule was corrupt, inept, and impotent, perhaps best illustrated by the speed with which he lost mainland China to Mao after World War II. Even the American military officials who advised him during World War II had no faith in him or in his Kuomintang (KMT) political party. As early as 1943, General Joseph Stilwell had disgustedly called the Chiang Kai-shek rule "a one party government supported by a Gestapo."

Though the mainland was not completely conquered by Mao until 1949, Chiang had established his cronies on Formosa (named by the Portuguese, meaning "beautiful") four years earlier. The native Formosans chafed under the Kuomintang rule, which had quickly monopolized the island's economy and government. In 1947, the natives, ardently pro-American, rebelled against the "occupiers" and pushed for greater autonomy.

If the Formosans were hoping for moderation from the Kuomintang or assistance from the Americans, they were soon disillusioned. Generalissimo Chiang Kai-shek may not have been able to defeat the communists, but the unarmed Formosans were a different story; under the cover of darkness, he rushed some twelve thousand of his Nationalist soldiers to the island. The massacres that ensued were indiscriminate and vast in scale.

"From an upper window," George Kerr, a State Department official in Formosa, wrote, "we watched Nationalist soldiers in action in the alleys across the way. We saw Formosans bayoneted in the street without provocation. A man was robbed before our eyes—and then cut down and run through. Another ran into the street in pursuit of soldiers dragging a girl away from his house and we saw him, too, cut down.

"This sickening spectacle was only the smallest sample of the slaughter then taking place throughout the city."[1]

Dr. Ira Hirschy, the chief medical officer in Formosa for the United Nations Rehabilitation and Relief Agency, was also a witness to the killings:

> In the city of Pintung where the inauguration of the brief people's rule was marked by the playing of the Star Spangled Banner on phonographs, the entire group of about 45 Formosans who were carrying on various phases of local government were taken out to a nearby airfield from which, later, a series of shots were heard. A Formosan, who, representing the families of these people, went to the military commander to intercede for their lives, was taken to the public square and, after his wife and children had been called to witness the event, he was beheaded as an example to the rest of the people not to meddle in affairs which did not concern them.[2]

After the initial wave of killings, which claimed the lives of most of Formosa's prominent businessmen, intellectuals, and political leaders, the Nationalists turned their attention to the younger generation. "We saw students tied together," Kerr reported, "being driven to the execution grounds, usually along the river banks and ditches about Taipei [the capital]. . . . One foreigner counted more than thirty bodies—in student uniforms—lying along the roadside east of Taipei; they had had their noses and ears slit or hacked off, and many had been castrated. Two students were beheaded near my front gate."

The March 1947 massacre took an estimated twenty thousand lives; the fledgling Formosan independence movement had been crushed and the way was paved for Chiang Kai-shek and his soldiers retreating from the mainland to establish a government-in-exile. The atrocity also proved the efficacy of total and unconventional warfare, a mode of combat the Nationalists would later teach to other anti-communists, often through the auspices of the World Anti-Communist League.

By 1949, nearly a million Nationalists had flooded into Formosa. There they established the Republic of China and imposed a rigid dictatorship over the indigenous population, which outnumbered them fifteen to one. The Formosans, now called Taiwanese under Chiang's decree, were completely shut out of the governing process, which became the domain of the Kuomintang. Businesses and factories belonging to natives were taken away and given to Chiang's cronies. Taiwanese suspected of harboring communist sympathies or of opposing Chiang's rule (to the government, the two were virtually synonomous) were executed or exiled to the prison on Green Island on the slightest pretext; this effectively crushed any opposition that remained.

Contrary to popular belief, and contrary to the pronouncements of the Kuomintang, the United States did not immediately support the new government in Taiwan. Throughout all branches of the American government, including the military, there was widespread contempt for Chiang Kai-shek and revulsion at the atrocities of his soldiers. Lieutenant General Albert C. Wedemeyer, generally considered something of a rightist and certainly no friend of Mao's communists, wrote in 1949:

> The Central Government [the Kuomintang] lost a fine opportunity to indicate to the Chinese people and to the world at large its capability to provide honest and efficient administration. . . . [They] ruthlessly, corruptly and avariciously imposed their regime upon a happy and amenable population. The Army conducted themselves as conquerors. Secret police operated freely to intimidate and to facilitate exploitation by Central Government officials.[3]

The man who would make the new regime in Taiwan palatable to the Americans was General Douglas MacArthur. One day in July 1950, while he was commander in chief of the United Nations forces fighting in Korea, MacArthur breezed into Taipei, met with Chiang Kai-shek, and promised him, in contradiction to President Truman's policy, that American expertise and weapons would soon be flowing to the island bastion. Appearing before the Senate Committee on Foreign Relations, the general extolled the virtues of the Kuomintang government.

> I superficially went through Formosa. I was surprised by the content-ment I found there. I found that the people were enjoying a standard of living which was quite comparable to what it was before the war. . . . I found representative government being practiced. . . . I went into their courts. I found a judicial system which I thought was better than a great many of the other countries in Asia. I went into their schools. I found that their primary instruction was fully on a standard with what was prevalent in the Far East. . . . I found many things I could criticize too, but I believe sincerely that the standard of govern-ment that he [Chiang] is setting in Formosa compares favorably with many democracies in the world.[4]

That MacArthur had achieved such a firm grasp of the state of affairs in Taiwan during a single day's visit was not questioned by the American legislators. Indeed, his promises of American support were prophetic. As the Korean War turned against the United States, Chiang Kai-shek, with his dream of returning to the mainland and defeating the communists, was seen as a potential pressure point against Mao. With the rise of Senator Joseph McCarthy and his "exposing" of communist sympathizers in the federal government, American officials muted or stopped their criticism of Chiang's rule. Suddenly the Kuomintang was respectable, and American aid began to pour in. The American Military Assistance Advisory Group (MAAG) in Taiwan grew from a handful of advisers in 1951 to 2,300 five years later. Economic aid and war materiel flowed in at a rate that the island could not possibly absorb. By 1961, military expenditures, nearly all provided by the American government, were three-quarters of the national budget.

Throughout, Chiang Kai-shek performed his appointed role. Every October 10, he emerged onto a balcony in Taipei's main square and, before hundreds of thousands of soldiers, students, and workers standing at attention, proclaimed that the return to the mainland was imminent.

At the end of World War II, Korea was a divided and shattered nation. The Soviets had seized the industrialized northern half of

Korea and established a puppet state. The Americans, occupying the southern half, brought in Synghman Rhee, a right-wing strongman who hadn't lived in Korea for thirty-five years, to rule their sector. Since Rhee had no power base, the military and the government of South Korea were both filled largely with rightists who had fought on the side of the Japanese during the war and who could thus be trusted as anti-communists. One of these was Park Chung Hee. Although the Asian People's Anti-Communist League was established during Rhee's reign, it was Park who would make it an important instrument of South Korean foreign policy.

When the Asian People's Anti-Communist League was formed in 1954, Taiwan and South Korea had much in common. Korea had lost half its territory, the most economically advanced part, to the communists, while Chiang's Nationalists had seen over 99 percent of theirs slip away. Both were in the front lines of the Cold War, completely exposed to their implacable enemies: the Korean capital was twenty miles away from the armies of North Korea, and Taiwan was ninety miles across the China Sea from the colossus of Communist China. Both harbored dreams of reunification through the defeat of communism, both were ruled by military dictatorships that kept order through perpetual martial law, and both were indebted to the United States for their survival and prosperity.

The Asian People's Anti-Communist League was born out of the desire of these two nations to cement ties with potential friends in other parts of the world, as well as to justify their own dictatorships. Although the Asian League has expanded to include other Asian countries in the American sphere of influence, ultimate power has always remained with Korea and Taiwan; the chairmanship goes to Taipei and the secretariat is housed in Seoul. In the 1970s, when other countries criticized Korea's iron-fisted internal policies and dropped their recognition of Taiwan in favor of mainland China, the Asian League, as well as the World Anti-Communist League, became virtual foreign policy arms of these two countries desperate to make, or at least maintain, relations wherever and with whomever possible.

From the beginning, the task of forming and perpetuating the Asian People's Anti-Communist League was entrusted to Korean and Taiwanese intelligence agencies. The composition of their league delegations was largely drawn from the intelligence and military communities. For example, Ku Cheng-kang, president of the Taiwanese chapter and currently "honorary chairman-for-life," had been a member of Chiang Kai-shek's Supreme National Defense Council during World War II, minister of interior and of social affairs, national policy adviser, senior adviser to the president, and a member of the Central Standing Committee of the ruling Kuomintang. Armed with an impressive array of posts and honors, Ku was, technically at least, the fourth most important official in the KMT government. The Korean delegations, on the other hand, were composed mostly of active and retired army officers or, beginning in the 1960s, Korean CIA agents.

The Chinese Nationalists established branches of the Asian League in ethnic Chinese communities in the United States. Korean CIA agents fanned out throughout Asia and the United States making contacts and arranging delegations for conferences, usually paying for the visitors' expenses. It was Park Chung Hee, Synghman Rhee's successor in South Korea, who was most responsible for this campaign of expansion and quiet influence.

Park, a slight man by Korean standards, was a master in the game of political musical chairs; he nimbly leaped from the right to the left, in whatever direction was most advantageous to his pursuit of power. He had been not just a Japanese sympathizer during the war; he had been trained by them. He had graduated from their Manchukuo Military Academy in occupied Manchuria and fought with them in China. That background did not, however, deter him from secretly becoming a high official in the Communist Party of South Korea while he was teaching at a military academy in 1946. When he was arrested by the government in 1948 and sentenced to death, his future looked bleak; it was time for him to move back to the right. Park cut a deal with the Rhee government: Spare my life, and I'll tell you everything. "His actions resulted in the purge of hundreds of army officers and the death of many former friends."[5]

Park's treachery kept him alive to lead the coup thirteen years later that would propel him to power as the strongman of a right-wing, anti-communist military dictatorship. At three o'clock on the night of May 16, 1961, the Korean army fanned out through the streets of Seoul. By the end of the day, the officers had formed a Military Revolutionary Committee, dissolved the National Assembly, closed all schools and newspapers, imposed a dusk-to-dawn curfew, and declared martial law. Before the end of the year, they had created the Korean Central Intelligence Agency.*

While he was the unbridled ruler of South Korea, Park transformed the Asian League. He replaced the Korean chapter leaders: High-ranking generals, admirals, and personal advisers to the president began attending its conferences. Through the League, the new ruling elite of South Korea could meet, confer, and negotiate informally with influential military officers and parliamentarians from throughout the world. In time, both the Asian People's Anti-Communist League and the World Anti-Communist League became instruments of the Park government's campaign to gain influence in other countries through the bestowing of gifts, money, or favors. The eventual revelations of this campaign culminated in the 1976–78 Koreagate scandal in the United States.

Just how important a foreign policy instrument Park considered Korea's League chapter to be, especially when directed at the United States, is illustrated by the fact that it was an American professor, David Rowe, who rebuilt it for him. "With the financial support of an American foundation," Rowe wrote in 1970, "and on the invitation of a Korean who is still today probably the second most powerful man in Korea [an apparent reference to former KCIA director Kim Jong Pil], I spent the summer of 1965 in the Korean Chapter of the APACL. I worked to establish training organizations and procedures for the anti-Communist struggle in Korea. . . . I accomplished almost single-handed the following: the then-head of the Korean Chapter was sacked and a younger and highly capable man took the job, albeit only for a limited time. The organization was thoroughly cleansed of its left-oriented infiltrators. . . . When I finally got to the President of the Republic of Korea, and outlined the rotten state of affairs then current in the Chapter and told him what had to be done, I can simply state for the record that within six months every one of my specific recommendations for the Chapter had been put into effect."[6]

The Korean president who acted on Rowe's recommendations, Park Chung Hee, ruled South Korea with an iron fist until 1979.

---

*Despite the similarity of names, there is no evidence that the American CIA was involved in the creation of the Korean CIA in 1961. In fact, American authorities were reportedly angered by the South Korean government's adoption of the identical title.

One evening in October of that year he was dining at the Kungjong, a government restaurant, with the KCIA director, Kim Jae Kyu. Sitting on the floor in traditional Korean style, the two men began quarrelling over the repressive methods that had been used recently to silence the oppositon. The climax of this "accidental argument" came when Kim Jae Kyu produced a gun, aimed it at the president's head five feet away, and pulled the trigger. Kim put two bullets into Park, then gunned down five other occupants of the room. (How the KCIA director fired at least seven bullets from a six-chamber revolver is a ballistic mystery that Korean authorities have never fully explained.)

Park Chung Hee was dead, but by that time the League could survive without him.

Although the U.S. government has denied the authors access to the pertinent records, it appears clear that the United States was largely behind the formation of both the Asian People's and the World Anti-Communist Leagues. Because the United States propped up the regimes of Synghman Rhee and Chiang Kai-shek, these rulers naturally initiated programs and pursued policies that their American advisers favored. Conversely, they could not easily embark on a project that the United States did not desire. Given the political realities of the time, it would be hard to believe that the Leagues were established without American assistance; after all, their stated objectives— to actively fight communism—were very much in keeping with American foreign policy objectives.

It is equally doubtful that the Taiwanese and South Korean governments footed the bills for the Leagues. Taiwan was still woefully poor in the 1950s, while Korea, devastated by the Korean War, was suffering famine in some provinces. Without enough money to feed their own people, where did the money come from to launch an international organization? The obvious answer is that it came from the United States.

If this is so, the financial assistance program was not overt; no bill was ever introduced in Congress for U.S. funding of the Leagues. Former intelligence officers suggest that the funds most likely came out of money already designated for economic or military assistance, CIA discretionary funds, or U.S. Embassy Counterpart Funds, and that it was done not out of Korea but out of Taiwan.

Since the Chinese Nationalists were in no position to repay the American assistance in the 1950s, an arrangement was made whereby the United States was given "credits" in the Taiwanese currency (NT) for its debts. Using this method, the Taiwanese then embarked on various programs dictated by the Americans as a means to lower their debt. Thus the much-hailed Taiwanese missions to Africa to teach farmers better agricultural practices were actually an American program, paid for by Counterpart Funds in the American Embassy.

These funds were not just numbers in a ledger book. They were actual sacks of money that sat in a safe in the American Embassy in Taipei. From the little-scrutinized Counterpart Funds account may have come the initial financing for the Asian People's Anti-Communist League in 1954 and the preparatory meeting of the World Anti-Communist League in 1958.

The most likely American conduit for the latter operation was a flamboyant Harvard graduate named Ray Cline. Having served as an intelligence officer for the U.S. Navy and for the Office of Strategic Services (OSS) in Asia during World War II, Cline was CIA station chief in Taiwan from 1958 to 1962. As such he had access to the Counterpart Funds account at the time when the first preparatory meetings were being held toward the establishment of the World League.*

Whatever the validity of this theory, Cline continues to have a close relationship with the League. Not only has he attended several conferences, including those of 1980, 1983, and 1984, but he is also a close friend of retired Major General John Singlaub; their relationship dates back to the 1940s, when both served with the OSS in China. Singlaub is currently chairman of the World Anti-Communist League.

Cline has contributed to the flourishing of the international ultra-right in ways more verifiable than his possible early work with the League. Despite his local notoriety in Taiwan for having built the gaudiest home on the island (dubbed "the Pink Palace"), Cline developed a deep and lasting friendship there with a man named Chiang

---

*Cline went on to become deputy director of intelligence for the CIA and is now a senior associate of the Center for Strategic and International Studies at Georgetown University in Washington and president of the National Intelligence Study Center.

Ching-kuo, who at the time was head of the obscure Retired Ser-
viceman's Organization.

Cline's friend and hunting partner was not just a low-level Kuomintang bureaucrat, however; he was the son of Generalissimo Chiang
Kai-shek and heir-apparent to the Taiwan dictatorship. He had an intelligence background similar in some respects to Cline's, except that he
had the added advantage of having been trained by the enemy.

Chiang Ching-kuo had graduated from the Sun Yat-Sen University
in Moscow in 1927. Deemed a "revolutionary cadre" by his communist instructors, he was appointed as an alternate member of the
Communist Party. He had also attended the Whampoa Academy, a
Soviet-run school in China that instructed its pupils, both communist
and Nationalist, in the art of political warfare. The generalissimo's
son put his instruction to good use; by the time of his affiliation with
Cline, he had already been in control of the Kuomintang's secret
police (or "Gestapo," according to General Stilwell) for at least a
decade and had personally overseen purges in which dozens of
Kuomintang officers were executed. Throughout his subsequent rise
to the top, from defense minister to premier and, finally, to president,
Chiang Ching-kuo had a steadfast ally in Ray Cline.

In the late 1950s they joined forces to create an instrument of war
that continues to have a hidden impact on events throughout the
world: the Political Warfare Cadres Academy. Today, much of the
international recruitment for this academy is coordinated through the
World Anti-Communist League.

Although the regime describes political warfare as a system "to
remove obstacles to national unity within and to resist aggression
from without,"[7] political warfare is actually the ideological base that
the Kuomintang has used to maintain Taiwan as a police state and
to infiltrate, expose, and liquidate any opposition that may be suspected to exist at any level of society, even down to the family level.
Through the use of political warfare, armed with the fiat of permanent martial law, the Nationalists have built what is probably one
of the most pervasive internal security and spying networks in existence. Fully one-fifth of the population is believed to be involved
in this warfare, in activities ranging from lecturing soldiers and workers in political "correctness" to surveilling one's own children, parents, and neighbors for the authorities. The tool used to perpetuate

this system is the Political Warfare Cadres Academy, housed on a hillside in Peitou, just outside the capital.

Patterned after the Soviet model of political officers, commissars, and informants, the academy is the training ground for the General Political Warfare Department, a branch of the Ministry of National Defense. Its primary function, as with the Soviet model, is to ensure party (in this case, Kuomintang) control of the military through political indoctrination. Kuomintang cells, called "political departments" and composed of graduates of the academy, are established in every military unit down to company size. These political commissars watch over troops as well as the non-academy officers, test their political awareness, and submit regular status reports to the General Political Warfare Department on each person. "The surveillance or inspection function of the company political officer is by far his most ominous duty. Each member of the unit has the responsibility to report on dissidence and deviant political attitudes which may be observed on the part of his comrades."[8] The commissars' primary loyalty is not to the military but to the Party, and according to former American advisers in Taiwan, in disputes between army and political officers, the latter always win.

The General Political Warfare Department conducts a vast array of operations. It runs radio stations, publishing houses, and even movie studios. It also has counterintelligence units to locate subversives and psychological warfare units to supervise political warfare campaigns and promulgate propaganda, as well as civic affairs units for the purpose of infiltrating behind enemy lines during an invasion to generate support for the Kuomintang. All of these different units undergo training at the academy.

Although it was created in the early 1950s, the academy took on new importance when Chiang Ching-kuo became director of the General Political Warfare Department and reorganized it in 1959, a move facilitated by American assistance. In fact, American military personnel, drawn largely from the Military Assistance Advisory Group stationed in Taiwan, taught at the academy.

One Taiwanese, a former Kuomintang Party member now living in exile, was selected from his university class to attend a two-month training course at the academy. "We were taught that to defeat communism, we had to be cruel. We were told to watch our commander, that if he showed weakness or indecision in combat, we were to kill him. They also had us watch fellow classmates who, of course, were watching us."[9]

The cadres are also instructed in how to spot potential communist or pro-Taiwanese-independence sympathizers and how to open letters with a pencil so that their tampering is undetectable to the casual observer. As the students progress and win the trust of the teachers, they are advanced to classes in psychological warfare and techniques of interrogation.

In keeping with the department's campaign to "resist aggression from without," graduates of the academy have also been active away from the island. "The political warfare system was involved in a wide range of international operations: personnel security; investigations; censorship; agent infiltration; front organizations; suppression of Taiwanese independence groups; and exploitation of overseas Chinese communities. These activities were carried out by a wide variety of agencies but overall planning and control was theoretically the responsibility of 'the intelligence agency of the nation's highest military organization,' " the Political Warfare Department.[10]

The most convenient cover for this international campaign of "organizational warfare" was, of course, the same cause that had gained the Kuomintang recognition in the first place: anti-communism. For this program, the Asian People's Anti-Communist League and, later, the World Anti-Communist League, were perfect vehicles.

Eventually, the Nationalists expanded their political warfare campaign into another sector. As nations dropped their diplomatic recognition of Taiwan in favor of mainland China in the early 1970s, the Kuomintang looked to their few remaining friends as the last threads connecting the island to the rest of the world. To the right-wing dictatorships in South and Central America, which represented most of the few real allies they had left, the Taiwanese could offer something more than trade; they could also offer political warfare training at their academy in Peitou. The legacy of the training at the academy, which the Americans in general and Ray Cline in particular helped to establish, can be found today in the "unconventional warfare" employed throughout Latin America. This transfer of expertise is, in large part, conducted through the offices of the World Anti-Communist League.

In the 1950s and 1960s the Asian People's Anti-Communist League remained a rather home-grown affair. While the preponderance of Taiwanese and Korean military and intelligence officers within its ranks may have caused some to take pause, as well as its representation of some of the most severe governments in the world, it was hardly the well-financed, nation-linking organization of the extreme right that it is today. Although it was able to get conservative American congressmen and senators to attend its meetings, it remained a rather benign and regional "paper tiger."

Other Asian nations placed varying degrees of importance on the League. In the capitalist bastions of Asia—Hong Kong, Macao, Singapore—League delegations consisted mostly of conservative businessmen and bankers. In Thailand, the military was represented at the League by General Prapham Kulapichtir. The Philippines chapter was filled with cronies of dictator Ferdinand Marcos and those drawn from his rubber-stamp National Assembly. Australia was represented largely by conservative members of Parliament (in 1978 one called the "international ecology movement" a communist ruse), interspersed with neo-Nazis, racists, and Eastern European immigrants whose roots lay in the fascist collaborationist armies of World War II. In Southeast Asia, the chapters were headed by members of the ruling elite like Prince Sopasaino of the Laotian royal family, or by the military, like Colonel Do Dang Cong, a military aide to South Vietnamese President Nguyen Van Thieu.

Although the League began to come of age during Park Chung Hee's reign, a much bigger boost occurred later in the 1960s, when it tapped into three Asians with powerful political connections and a lot of money. The League's benefactors were two former Japanese war criminals who controlled Japan's underworld and a Korean evangelist who thought he was God.

FIVE

I am the world's wealthiest fascist.

Ryoichi Sasakawa

IN AUGUST 1945, thirteen Japanese fascists climbed to a hilltop above Tokyo. From the hill, they looked out at shimmering Tokyo Bay and saw the surrounding snowcapped mountains, the brilliant green of the rice paddies, and the tiny hamlets whose coal fires sent little black spumes into the blue sky. But the men hadn't come to admire the view. The empire they had spent their lives creating lay in ruins. Hiroshima and Nagasaki had been obliterated by atomic bombs. American troops were massed just over the horizon, ready to invade. The talk in Tokyo was of surrender. For the men on Atagoyama Hill, that would be the ultimate disgrace. Better to die than bear witness to the final humilation.

As thousands of their countrymen throughout Japan and on untold numbers of islands in the Pacific had already done, twelve of the men, members of the ultra-right Sonjo Doshikai ("Association for the Reverence of the Emperor and the Expulsion of the Barbarians") had come to the hill to commit suicide. The thirteenth member of their party was apparently there to dissuade them. It was to no avail; the men on Atagoyama held hand grenades to their stomachs and pulled the pins. Only one man, Yoshio Kodama, came down from the hill.

Kodama had a lot to live for. Thanks to the war and the patronage of a political leader, Ryoichi Sasakawa, he was sitting on a fortune of over $200 million. In the years ahead, he would help create the dominant political party of Japan, make and destroy prime ministers, fund the World Anti-Communist League, and be the principal figure in the greatest scandal in modern Japanese history. Working alongside him would be Sasakawa, his old mentor.

The lives of Kodama and Sasakawa, the pre-eminent fascist leaders in postwar Japan, are closely intertwined. Born in 1899, Ryoichi Sasakawa, the son of a small *sake* (rice whiskey) brewer, became a millionaire at thirty by speculating on rice futures. In 1931, he formed the Kokusui Taishuto, a militarist political movement and, according to a U.S. Counter-Intelligence Corps (CIC) report after World War II, was "one of the most active Fascist organizers prior to the war."

Yoshio Kodama started life more abjectly. An orphan who had survived by toiling in sweatshops, he found his calling among the various right-wing movements that sprouted up throughout Japan in the 1930s. Often these *yakuza* groups functioned more as criminal bands than as genuine ideological movements; modeling themselves after the legends of the samurai warriors, they displayed their allegiance to a particular leader by covering their bodies with tattoos; they repented errors by cutting off the tips of their little fingers. Bankrolled by conservative businessmen and politicians, these private *yakuza* armies broke up labor unions, "protected" factories and offices from vandalism, and assassinated opposition leaders. The young Kodama excelled at these activities and by the time he was fifteen was a terrorist leader in his own right. In 1931, he sent a dagger to a former Japanese minister of finance. "Allow me to present you with this instrument," the accompanying note read, "so appropriate for our troubled times. I leave you to make up your mind as to how to use it—to defend yourself, or to commit ritual suicide."[1]

The threat landed the twenty-year-old Kodama in jail, but it was not in vain; the day he was released, another *yakuza* succeeded in killing the former minister.

In the 1930s both of the future League benefactors ran afoul of the law and were imprisoned, Sasakawa for plotting the assassination of a former premier, Kodama for another murder plot, this time against the prime minister.

As the forces of fascism took over Japan and as the war in Manchuria got under way, the talents of men like Sasakawa and Kodama were suddenly needed. Both were released in order to further the cause of the empire—Kodama to carry out intelligence missions in China and Sasakawa to resurrect his Kokusui Taishuto movement, whose followers were now clad in blackshirts, the symbol of international fascism; they were to rally forces behind the government's plans to rule Asia. Sasakawa even flew to Rome for a personal audience with Mussolini, a man he would later describe as "the perfect fascist." In 1942 Sasakawa was elected to the Japanese Parliament (Diet) on the promise of expanding the war throughout Asia.

In the meantime, Kodama was making a name for himself in China. Entrusted with the task of keeping the Japanese navy supplied with raw materials, Kodama made a fortune of at least $200 million by seizing materiel, often at the point of a gun, and then selling it back to his own government at exorbitant prices.

At war's end, both men were sent to prison by the American Occupation Forces, classified as Class A war criminals. "Sasakawa," a CIC report concluded in 1946, "appears to be a man potentially dangerous to Japan's political future. . . . He has been squarely behind Japanese military aggression and anti-foreignism for more than twenty years. He is a man of wealth and not too scrupulous about its use. . . . He is not above wearing any new cloak that opportunism may offer."[2]

Yoshio Kodama was, in the eyes of the Americans, just as potentially dangerous: "His long and fanatic involvement in ultra-nationalistic activities, violence included, and his skill in appealing to youth make him a man who, if released from internment, would surely be a grave security risk. . . . Persistent rumors as to his black-market profits in his Shanghai period, plus his known opportunism, are forceful arguments that he would be as unscrupulous in trade as he was in ultra-nationalism."[3]

But just as they did with the Nazis in Europe, the American occupation authorities had a change of heart about Japan's war criminals. As the Cold War began, the enemy was no longer the fascists but the communists. In Japan, as for example in Italy, the political left emerged from the war as a major power bloc with the potential for becoming the dominant political force and even, it was feared by the Americans, for leading the nation into the Soviet camp. Sasakawa, Kodama, and other prominent Japanese war criminals were quietly released from prison in 1948 and became some of the prime movers, organizers, and funders of the Japanese Liberal Democratic Party, a conservative pro-American party that has controlled the political life of Japan ever since. Through this maneuver, the old ruling circles of Japan, the men who had allied with Nazi Germany and plunged their nation into a war of military imperialism throughout Asia, were resurrected and brought back into leadership roles.

Many observers feel that a deal was struck, in which the United States released the war criminals in return for use of their connections and money to undercut the growing left. There is some evidence of this change of heart in declassified American documents from the period. Frank O'Neill, an American lieutenant attached to the International Military Tribunal, concluded in 1946 that Kodama "committed numerous acts of violence in China in the acquisition by foul means or fair of commodities and goods [belonging to] the Chinese"; in 1948, the same Mr. O'Neill predicted that "ten years from today this man Kodama is going to be a great leader of Japan."[4]

Besides being two of the prime backers of the Liberal Democratic Party, Sasakawa and Kodama extended their influence to other fields. Sasakawa rebuilt his personal fortune through the establishment of the Japan Motorboat Racing Association* and maintained his contacts in the right-wing underworld through an organization called the National Council of Patriotic Organizations, or Zenai Kaigi. On the board with him were "several *yakuza* bosses and at least three right-wing terrorists convicted of the assassinations of Prime Ministers in the 1930's."[5]

Kodama, meanwhile, added to his wealth by becoming one of the supreme bosses of the Japanese underworld, mediating disputes between rival *yakuza* and receiving protection money from Japanese industry. He, too, had his own organization, the Sheishikai, nicknamed "Kodama's Club," which was composed almost entirely of underworld groups.

If the backgrounds of Sasakawa and Kodama are less than illus-

*Sasakawa got a bill passed through the Diet in 1959 establishing this monopoly with himself as head. The prime minister at the time was Kishi Nobosuke, another former Class A war criminal and Sasakawa's cellmate at Sugamo Prison. Kishi was the prime mover in the establishment of APACL–Japan and was active in the WACL throughout the 1960s, including serving as chairman of the planning committee in 1970.

trious, that of the Reverend Sun Myung Moon is downright bizarre. The son of middle-class parents from what is now North Korea, Moon's life took a dramatic turn when, walking through the hills around his village, he was visited by Jesus Christ. "You are the son I have been seeking," Christ informed the startled sixteen-year-old, "the one who can begin my eternal history."

Moon clearly took this sign from heaven to heart; today his Unification Church, operating under a bewildering maze of religious, cultural, political, and economic front groups, spreads the word and influence of the "Heavenly Father" on five continents.

Unification theology is a potpourri of Christianity, Confucianism, mysticism, patriotism, anti-communism, and Moon's own megalomania. In Moon's eyes, Christ technically falls into the category of a failure, for although he established a spiritual kingdom, he didn't establish a physical or political one. Moon is here to rectify that oversight; he is anointed as the man to complete Jesus' original mission.

Because it rejected Jesus, Israel is no longer God's chosen land (though the Jews were finally cleansed by suffering six million dead in World War II); God had to find a new Messiah and a new Adam country. Moon and Korea were uniquely designed for this purpose, for one of the most original aspects of Unificationism is its attribution of spirituality and gender to nations based upon their topography. "It [Korea] is a peninsula, physically resembling the male. . . . Japan is in the position of Eve. Being only an island country, it cannot be Adam. It yearns for male-like peninsular Korea on the mainland. . . . America is an archangel country. Its mother is England, another island country in the position of Eve."[6]

Today, Unification Church disciples, or "Moonies," are, according to former members, "love-bombed" upon induction, fed high-carbohydrate diets, and kept awake for long periods. These are basic forms of brainwashing designed to lower a person's resistance to coercion or suggestion. Initiates are kept under close surveillance, told to report their every action, even their dreams, to their leaders, and, when finally trusted, offered "redemption" by going out to raise funds for the Church. The fund-raisers, called "Mobile Teams," best known for relentlessly selling flowers, American flags, and magazines in airports, send to headquarters a payment of ten percent "for family support."

Virtually every action a Moonie makes is scrutinized, analyzed, and regulated. Moonies are constantly berated to save money, to tighten their belts, and to function on little food and sleep. "It's a sin to call long distance necessarily," Moon proclaimed in a confidential 1983 paper entitled "Instructions from Father." "When you are going to call, first, write down each point you wish to convey. Then, record the response. After you acknowledge the message, say good-bye and quickly hang up. I seldom call. If you misuse phone calls, you are commiting the crime of misusing your brother's blood."

Throughout Moonie indoctrination, the "Heavenly Father" holds himself up as an example to be emulated. "Initiate an austerity program," the instruction memo goes on. "In eating, be tasteful, not excessive. I never eat snacks. You don't need any snack. Also, we never eat as we walk. It's unhealthy. Divide the eating, walking and talking time. I abhor eating and walking at the same time. I never carry food in my pocket or buy chewing gum. . . . I'm not fat. I have a special muscle for speaking long periods of time."

Moon never would have developed that "special muscle" if it hadn't been for the intervention of the Korean CIA or the financial largesse of Japanese underworld bosses Sasakawa and Kodama.

After studying electrical engineering in Japan during World War II, Moon returned to Pyongyang (now the capital of North Korea) to found his first church. "It was no different from many other unorthodox Christian sects except for the ritual of 'blood separation,' involving female members of the Church. They were required to have sexual relations with Moon, to clear themselves of 'the taint of Satan.' "[7]

Moon was arrested by the communist authorities twice and in 1947 was sentenced to five years in Hungnam Prison. Although he maintains that this was just another example of communist persecution of religion, other sources, including former Korean government officials, say the charges were in response to the Church's reported orgiastic practices.

Eventually freed by United Nations troops in their advance north during the Korean War, Moon fled to Pusan, in South Korea. There he founded the Holy Spirit Association for the Unification of World Christianity or, simply, the Unification Church.

Moon's ministry found quite a few converts among the homeless and impoverished refugees who flooded Pusan, but the strange tenets he espoused were met with suspicion and hostility by both the rulers of South Korea and the established Catholic clergy. Moon could count among his disciples, however, a number of well-connected young army officers. When he was again arrested in 1955, this time on a morals charge for staying the night in a "love hotel" with a follower, Moon's military contacts managed to get the charge changed to violation of military conscription law and it was eventually dropped.

A major boon for Moon's Church came in 1962 when Kim Jong Pil, director of the newly formed Korean Central Intelligence Agency, went to the United States on an official visit. His interpreter was Kim Sang In, a Moon lieutenant. Coordinating his visit from the Korean Embassy in Washington was Colonel Bo Hi Pak, who is today Moon's chief aide.

Impressed by Pak's access to influential American government officials, Kim Jong Pil held a secret conference with Unification Church leaders in the United States at the St. Francis Hotel in San Francisco. According to Robert Boettcher, former staff director of the House Subcommittee on International Relations, which investigated Moon's ties to the KCIA, Kim Jong Pil "decided the Unification Church should be organized satisfactorily to be utilized as a political tool whenever he and KCIA needed it. . . . It was a situation favorable both to Moon's plan for expanding via the good graces of the government and to Kim Jong Pil's plans for building a personal power base."[8]

This was the attainment of one of Moon's most important aims.

> In order to rule the world, Moon had to start with Korea. It was essential that he have loyal cultists inside the government. They had to be well placed so they could sway powerful persons and become influential themselves. They must be skillful in portraying the Unification Church as a useful political tool for the government without revealing Moon's power goals. By Moon's serving the government, the government would be serving him. . . . The government could come to need him so much that he would be able to take control of it.[9]

In order to gain greater influence and to serve the Korean government, it was necessary to expand Unification activities in the United States. Entrusted with this program was Colonel Bo Hi Pak, KCIA agent, member of the Unification Church since 1957, and assistant military attaché in the Korean Embassy in Washington.

Pak returned to Korea in 1963 and retired from the army. Although he was now a private citizen and thus subject to South Korea's strict passport laws, he was able to return to Washington on a diplomatic visa with a letter from the National Defense Ministry stating he was on a diplomatic mission.

Upon his return, Pak created the Korean Cultural and Freedom Foundation (KCFF), an organization ostensibly dedicated to furthering cultural ties between the United States and Korea. Pak quickly lined up an impressive list of names for the letterhead, including former Presidents Truman and Eisenhower, as honorary presidents, and Richard Nixon as an adviser. What these and many other prominent Americans did not know was that the foundation was actually a front behind which the Unification Church and the KCIA gained access to American policymakers.

The foundation scheduled tours of the Little Angels, a Korean singing company and "unofficial goodwill ambassadors," an idea Pak got after watching a concert of the Vienna Boys' Choir. Although the tours also served the Koreans' goals of winning influence abroad (the Little Angels gave a private performance for former President Eisenhower in Gettysburg and appeared at the United Nations and before Queen Elizabeth II), there was another, hidden bonus for Bo Hi Pak.

> He discovered the Little Angels could be convenient vehicles for bringing cash for the KCFF into the United States. . . . Large amounts could be divided among members of the company before passing through Customs. . . . In 1972, a little Angels travelling group delivered 18 million yen [$58,000]."[10]

Pak had also mastered the art of lining up prominent Americans for seemingly legitimate causes, then using the respectability that those Americans lent to raise money for the Unification Church. A particularly bold example was the launching of Radio of Free Asia (ROFA) in 1966. Contacting anti-communist American supporters for a radio station that would broadcast propaganda from South Korea into North Korea, mainland China, and North Vietnam, Pak placed these Americans in the directorship and put their names on the ROFA letterhead, which was sent out in mass mailings across the United States asking for donations. Pak maintained actual control of the project, neglecting to tell the American chairman that the Korean government had already agreed to the free use of transmitters or that the operations director in Korea was a KCIA agent. In this way, Americans continued to send in financial contributions to Radio of Free Asia, a KCIA operation, for nine years; most of their money was diverted to the Unification Church, which used it to finance its increased proselytizing activities in the United States.

It would appear, then, that along with ardent anti-communism and nationalism, the Reverend Moon also shared with Sasakawa and Kodama, his future Japanese underworld benefactors, a lack of reverence for legitimate business practices.

One Moon mission was to rally anti-communist, pro-Korean forces in Asia. With the backing of the Korean government and with funds coming partly from his share in state-controlled Korean industries, including the Tong-il Armaments Company, an armaments manufacturer, Moon established the International Federation for the Extermination of Communism. Although the dramatic name probably endeared him to the Korean military, it was a little much for other countries; the U.S. branch was called the Freedom Leadership Foundation.

It was in Japan that Moon found his bonanza. Membership in the Japanese Unification Church had quickly surpassed that of the original Church in Korea. Even today, with Church membership declining rapidly in the United States and the Korean chapter virtually dormant, the Unification Church in Japan remains a powerful force.

Ryoichi Sasakawa was the first Japanese leader to see the advantages of the Unification Church. In 1958, the Unification Church was begun in Japan under the name Genri Undo by a man named Nishikawa Masaru. It soon turned out that Masaru was not Japanese at all but was rather a Korean, Choi Sang Ik, who had entered Japan illegally. During Choi's subsequent immigration trial, Sasakawa interceded as his legal guarantor. From that time on, Sasakawa played an important role as adviser to Genri Undo.

Neither Moon nor Sasakawa was content merely to promote a church, however; in keeping with Sasakawa's lifetime involvement in ultra-nationalist activities and Moon's holy quest to establish a "physical mission" on earth, it was necessary to establish a political arm or, even better, to take over an existing one, like the World Anti-Communist League.

In July 1967, Sasakawa arranged a secret cabal at a building he owned on a lake in Yamanashi Prefecture. Among those attending were Reverend Moon, Shirai Tameo, and Osami Kuboki. Tameo was an underworld lieutenant of Yoshio Kodama and secretary of the innocuously named Japan Youth Lectures, a Kodama organization that indoctrinated and trained young members of the *yakuza* gangs. Kuboki was secretary-general of Japan's Genri Undo; he also served as an adviser and lecturer to Kodama's Youth Lectures.

The purpose of the meeting was to create in Japan a Korean-style anti-communist movement that could operate under the umbrella of the World Anti-Communist League and that would further Moon's global crusade and lend the Japanese *yakuza* leaders a respectable new facade. Shokyo Rengo, or "Victory Over Communism," was born. Ryoichi Sasakawa was made overall chairman of Shokyo Rengo, and Yoshio Kodama its chief adviser.[11]

In April 1968, Shokyo Rengo was chosen as the official Japanese chapter of the League. While theoretically unaffiliated with the Unification Church, virtually its entire membership came from Moonie ranks or the *yakuza* minions of Kodama and Sasakawa.

> It was in the months preceding the 1970 (WACL) Congress that the general public in Japan first became aware of the existence of Shokyo Rengo, when its activists carried out a nation-wide campaign in the streets publicizing the congress, passing out leaflets, collecting donations, etc.[12]

At the 1970 League conference, held in Kyoto and Tokyo, Osami Kuboki was named chairman of the finance committee, and Sasakawa, the overall chairman. Shokyo Rengo sponsored the conference; its monetary generosity was considered the chief reason for this being the biggest gathering in League history.

After their sponsorship of the 1970 League conference, both Sasakawa and Kodama stayed in the spotlight. Although Sasakawa no longer plays a visible role in the League, he remains a firm believer and important financier of both the Unification Church and Shokyo Rengo in Japan. In 1974 he created the World Karate Federation with Jhoon Rhee, another Moon lieutenant. Because of his philanthropy, Sasakawa has been honored with the Helen Keller International

Award, the Linus Pauling Medal for Humanitarianism, and the United Nations Peace Medal. Now he is reportedly angling for a Nobel Peace Prize.

Yoshio Kodama remained one of the most powerful of Japan's *yakuza* bosses. In the 1970s, he was also the Japanese and Korean agent for the Lockheed Aircraft Corporation; his bribery efforts to get the Japanese government to buy Lockheed airplanes made him the central figure in the Lockheed scandal in 1978. The scandal pulled down the government of Prime Minister Tanaka but left the gangster, until his death in 1985, at least $7 million richer with which to expand his domain. Today it seems that his *yakuza* successors might consider the United States part of that domain.

In 1985, "federal immigration inspectors at Honolulu International Airport, on special alert for Japanese gangsters, noted a curious similarity among some of the hundreds of tourists arriving from Japan each week: a little finger had been partly amputated."[13]

SIX

I suspected the Tecos were involved. If they're fighting the communists, they must have links to the death squads. For fear of being caught, they've compartmentalized their thing.

Former League member

IN EARLY APRIL 1970, heavily armed police in the northern Mexico city of Hermosillo sealed off a section of Calle 14 de Abril and, with guns drawn, stormed one of its buildings. In its cluttered rooms, they discovered Nazi magazines and leaflets, piles of Hitler's book, *Mein Kampf,* and code books. Most intriguing of all were a half-dozen grotesque papier-maché masks.

The masks were props used at initiation ceremonies for one of Mexico's most violent and feared secret societies. The raid was a strike against the Tecos, a network of some three or four hundred neo-Nazis whose members were divided into cells and took oaths of blind obedience to their leaders. But the Tecos were not young swastika-clad misfits who plastered their bedroom walls with posters of Hitler; they were some of Mexico's most influential leaders—industrialists, bankers, and college professors—and had been accused of coordinating innumerable acts of violence, including dozens of political assassinations, in previous years.

The Hermosillo raid did not result in a large government investigation or dissolution of the Tecos. In Mexico, where corruption is rife and where the institutionalized ruling political party has a long tradition of tolerating—and playing off—extremist movements of both the left and right, the Tecos were able to control the damage done by the 1970 raid and continue their activities. They were still in place when the World Anti-Communist League came looking for a Latin American affiliate in 1972.

Not only were the Tecos allowed to establish the Mexican League chapter, they were given a mandate to form the entire South and Central American regional organization of the League. Naturally, they chose kindred spirits, quickly making the Latin American Anti-Communist Confederation (CAL) one of the region's most powerful and deadly ultra-right federations. As "Lobo," the Honduran doctor/assassin, told one of the authors in 1983, it was a federation that served as a coordinating body for death squads throughout the region. In recent years, the slogan of the once-obscure Tecos, *Contra la guerrilla roja, la guerrilla blanca* ("Against the red guerrilla, the white guerrilla"), has been put into practice throughout the continent.

Ironically, this prestige and influence, this "miracle," to quote the Tecos, would probably have never occurred if it hadn't been for the financial assistance of the U. S. government and some of America's largest philanthropic foundations.

The Tecos trace their historical roots to the Mexican Revolution of the 1910s. Mexico was in the grip of a violent civil war that was greatly exacerbated by government anti-clerical campaigns. The Catholic Church, which owned vast tracts of the country, bore the brunt of the revolutionary zeal of a wide range of groups, ranging from impoverished and landless peasants to leftist intellectuals. Priests were murdered and churches were bombed or sacked.

To defend the Church and fight back, the Legion of Christ the King, or Los Cristeros, was formed. The counterrevolutionary Cristeros were a secret army that, like the Holy Crusaders they emulated, rode into battle with the blessings of priests. For them, this wasn't a revolution but a holy war, and they were fully prepared to die for their God and the Virgin against the "Satanists." In the ensuing strife, which took tens of thousands of Mexican lives, the Cristeros played their role.

Upon the success of the Mexican Revolution, the Cristeros were officially disbanded. In the 1930s a French Jesuit priest, Bernardo Bergoend, sought to unite the Mexican Catholic opposition to counter the anti-Church government that had been installed.

Bergoend advanced a scheme for double organization; one group was to concern itself with political mass action, the other was to be a section devoted to social action. Bluntly, the mass organizations were to be directed from above by a select leadership, i.e., a secret society.

Tecos ... represented the effective leadership of this entire complex. ... The members, especially the younger ones, were expected to fight, wherever and whenever this was indicated, for the interests of the Church and the country.[1]

In these early days, the Tecos were not strictly a fascist organization; they were basically devout Catholics and traditionalists who took up arms to defend the old, established order. That changed, however, after World War II. Through the efforts of two men, a Mexican Nazi who had spent World War II in Germany and an Argentine Jesuit priest who admired Hitler, the Tecos became the spiritual mentors for many of the continent's neo-Nazi movements and, eventually, the coordinators of death squads throughout Central America.

Carlos Cuesta Gallardo, the creator of the modern-day Tecos, spent World War II in Berlin. His exact role or function there is unknown. Some say he was a secretary to Hitler; others say he was a confidant of Alfred Rosenberg, the Nazi ideologue who formulated the German anti-Jewish policy and who was executed at Nuremberg. Whatever his role, Cuesta Gallardo was almost certainly used by the Germans in the hope of establishing a private Mexican army that would be sympathetic to Nazi goals on the United States's southern border. When Germany's plan for global conquest didn't work out, Cuesta Gallardo returned to Mexico but remained an ardent fascist and anti-Semite.

Cuesta Gallardo settled in Guadalajara, the financial center of Mexico and its second-largest city; it is as well the historical home of the Cristeros. According to a report by an American League member in 1973, "Today he leads a most secluded life in Guadalajara, never appearing in public. His house is a disguised fortress, well-guarded all the time."

Cuesta Gallardo was not idle in his Guadalajara lair. He envisioned a renaissance of the Tecos, this time committed not only to fighting the anti-clerics in Mexico but also to battling all enemies wherever they existed throughout the world. Those enemies included the

United States, Jews, Freemasons, and most of the hierarchy of the
Vatican Church, for they were all, according to Cuesta Gallardo,
conspirators in the Jewish-Freemason-Communist plot to take over
the world.

When Cuesta Gallardo embarked on this mission in the late 1940s,
he could count among his allies the "Nazi priests" whom he had
met while he was in Germany. These Catholic clerics had collaborated with Germany and its allies during the war; many were not
priests but were regular war criminals who, with Church assistance,
had donned robes to facilitate their escape. They were now scattered
throughout Western Europe and Latin America. The Tecos' present
ties to the "religious leaders" of the Croatian Ustasha and the Romanian Iron Guard most certainly date from their leader's tenure in
Berlin.*

Cuesta recruited a young Mexican intellectual, Raimundo Guerrero, to his cause. Guerrero succeeded in drawing other right-wing
students and academics into the Teco cabal and in time assumed its
overt leadership. The real power, however, would always remain
with the shadowy Cuesta.

From the old Mexican Nazi's standpoint, Guerrero was a good
choice as protégé. In 1952, Guerrero was dispatched to Buenos
Aires to represent Mexico at a conference of the World University
Organization. There he made contact with other neo-Nazi student
groups from around the world. In addition to forging a lasting
relationship with the anti-Israel Arab League, it was in Buenos
Aires that Guerrero came into contact with the Jesuit priest Julio
Meinveille.

Meinveille was an ultra-right Argentine ideologue who launched
vitriolic literary attacks on the world's "plagues": Jews, Freemasons,
and liberal elements of the Catholic Church. By 1952, Meinveille was
already the spiritual leader of the Tacuaras, an Argentine secret society of neo-Nazis, and he would become the same for the Tecos.
His hate books, including such tracts as *The Jew, The Cabal of Progres-
sivism,* and *Among the Church and the Reich,* became the Tecos' Bibles.
The Mexicans frequently distributed Meinveille's books at World

*In particular, the Tecos have close ties with the Romanian Iron Guard fascists
of Horia Sima in Spain, and it could be more than coincidence that Teco "cells"
are composed of thirteen followers, the same number as in the Iron Guard
"nests."

Anti-Communist League conferences, and the aging priest was even invited to be the main speaker at the first CAL conference in Mexico City in 1972.

Stefan Possony, a professor emeritus at the conservative Hoover Institute at Stanford University and a longtime American League member, investigated the Tecos in the early 1970s. Pointing out Meinveille's importance to the Mexican neo-Nazis, he nonetheless portrayed the Argentine in a favorable light:

> He is a theologian with knowledge in the social sciences, and he is far more scholarly and also more moderate than the rest. He is knowledgable on many aspects of Communism, about which he wrote with wisdom and insight. He produced the overarching interpretation of history on which the reasoning of the Tecos literature is based. But he has also been the victim of obsessive ideas, especially anti-Semitism, in the pursuit of which he resorted to questionable methods.[2]

Despite Possony's characterization of Meinveille as a scholarly moderate, the "interpretation of history" that he gave the Tecos was one of violence, hatred, and paranoia. To them, practically all established leaders, whether in the religious, economic, or political fields, were traitors and tools of international Zionism. Franklin Roosevelt, Harry S. ("Solomon," according to the Tecos) Truman, and Nelson Rockefeller, they believe, were all Jews. So, too, were several leaders of the Spanish Carlists, a movement best known for its ardent Catholicism and unwavering support of Generalissimo Francisco Franco, and so were conservative and Catholic politicians throughout South and Central America. The Tecos saw, and continue to see, all their enemies as performing assigned roles toward the secret Jewish plan of global domination.

And their "enemies" quickly became an even larger bloc upon the inclusion of the Vatican Church under Pope John XXIII. Although many conservative Catholics were disturbed by what they saw as the liberal bent of the Pope and by the decrees that emerged from Vatican Council II in 1962, none reacted as bitterly or as blasphemously as the Mexican Tecos did in authoring the *Complot contra la Iglesia* ("Conspiracy Against the Church").

The *Complot* remains one of the most scathingly anti-Semitic and unabashedly pro-Nazi tracts ever written. Translated into a half-dozen languages, it was supposedly the work of one "Maurice Pinay," a fictitious name. The Italian edition was distributed at Vatican Council II, causing a minor uproar.

> We must join forces against Jewish imperialism and liberate our own peoples, all who are being kept captive by Jews, so that after victory over the worst imperialism the world has ever seen . . . all countries can form a world organization.

That world organization was clearly not to be the United Nations, for the UN is "controlled by the secret power of Jewry and Freemasonry and used for the purpose of securing the triumph of the imperialist schemes hatched by the Synagogue."[3]

The *Complot* went a step further than other apologists had in lamenting Nazi Germany's failure: "If they had confined themselves to saving their nation and Europe from the deadly threat [Judaism] they could not be blamed, and perhaps their commendable enterprise might have succeeded."

Many journalists and shocked Church leaders attempted to discover the true identity of the author of the *Complot*; they came to the conclusion that it was a collaborative effort of European neo-Nazis and Latin American fascists. Actual responsibility, however, belonged to the Tecos, specifically Cuesta Gallardo and Garibi Velasco, another Teco leader; they were its major authors.

The Tecos' front man for the hate campaign at Vatican Council II was their theologian, Father Saenz y Arriaga, a Jesuit priest. At the close of the council, he issued a press release "signed" by twenty-eight conservative Catholic leaders that attacked the council for having "yielded to the pressures or to the money of Judaism." Most of the signatures were forgeries, and Saenz y Arriaga was later excommunicated.

Some of the more moderate Tecos, disgusted at the group's actions, broke away to form the Group of Puebla in 1964. The parting was not amicable. To the Tecos, the Pueblas had now proven themselves to be part of the Jewish conspiracy. According to a South American rightist who has followed the Puebla-Teco split, "They've been killing each other ever since. Neither group is composed of saints."[4]

The rift between the Tecos and the Group of Puebla helped to bring some aspects of the secret society into the open. Mexican Church leadership, even some of its extremely conservative members, criticized the Tecos. The cardinal of Guadalajara, Garibi y Rivera, issued a letter in 1964 warning "students so that they would not go astray by those who, with the pretext of fighting errors like Communism, built secret organizations in which it is demanded under oath of strict secrecy and obedience to unknown leaders and even with clear menaces to those who would break the orders given."[5]

Such denunciations did not destroy the secret society. Rather, the Tecos launched a public relations campaign, created political front groups, and established links with other neo-Nazis throughout Latin America, the United States, and Europe. One of their most successful operations, probably inspired by Raimundo Guerrero's involvement in the World University Organization in the early 1950s, was in gaining influence and funding through the academic world.

Throughout Latin America, there is a tradition of "autonomous universities." Theoretically at least, autonomous schools are legally allowed complete academic freedom, including immunity from repercussions for teaching subjects like Marxism that could never safely be discussed outside the campus. Neither the army nor the police are allowed onto university grounds; security details are handled by university-selected personnel. This system has led to a dramatic irony: liberal or Marxist professors teach classes under the protection of campus autonomy in nations where liberals and Marxists are routinely arrested, tortured, and/or murdered.

The Tecos saw the Latin American autonomous university system, which was traditionally the domain of leftists, as a potential tool for themselves that could be used to propagate their views of communism and the international Jewish conspiracy; it could also be a funding source for their secret operations. The springboard for this goal of continental influence was the Teco-controlled Autonomous University of Guadalajara (UAG).

Founded in 1935 by Carlos Cuesta Gallardo, the Guadalajara school had always been an understaffed and underfinanced institution. In 1960, the school had a budget of fifty thousand dollars and consisted of a few disheveled buildings and a dusty campus. Then things changed: by 1962, when the Tecos turned their attention to this latent weapon at their disposal, they had already endeared themselves to American officials whom they could count on for support.

"After years of financial starvation, Guadalajara [UAG] received money from the Rockefeller, Ford and Carnegie Foundations as well as from the Agency for International Development (AID). This happy change was accomplished by Luis Garibay, rector of the university and Guerrero's compadre."[6]

According to a confidential report prepared by Tradition, Family and Property (TFP), an ultra-conservative Catholic organization based in Brazil that has long been at odds with the Tecos, the man most responsible for putting the Tecos' university on the map was Oscar Wiegand, the U.S. consul in Guadalajara. "He was so interested in the development of the small university, that he moved to Guadalajara to follow up the process. Dr. Wiegand himself took Dean Garibay to visit 12 American universities to introduce him and his plans and to solicit 'donations.' "[7]

By 1975, the Autonomous University of Guadalajara had a budget of ten million dollars, in what Vice-Dean Antonio Leaño, a high-ranking Teco, called a "miracle" of American and Mexican philanthropy. That miracle was the result of the funds provided by the U.S. government through the Agency for International Development (AID) and American philanthropic foundations. Between 1964 and 1974, they had bestowed nearly twenty million dollars in grants to the Tecos' university.

In all probability, some of the foundation and government officials responsible for clearing the grants to the university were not aware that it was dominated by the Tecos. Yet it is a rather glaring oversight. Within the various university departments could be found most of the Tecos' top leaders, men responsible for previously delivering scathing attacks on the Vatican Church, Judaism, and, in fact, the United States. Further, "American money flowed only *after* Tecos, or related group, already had spent considerable amounts on the preparation, publication, translation and distribution of costly books, notably *Complot*."[8]

With the influx of American financial assistance, the Tecos at the Guadalajara campus were able to finance their nonacademic programs. According to a Mexican political analyst who infiltrated the Tecos and attended their secret meetings, the grants and scholarship funds received from the United States were laundered through the university for Teco use. "Much of this money went to support the Teco 'political' activities," he said.

Their political activities were many. In addition to furthering their ties with neo-Nazis in Europe and South America and subsidizing the publication of their anti-Semitic magazine, *Replica,* the Tecos also now had the funds to establish political front groups, such as FEMACO (Mexican Anti-Communist Federation) and the IACCD (Inter-American Confederation of Continental Defense), to serve as liaisons to right-wing death squads; they became part of the World Anti-Communist League in 1972.

Operating under the front group FEMACO, the Tecos' power within the League became enormous. Not only was Raimundo Guerrero made an executive board member but the Mexicans proceeded to draw in their violent brethren from throughout Latin America with little or no review by the League's Asian godfathers. Since they had created the entire Latin network, the Tecos naturally assumed leadership of the Latin American Anti-Communist Confederation (CAL).[9]

Helped by their League credentials, the Tecos intensified their *Replica* hate campaigns. In freely reprinting articles from other League-affiliated magazines, such as the *Canadian Intelligence Service* and the Taiwan-based *Asian Outlook, Replica* remains today a forum wherein conspiracy theorists and neo-Nazis can rail against the Jewish-Freemason conspiracy. At the 1978 World Anti-Communist League conference, the Tecos handed out reprints of an article attacking the television miniseries *Holocaust* as "Jewish propaganda."[10]

Their inclusion in the World Anti-Communist League also gave the Tecos a platform for airing their philosophy internationally and winning the notice and support of neo-Nazis everywhere. When Aktion Neue Recht ("New Right Action"), a German Nazi group, held a congress in Munich, Guerrero sent them a congratulatory telegram. The fascist Norwegian Norsk Rikt party heaped praise on the Mexican League chapter. In the late 1970s, when the chairman of the American chapter of the League tried to fill the European delegations with neo-Nazis and former SS officers, the Tecos under Guerrero were among his principal supporters.

Today, the Autonomous University of Guadalajara is a thriving institution of higher learning. It confers nearly sixty professional degrees, and its president, Dr. Luis Garibay Gutierrez, was president of the International Association of University Presidents in 1985. Still, many of its professors and students have secret memberships in the Tecos. Raimundo Guerrero is now a department dean. The Tecos so dominate the university that they have lent their name to its soccer team. Rallies are held in which, according to former students, swastika armbands are worn and allegiance to Nazism sworn. The Tecos operate their own armed university security police, and students are fed a heavy and steady diet of anti-communism and anti-Semitism. Visitors are required to have a special pass and are led about the campus by a "companion."

An American former professor at the university and a Teco loyalist inadvertently revealed much of its inner workings. In an anonymous phone call to Dale Van Atta, an associate of syndicated columnist Jack Anderson, he defended the university but went on to explain the required loyalty pledges, the pressure on professors of all nationalities to join the secret society, and the divisions of the Tecos' labors.

> There's basically three branches, the school administrators and professors, the prefects, students who watch over other ones and analyze their political orientation, and the *tecos de choque* [shock Tecos].
> And could the shock Tecos be involved in death squads?
> I don't know. It—it wouldn't surprise me.[11]

He then hung up.

When one of the authors exposed the Teco control of the Autonomous University of Guadalajara and its links to Central American death squads in January and February 1984 in a series of articles with Jack Anderson, the school and its allies reacted heatedly. In addition to running a defending advertisement in *The Washington Post*, they denounced the Anderson columns in Mexico and Guatemala. One of the most amusing counterclaims made by the university was that the word *Teco*, or "owl," referred to "the students' devotion to late-night academic studies."

The daughter of a Teco laughed at the explanation. "Yes, it does mean owl. Los Tecos are owls whose eyes are red. The members of the group are called Los Tecos because they are up all night doing their thing."

"In CAL we are not pluralistic; we cannot be," Teco emissary Rafael Rodríguez declared to the World Anti-Communist League conference in 1980. "The values of our faith, of our culture, of our civilization and of our nationalism are the only truth for which we live our anti-communism. Communists, Marxists of any label, can only be situated in the enemy trenches. Our real mission is not to talk about communism but to fight communists."

SEVEN

The communists have already roughly decided that the time for conquering the world will be in 1973.

> *Fred Schwarz,*
> *American League member,*
> *1971*

BECAUSE OF ITS FINANCIAL resources and its status as the richest and most powerful nation in the West, the United States has always been a major power within the World Anti-Communist League. U.S. chapters have historically been composed of mainstream conservative academics, retired military officers, and members of the so-called New Right. But not only have they permitted anti-Semitism and racism within their own regional branch, they have also consistently, through their silence and timidity, given tacit approval to the most reactionary and vicious elements within the League as a whole.

The South and Central American chapters of the League have never concealed their theory that Jews are behind a global communist conspiracy. The South Africans have never made secret their staunch support of the racist policy of apartheid in their country, and the Arab chapters have never modified their militant diatribes against Israel and Zionism.

These facts are known to the Americans. Their claims of ignorance are rather silly, since American members have consistently been responsible for uncovering much of the darker aspects of the League, then failing to act on the information until forced to do so.

It was the Americans who revealed the Nazi nature of the Mexican Tecos in 1972. Not only did they not publicize their findings, but they remained in the League for another two years. In fact, many who eventually left have since rejoined, including the author of the Teco investigation.

American League members were alerted as far back as 1973 to the rabid racism of Donald Martin and Ivor Benson, chairmen of the British and South African League chapters respectively, and both listed as foreign correspondents for the anti-Semitic, California-based Liberty Lobby. Yet both men were honored guest speakers at the North American regional League conference in 1984.

The Americans were well aware of the allegations of death squad involvement among the Latin American affiliates, yet those elements were not expelled until 1984, after one of the authors helped to expose them in the press. Their alleged explusion notwithstanding, several of these Latins were present at the 1984 and 1985 conferences sponsored by the American League chapter.

The Americans who have belonged to the World Anti-Communist League consistently contend that they have attempted to be a moderating influence or that they were unaware of the unsavory nature of other League chapters. The evidence, however, much of it compiled by the Americans themselves, shows that they knowingly belonged to a federation of death squad leaders, Nazi war criminals, and neo-fascists. At best, they are showcases of naïveté; a more critical observer would say that they are showcases of far worse.

The first American League Chapter was the American Council for World Freedom (ACWF), founded in 1970 in Washington, D.C. The main force behind its creation, and its first secretary, was Lee Edwards, head of a public relations firm and former director of Young Americans for Freedom, the youth arm of the John Birch Society.

Edwards was a stalwart of the emergent New Right in American politics and brought his own questionable background and motives into the World Anti-Communist League as a professional fund-raiser. Along with a handful of other New Right fund-raisers such as Richard Viguerie and Patrick Gorman, Edwards was in the business of raising donations for charitable or nonprofit organizations and then keeping a large chunk of the money, sometimes over ninety percent, for his "operation expenses." His induction as the American League chairman in 1970 did not divert his energies from these endeavors; in 1971, he joined forces with Patrick Gorman to create Friends of the FBI.

By that time, Gorman had already achieved a certain notoriety by operating the United Police Fund. The fund's aim, to aid the relatives of slain policemen, had succeeded in tugging at the heart- and purse-strings of those who received its brochures by displaying photographs of the grieving families standing beside the fallen officers' graves. "In two years," according to Alan Crawford in *Thunder on the Right,* "the project netted a reported $110,000, almost 90 percent of which went to fundraiser Gorman."

Friends of the FBI was established to rally support for the agency and its director, J. Edgar Hoover; the recipients of its brochures were told that there was no better way to express that support than by sending donations to Edwards and Gorman. With the aid of an endorsement letter signed by Efrem Zimbalist, Jr., star of the television show *The FBI,* they raised nearly $400,000 dollars in four months, 64 percent of which went toward "operation expenses"; the rest was divided up between Gorman and Edwards and their lieutenants. "Soon Zimbalist became suspicious, claiming he had been 'used' by the partners; and his lawyers told the group to stop using their client's name, accusing them in a letter of 'fraud and misrepresentation'."[1]

Edwards lined up an impressive array of conservative American leaders for the American Council for World Freedom to appear on its letterhead and to attend World Anti-Communist League functions. Lev Dobriansky, a former OSS officer in Germany during World War II and chairman of the National Captive Nations Committee (and currently ambassador to the Bahamas), joined, as did Dr. Walter H. Judd, former Republican congressman from Minnesota; John Fisher, executive director of the American Security Council; and Reed Irvine, a longtime fixture of the far right. A year earlier, Irvine had established Accuracy in Media, "a watchdog of the media by promoting accuracy and fairness in reporting." ACWF's eventual president was retired Army Major General Thomas Lane; Eleanor Schlafly represented the Cardinal Mindszenty Foundation.[2]

The Unification Church in the United States was also involved; Neil Salonen—president of the Church in the United States, secretary general of the Freedom Leadership Foundation, and a director of the Moonie-owned Tong-il Armaments Company in Korea—was on the ACWF board. In 1973 Salonen achieved fame of sorts by joining the Reverend Moon on the Capitol steps for a three-day fast and prayer vigil beseeching God not to allow Richard Nixon's impeachment.

Through the prominent conservatives who made up the American Council for World Freedom, the League was able to get American senators and congressmen to attend conferences and serve as guest speakers. Strom Thurmond, Republican senator from South Carolina, and Robert Dornan, Republican congressman from California, both spoke at League conferences in the early 1970s.

Not all the council members were ecstatic over its joining the League. One, David Rowe, the man who had been sent to reform the Korean chapter of the Asian People's Anti-Communist League in 1965, actually quit over his objections to the League's Taiwanese chairman, Ku Cheng-kang.[3]*

Despite Rowe's objections, the ACWF did join the League, largely through the efforts of Stefan Possony, professor emeritus at the Hoover Institute at Stanford University. Ironically it was also Possony who would eventually launch an investigation which would discredit not only the Latin American chapters of the League but also the American Council for World Freedom.

At the 1972 League conclave in Mexico City, it was decided that the next League conference would be held in London. In accordance with one of the League's more peculiar rules, the international chairmanship for the following year automatically went to the sponsor of the preceding conference, that is, to the Mexican chapter; this was the Mexican Anti-Communist Federation, or FEMACO, headed by Teco professor Raimundo Guerrero.

In reaction to the persistent rumors of extremism within FEMACO, the Americans sent Possony to investigate their Mexican League counterpart. It was soon apparent that FEMACO was merely a cover for the Teco secret society.

Tecos is not only anti-Semitic, it is also anti-American and opposes

---

*Despite his animosity for Ku Cheng-kang, Rowe rejoined the WACL and attended League conferences in 1983 and 1984, while Ku Cheng-kang was still honorary chairman.

most of the goals ACWF stands for, e.g., freedom. It claims to be *la legion de Cristo Rey,* which is fighting for the re-establishment of a Christian order, but it regards the Church as infiltrated by Jews and Masons, and wants Pope Paul VI—supposedly a concealed Jew and drug addict—to be deposed as a heretic.

Although the *cristero* movement predates the various nazi and fascist movements, Tecos has personal and ideological links with the remnants of the Rumanian [sic] Iron Guard and possibly the Croat Ustashis. It seems to be connected with several neo-fascist movements. Nazi traces are visible. . . . I found no references to representative government, none to democracy or national self-determination.

In the conclusion to his confidential report to the ACWF, Possony warned, "It would be a mistake to forget that anti-Semitism and anti-masonism serve to conceal anti-Americanism" and that "ACWF association with enemies of the United States is unacceptable."[4]

Confronted with this detailed investigation by one of its own most respected members, the ACWF met in Washington in April 1973 to discuss what should be done about the Mexicans. The meeting was a study in cowardice.

One council member felt that something had to be done about anti-Semitism in the League and urged the ACWF to go on record that "anti-Semitism is incompatible with anti-communism." Another dissented, holding that "the motion would be a political mistake as it would imply we have a guilty conscience."

Finally, "Mr. [Reed] Irvine proposed the following amendment: 'Anti-Semitism is incompatible with enlightened, civilized conduct and we condemn the communist states for the practice of it.' "

Irvine's motion passed overwhelmingly. Thus the ACWF, after gathering firm evidence of the neo-fascist sentiments of its Mexican counterpart, did nothing. The ACWF remained in the League and would perhaps still be there if it weren't for its own carelessness: The council initiated its self-destruction in 1973 when it sent a copy of Possony's report to Geoffrey Stewart-Smith, the head of the British League chapter and the proposed sponsor of the upcoming League conference.

Stewart-Smith was a staunch anti-communist who saw the need for nations and private groups to work together to combat what he saw to be the Soviet strategy for global domination; the World Anti-Communist League appeared to be a good vehicle toward this. He was not prepared, however, to count among his comrades in the struggle Nazis, anti-Semites, and "Kuomintang geriatrics."

A former Conservative member of Parliament, Stewart-Smith was also the director of the Foreign Affairs Circle, a think tank located outside London that published conservative monographs on foreign policy matters. Under Stewart-Smith, the Foreign Affairs Circle joined the League and was the official British chapter from 1972 to 1974.

The planning for the 1973 conference in London was already in trouble before Stewart-Smith received the Possony memos, for the Foreign Affairs Circle was being less than acquiescent to the wishes of the League leadership.[5] Stewart-Smith was refusing to invite the European Nazis that the Latin American and Asian chapters had asked to attend, and he fired off angry letters to the chapters responsible.

One case that particularly galled the Briton was that of Jesus Palacios, Spanish representative of the World Youth Anti-Communist League, the League's youth arm. Since Palacios had attended the 1972 League conference, and since his organization, the Anti-Marxist Intellectual Group of Spain, was a full associate member, he was entitled by League rules to attend the London conference. Parliamentary technicalities notwithstanding, Stewart-Smith balked.

Palacios was also a founder of an ultra-rightist shock troop called the Spanish Circle of Friends of Europe (CEDADE). Founded in Barcelona in 1969, CEDADE declared itself to be a "national-revolutionary" force with an aim "to oppose the tendency of defaming the positive aspects of the National Socialist Movement." As head of the group's Madrid chapter, Palacios, clad in a brown shirt and black tie, reminded his listeners that Marxism was simply a tool to "install the tyranny of the Jews." CEDADE published monographs such as *The Myth of Christ's Judaism* and *Hitler and the Church: The Lie of Hitler's Atheism* and concluded its meetings with a Nazi salute and a cheer for the fallen idols, Hitler and Mussolini. "It would seem beyond reasonable doubt," Stewart-Smith wrote Ku Cheng-kang in May 1973, "that Jesus Palacios is a neo-Nazi."

When no response was forthcoming, the Foreign Affairs Circle director wrote to Dr. Bastolme Puiggros, the head of the Spanish League chapter. "If you need references concerning Señor Palacios," Puiggros responded, "Mr. Ku Cheng-Kang through his government can ask for a report from the Taiwan Delegation in Madrid; and they will certainly inform you of the cordial relationship between the said Delegation and Señor Palacios."[6]

It was now apparent that Stewart-Smith was sending warnings about Nazism in the League to the very people who were coordinating it, and the coordinators were not pleased. Finally tiring of the British chapter's obstructionist attitude, the League leadership canceled the London summit at the last minute, sticking the Foreign Affairs Circle with a bill for eighty-four thousand dollars. Their efforts to recover the money are still tied up in international courts thirteen years later.

"The World Anti-Communist League," Stewart-Smith now says in retrospect, "is largely a collection of Nazis, Fascists, anti-Semites, sellers of forgeries, vicious racialists, and corrupt self-seekers. It has evolved into an anti-Semitic international. . . . The very existence of this organization is a total disgrace to the Free World."

Stewart-Smith was the first League member to realize the League's nature and attempt to reform it. When he obtained the Possony memos describing the anti-Semitic history and violent nature of the Mexicans, whose chapter was the most powerful in Latin America, he realized the true face of some of the "anti-communists" he was associated with. Even more, he was outraged that the American chapter, the source of the memos, had not only made no move to publicize their findings or leave the League but were going ahead with their plans to host the 1974 conference. "Anti-Semitism and political extremism," Stewart-Smith wrote Lee Edwards in June 1973, "could destroy WACL. [If they are not expelled] the organization will remain a collection of fringe ultra-rightists, religious nuts, aging ex-Nazis, emigres and cranks."

The Americans did not respond to the letter. Stewart-Smith was not prepared to assume the see-no-evil stance of the Americans; he did some investigative work on his own. In January 1974, he wrote Edwards again, this time threatening media exposure if the ACWF did not cancel its conference sponsorship. "The results of a very thorough piece of research by this organization reveals that some of the Chapters, associates and observers are drawn from neo-Nazi, ex-Nazi, fascist, neo-fascist and anti-Semitic groups."

"You know very well," Thomas Lane, president of the ACWF, responded, "that WACL had its origins in the struggles of the free peoples of Asia who are on the front lines of the resistance to Communism. . . . As to the alleged anti-Semitism of other chapters of WACL, your evidence seems to be based on guilt by association and by an alleged association at that. . . . We shall, of course, proceed under full sail to prepare our WACL conference in Washington."[7]

But Stewart-Smith had powerful ammunition. He sent six hundred copies of a report, *WACL and Anti-Semitism,* to all League chapters and to every associate of the American Council for World Freedom. By including the Possony memos along with his own findings, his report gave the appearance that the ACWF had joined forces with the Foreign Affairs Circle against the Mexicans. It placed Thomas Lane in the unenviable position of refuting the evidence of his own organization. "You have apparently seriously misread the evidence you offer," he wrote Stewart-Smith. "The chief piece, called an 'ACWF report' is not an ACWF report at all. It is on its face the statement of one individual. . . . This 'report' does not pertain to the Mexican chapter of WACL but to a secret organization thought by the writer to have interlocking membership with the chapter."[8]

But the damage had been done, and the ACWF, despite its desperate attempts to maintain its position within the League, could not last. Ironically, by including the Possony memos in his mass mailing, Stewart-Smith helped destroy not the WACL but the ACWF. In the eyes of the Latin chapters, the Possony memos showed the American Council for World Freedom to be not only an enemy of anti-communism but, worse, Zionist. They rallied around the maligned Tecos of Mexico. "Both Stewart-Smith and the American Council for World Freedom," the Uruguayan chapter wrote in March 1974, "with these documents and other attitudes are doing communism the enormous service of attempting to create divisions and problems in the WACL, acting as if they were cryptocommunists infiltrated in the anticommunist ranks to carry out sabotage."

The Bolivian chapter was even more forceful, if less grammatic: "The absurd memorandum of the American Council for World Freedom sent to us by Stewart-Smith in addition to being obviously a pro-Zionist document proves what has been said that the American council is one of the instruments of Zionism to control the WACL and use it for benefit of Zionist interests that use the myth of anti-Semitism to frighten or attempt to paralyze those who refuse to become puppets of Zionism."[9]

Still, the ACWF wasn't ready to give up. Although bearing the brunt of venomous diatribes from the Latin League chapters, it went on to host the 1974 conference. There it made a feeble attempt to give the League at least the appearance of respectability: the ACWF introduced a motion to declare the League against anti-Semitism and extremism. The Latins were outraged.

It was decided, the Tecos reported afterward, "through an overwhelming majority of votes to suppress for the time being any reference to these problems, which are totally alien to the anticommunist fight; later on . . . very plainly and also with overwhelming majority it was agreed to reject the project, with the result that it was not even presented for consideration to the General Assembly. . . . A completely different resolution condemning the defamation activities and the attacks of Geoffrey Stewart-Smith against WACL was unanimously approved."[10]

Although some former council members state that they finally left in January 1975 because of the extremism in the League—extremism they had failed to modify—at least as important a reason was that they were no longer trusted by the Latin fascists.[11]

The American Council for World Freedom withered; its officers went off to join other New Right organizations.

Perhaps the greatest success story among former ACWF officials is Lee Edwards. Joining forces with Richard Viguerie, the "king of fund-raisers," he served as editor of *Conservative Digest* upon that magazine's founding in 1975. Edwards also was the chief fund-raiser for the Underground Bible Fund. According to Democratic Representative Lionel Van Deerlin, the fund "undertook to persuade prospective donors that for every $2 that came in there would be five Bibles [delivered] in the native tongue of an Iron Curtain country . . . [but] we couldn't ascertain whether one single Bible had ever been delivered to one single person behind the Iron Curtain, despite more than $200,000 that had been collected."[12]

Edwards is believed to have made off with over eighty percent of the funds and probably nearly as much through his next operation, "Save Our Symbol," purportedly a campaign to protect bald eagles.

Perhaps Edwards's true colors—and the reason why he never seemed to be very upset by anti-Semitism within the World Anti-Communist League—were shown when he joined Viguerie in an attempt to take over the virulently racist American Independent Party (AIP) in 1976. Aided by New Rightists Howard Phillips and Paul Weyrich, they sought the nomination of Robert Morris (currently on the board of directors of the new American League chapter) as AIP's presidential candidate, with Viguerie for vice-president.[13]

Although the move failed and the AIP's perennial nominee, Lester Maddox, the bigoted former governor of Georgia, remained at the helm, the venture serves as another example of just how far men like Lee Edwards would go—and what they would overlook—in their search for allies. Bankrolling themselves by running "charities" with exorbitant operating costs, they sought out others who shared their apocalyptic vision of the takeover of the world by communists and their "fellow travellers," whether in the American Independent Party or in the World Anti-Communist League. Today Edwards is president of the Center for International Relations, a conservative think tank funded by the Reagan Administration.

Evidence suggests that several American members of the World Anti-Communist League were not as disgusted by the neo-Nazism as they contend they were. Stefan Possony, Lev Dobriansky, and Jay Parker, all original ACWF members, returned to the League fold later, this time under the banner of the United States Council for World Freedom. They rejoined at a time when the Mexican Tecos, whose presence had supposedly spurred their exit the first time, were still very active. Even Edwards seemed to have a soft spot for the organization; as late as 1982, seven years after his official departure, his public relations firm was the registered foreign agent for the World Anti-Communist League.

However unfounded the fears of the League's Latin representatives that the ACWF was part of the "Zionist conspiracy" seem, they would have no such troubles with the next American chapter.

With the resignation of the American Council for World Freedom in 1975, the door was open for an energetic neo-Nazi to transform the face of the League in the United States and Europe, plunging it even further into the depths of fanaticism.

EIGHT

Western Destiny's *duty remains to carry the message of true White, Western Culture further afield to more and yet more members of our race. . . . Our Race can only survive if we can prevent them [Jews and blacks] from capturing the minds, morals and souls of our children.*

Roger Pearson,
Editor of Western Destiny,
1965

THE LETTER from President Reagan is a source of pride in Roger Pearson's small office in downtown Washington, D.C.

You are performing a valuable service in bringing to a wide audience the work of leading scholars who are supportive of a free enterprise economy, a firm and consistent foreign policy and a strong national defense.

Your substantial contributions to promoting and upholding those ideals and principles that we value at home and abroad are greatly appreciated.[1]

The letter had been a boon for Pearson, who used it in soliciting donations and subscriptions to his magazines and to show the approval of conservatives, up to and including the president, of his myriad activities. Indeed, Pearson has traveled in New Right circles for many years, formerly as an editorial associate for such mainstream organizations as the Heritage Foundation and the American Security Council, and currently as chairman of the Council on

American Affairs and editor of *The Mankind Quarterly* and *The Journal of Social, Political and Economic Studies*. He has also maintained an interest in international politics, as evidenced by his three years as head of the American chapter of the World Anti-Communist League.

In fairness to Reagan, the president was probably not aware of some of Roger Pearson's past activities. Yet when White House officials were told of Pearson's background, they neither disavowed nor repudiated the letter. What the president had done was offer his support—and provide a very useful fund-raising tool—to one of the most persistent neo-Nazis in the world.

For Roger Pearson is a man of several personalities. On the one hand, he is a mainstream conservative, hobnobbing with officials of the New Right, publishing articles written by senators and congresspeople in his journals. On the other, he is a white supremacist who warns of the dangers of whites breeding with "inferior" stock, advocates the measurement of craniums to determine intelligence, and once bragged to an associate about his alleged role in hiding Nazi doctor Josef Mengele, the infamous "Angel of Death" of the Auschwitz extermination camp. He is also the man who, as world chairman of the World Anti-Communist League in 1978, was responsible for flooding the European League chapters with Nazi sympathizers and former officers of the Nazi SS.

Now active in American conservative political causes and residing in Washington, Pearson is a Briton who lived for twenty years in India. Before Indian independence in 1947, he served as a colonial Indian army officer, then as manager of a tea plantation in what is now Bangladesh.

Obtaining his bachelor of science degree in anthropology from the University of London in 1951 and his master's in economics in 1954, Pearson showed an early interest in eugenics, a pseudoscientific study first made popular by the Nazis that holds that a human racial stock can be improved by selective genetic breeding. Likewise, a racial stock can be diluted by the introduction of an "inferior" breed. He wrote several books on the subject, including *Eugenics and Race* and *Race and Civilization* (the latter of which credits Professor Hans F. K. Gunther, a Nazi racial theoretician, for its inspiration). Both books are still sold by the American Nazi Party.

Only by tracing descent through several generations can one be sure that a stock is healthy, and does not contain bad elements. It must be possible to show that the donor has a "pure" and "healthy" genetic constitution. . . . This means that he must be "racially" pure—capable of breeding true to the healthy lines required. If in his family history there are inherited faults present in his genes, due to earlier crossing with unhealthy stock, then the individual cannot be allowed to donate either egg or sperm. . . . When that is achieved we shall have a "pure race."[2]

But Pearson was not content to air his theories in obscure books; he wanted to form an alliance with like-minded men whereby the tenets of racial purity could, as in Nazi Germany, be put into practice. Toward that end, in 1957 he helped establish the Northern League for Pan-Nordic Friendship, an umbrella group for historical revisionists, scientific racists, and old Nazis from the "Aryan" nations of the world. Billed as an organization to instruct peoples of Northern European descent about the vitality of their ancestral heritage, namely pre-Christian Nordic paganism, one basic tenet of the Northern League was that "further human progress can only be sustained if the biological heritage is preserved, and a cultural decline must inevitably follow any decay in the biological heritage or falling-off of genetic quality."[3]

The Northern League established contacts with other groups in Sweden, Denmark, and Germany and opened a branch in Sausalito, California. Attending its first conference in Detmold, West Germany, was Colin Jordan, a British neo-Nazi, and Wilhelm Landig, a former SS officer. According to an internal WACL document, "The program and manifest from the Conference was described by German authorities as 'national socialism revived'. The Detmold Conference decided that members should use the conspiratorial method of expanding the influence of the Northern League."[4]

Under pressure from various Western European governments, the Northern League never received the recognition Pearson sought. By the 1960s, however, Pearson's racial writings and activities in Europe had come to the attention of an American named Willis Carto. A historical revisionist (believing the Holocaust to have been a hoax perpetrated by the Jewish-controlled press) and a rabid racist, Carto headed the California-based Liberty Lobby. In 1960, Liberty Lobby had praised the American Nazi Party and its leader, Lincoln Rockwell, who was later murdered in Arlington, Virginia, by a rival Nazi. Carto apparently saw in Pearson a "fellow traveller" with a gift for words and persuaded Pearson in 1965 to relocate to the United States and become editor of Liberty Lobby's magazine, *Western Destiny.*

Pearson worked briefly with *Western Destiny,* writing several books on race and eugenics for Liberty Lobby's publishing arm. After an amicable parting with Carto, Pearson immersed himself in the academic mainstream of his adopted country, teaching anthropology at Queens College in North Carolina and at the University of Southern Mississippi before becoming dean of academic affairs at the Montana College of Mineral Science and Technology. By 1975, he was ready for another career move, this time to Washington, D.C., to become founder and president of the Council on American Affairs (CAA).

The council, which is still in existence, is typical of many backroom councils and organizations operating in the nation's capital that solicit funds and sell subscriptions for a wide variety of causes and publications using different names and post office boxes, but all emanating from a single entity. From his office just off Logan Circle, Pearson not only accepts funds for the Council on American Affairs but also peddles *The Mankind Quarterly,* the *Journal on Social, Political and Economic Studies,* and the *Journal of Indo-European Studies,* a highly technical linguistic quarterly.

Besides being a means to keep himself financially solvent in the mid-1970s, the CAA gave Pearson the opportunity to collaborate with leaders of the New Right and elicit the support of conservative congressmen and senators. In short order, he was on the editorial board of the Heritage Foundation, the Foreign Policy Research Institute, and the American Security Council. Senators Jake Garn (R–Utah) and Carl T. Curtis (R–Nebraska) wrote articles for monographs published by Pearson's council. Senator Jesse Helms (R–North Carolina) and Representatives Jack Kemp (R–New York) and Philip Crane (R–Illinois) contributed to the *Journal of Social and Political Studies* (renamed *Journal of Social, Political and Economic Studies* in 1980).

Pearson had carved his niche into New Right political circles and had been accepted by 1976, just in time to come to the attention of the World Anti-Communist League when it was looking for a new American affiliate. When the American Council for World Freedom quit, the League turned to Roger Pearson and his council to rekindle the flame in the United States.

It was a responsibility that Pearson clearly took to heart. In the next three years, he was the man most responsible for turning the League into a platform for Norwegian neo-Nazis, German SS officers, and Italian terrorists wanted for murder.

When Pearson looked at the World Anti-Communist League in 1976, he saw a strong international federation, with one major exception.

The Latin American affiliates were firmly controlled by the Tecos of Mexico; the Australian and South African chapters were composed of historical revisionists, anti-Semites, and Eastern European emigrés drawn largely from the Romanian Iron Guard and the Croatian Ustasha; the Eastern Europeans, under the Anti-Bolshevik Bloc of Nations umbrella, had not swayed from the course; the Asian delegations were primarily government ministers and high military officers from their respective anti-communist governments who could not be touched anyway since they were the League's founders. Where Pearson saw the weak link was in Western Europe.

There the chapters were run by prominent mainstream conservatives, some of whom had fought against the Nazis during World War II. They were clearly the odd men out, and Pearson set about planning their replacement with "true" anti-communists. Pearson saw in the League the chance to close the circle, to unite the neo-Nazis of Europe under the banner of the World Anti-Communist League, which he had failed to do fifteen years earlier with the Northern League.

As head of the new American chapter of the League, Pearson immediately reshaped the European affiliates. He turned not only to his old cohorts in the Northern League but also to those who fell under the leadership of an aging Swedish fascist named Per Engdahl.

According to a confidential internal League document, "Engdahl is the 'grand old man' of Swedish and European Fascist ideology. He first belonged to 'Sweden's Fascist Struggle Organization', then he held positions in various Fascist and pro-Nazi organizations and political mini-parties during the 1930's and 1940's."[5] He was also the coauthor of a book, *Germany Fighting,* that has a swastika emblazoned on its cover and features a photo of Hitler on an inside page.

More important, in 1950 Engdahl had joined forces with Giorgio Almirante, the leader of Italy's fascist party Italian Social Movement

(MSI), to form the European Social Movement, a fascist federation with chapters throughout Western Europe. Known by its German acronym, ESB, the European Social Movement was probably the largest European ultra-right union operating after the end of World War II; it reached into twelve countries. The head of the British chapter was Oswald Mosley, the leader of the British National Front; he had attired his followers in Nazi-style uniforms and urged peace with Hitler during the war. The Hungarians-in-exile were represented by the Hungarist Movement of Arpad Henney, the second-in-command of the 1944 Hungarian government that had seen to the liquidation of over a half-million of its nation's Jews. The German chapter was led by Karl Heinz Priester, a former SS officer and former press and propaganda chief of the Hitler Youth. Austria was represented by Wilhelm Landig, "a former SS officer with cultural interests," according to Per Engdahl.

It was to these men and their younger followers that Pearson turned in 1977 for help in reforming the European affiliates of the World Anti-Communist League. With the support of the Mexicans and the new extremist British chapter, he oversaw their induction into the League.

At the 1978 League conference in Washington, D.C., which was organized and officiated by Roger Pearson, there were some new faces among the delegations from Europe. Sitting in the Belgian delegation was dapper St. C. de Berkelaar. Representing Norway was a handsome black-haired man with a handlebar moustache named Tor Hadland. Ake Lindsten, a stoop-shouldered old man with white hair, sat nearby, heading the Swedish delegation. From Austria was Wilhelm Landig; from Germany, Heinrich Hartle; and from Italy, Giorgio Almirante. All these observers were there upon the personal invitation of Roger Pearson.

St. C. de Berkelaar was a former Dutch SS officer; his organization, Sint Martinsfonds, was a brotherhood of three to four hundred former Nazi collaborators in the Netherlands. It published a magazine, *Berkenkruis,* whose name (literally, "birch cross") refers to the SS custom of placing crossed birch branches on the graves of fallen comrades.

Tor Hadland was head of the Norwegian Front, a right-wing shock troop that had first gained notice by holding a commemoration on the thirtieth anniversary of Vidkun Quisling's death. Quisling, whose name is now a synonym for "traitor," was the Nazi puppet leader of Norway during World War II; he was executed in 1945 for war crimes.

Chairman of the Swedish National League, Ake Lindsten had a fascist history dating back to World War II, when he advocated alignment with Nazi Germany. The secretary general of his organization, Ola Albinsson, had recently been arrested and sent to a psychiatric institute.

Heinrich Hartle was a former Nazi official and an associate of the notorious Nazi ideologue Alfred Rosenberg; Wilhelm Landig, the "former SS officer with cultural interests," was president of the Austrian chapter of the European Social Movement.

Giorgio Almirante, once a minor official in Mussolini's Black-shirts, was head of the Italian Social Movement (MSI), whose youth groups and organizational offshoots were blamed for much of the wave of rightist terrorism in Italy during the preceding five years.

Almirante was the most important of the League newcomers, perhaps in the League as a whole that year. As chief of Italy's fourth-largest political party, Almirante had risen to prominence by capitalizing on and fueling Italy's ongoing "civil war of terror."

> Almirante's strategy follows Mussolini's early tactics: During times of crisis, violence should be employed to arouse and polarize the public. . . . Neo-Fascists murdered innocent people in the streets, and leftists retaliated with arson attacks. All attempts to outlaw the MSI have failed, despite an official report which states that the party "glorifies the goals of Fascism" and employs "violence as a political weapon."[6]

Almirante had earlier joined forces with Pino Rauti. Rauti, a journalist in horn-rimmed glasses, had authored such books as *Fundamentals of Fascist Racial Theory* and formed the ultra-right Ordine Nuovo ("New Order") in 1956. Borrowing the SS slogan "Our honor is our loyalty," Ordine Nuovo was one of the most violent of the rightist groups operating in Italy and was responsible for dozens of murders. Rauti was arrested in 1972 on charges of organizing a series of 1969 bombings in which at least sixteen people were killed. Finally, Italian authorities outlawed Ordine Nuovo in 1973, and Rauti, back on the streets, joined Almirante; he later became a Deputy of Parliament under the MSI banner. In 1980 the Armed Revolutionary Nuclei, an offshoot of his Ordine Nuovo, was blamed for the Bologna railway massacre in which over eighty innocent people died.

The Pearson coup in Europe was not accepted with resignation by the less-radical chapters that had been usurped; they fought the infusion of European fascists into the League. "As you will read in this letter," Dr. Broekmeijer, president of the pre-1978 Dutch League chapter, wrote to the Danish chapter in March 1979, "there is in the Netherlands as well an organization of 300 to 400 former Dutch SS-traitors, closely related to a similar organization in Germany. Already one and a half years ago, I warned [WACL] of this Dutch SS-organization and particularly for [sic] Dr. de Berkelaar, the chairman of that organization.

"WACL has already made a big mistake by inviting Dr. de Berkelaar during the WACL conference in New York [actually Washington]. He was at that time in New York and Dr. Ku [Cheng-kang] liked to have a Dutchman as observer and representing the Netherlands. . . . I made an investigation and found that he was the leader of a former Nazi group. He had a recommendation letter of Dr. Pearson."[7]

Broekmeijer's complaints were ignored by Ku Cheng-kang and heads of other League chapters. The message was clear: the World Anti-Communist League espoused "active" anti-communism. It didn't want old men and their theories and monographs. It wanted men of action who were willing to fight for their convictions and who had support among the youth. If those men were also former SS officers who held rallies in European forests, whose followers threatened and attacked Jews and leftists, it was a small price to pay for global brotherhood.

Besides, Pearson had powerful friends within the League hierarchy. Donald Martin, British correspondent for Carto's *Liberty Lobby,* author of racist books, and peddler of the forged *Protocols of the Elders of Zion,* was a close ally. (Martin was also chairman of the British League of Rights, a racist, anti-emigration outfit that became the new League chapter after the resignation of the Foreign Affairs Circle.) The Tecos in Mexico, as well as the Ustasha in the Croatian Liberation Movement, also liked Pearson's stand on matters. With their support, he was able to pursue his program of remaking the League in Europe to his own suiting.

In November 1978, Pearson organized a conclave of Nazis and

their sympathizers from throughout Europe in Vienna. Now, he told them, was the time to go truly international under the banner of the World Anti-Communist League; by April, seventeen groups had applied for admission. The names on the petitions, most of which were submitted on the recommendation of Pearson and seconded by Donald Martin, represented one of the greatest fascist blocs in postwar Europe.

Some of the applications were contradictory and overlapping. St. C. de Berkelaar, for example, applied both under Sint Martinsfonds and under *Berkenkruis,* the Sint Martinsfonds newspaper. Other proposed chapters were little more than hastily created "organizations" operating out of post-office boxes. What most of the petitioners had in common was that they were former collaborators with Nazi Germany. Along with the men who had attended the 1978 League conference as observers were some new names, including Erno (Gyula) Gombos, the new head of the Hungarist Movement, and Roeland Raes, head of the Dutch Voorpost. "They are actionists," an internal League document stated about the Voorpost, "very often appearing as para-military units, in helmets and jack-boots."[8]

But this time Pearson and his allies had gone too far. Groups on the European right rallied together to combat the Nazi influx. The World Anti-Communist League was deeply divided, with most of the Latin chapters rallying to Pearson's side, the Asians ambivalent, and the pre-Pearson European chapters threatening to quit. Ku Chengkang called a hasty League executive committee meeting, and an agreement of sorts was reached: the old European chapters would not be expelled as Pearson wanted, but the new applicants would be invited to attend the upcoming 1979 conference in Asunción, Paraguay, as observers.

At least one of those new Europeans who attended came away very impressed, seeing the League as a possible source of funding for his group back in Europe: Tor Hadland of the fascist Norwegian Front, whose journey to Paraguay was reportedly subsidized by the leader of the Arab contingent, Sheik Ahmed Salah Jamjoon, gave a glowing report upon his return. "The World Anti-Communist League (WACL)," a Norwegian Front memo of May 1979, stated, "has previously been accused of being in the services of reactionary elements and to be CIA-financed. The truth, however, is that WACL today stands forth as a world-wide and powerful movement of organizations that are united in the battle for the freedom of the peoples and the nations from both World Communism and the international financial-imperialism."[9]

In Asunción there were also some new personalities from Southern Europe. Blas Piñar, chief of the Spanish fascist party Fuerza Nueva, was there in the company of his friend Giorgio Almirante. Piñar had started a fascist minileague in 1977 by forming Eurodestra, an umbrella for the Fuerza Nueva, Almirante's MSI, and the French Forces Nouvelles. He was the spiritual leader of most of Spain's rightist thugs. In 1977, two of his followers had murdered the five lawyers on Calle Atocha, while another had shot a schoolgirl in the head in the belief that she was a leftist.

Even more intriguing among the European delegations at Asunción was the presence of Elio Massagrande. As Pino Rauti's deputy chief in Ordine Nuovo, Massagrande had ignored the 1973 ban of his organization by the Italian government and had gone on to leave his mark on France and Italy through robbery and murder.

On August 4, 1974, the *Italicus* express train from Rome to Munich was passing through a long tunnel south of Bologna when a bomb ripped one of its cars apart. Twelve bodies were found amid the twisted metal, along with forty-eight injured. An Italian magistrate, Vittorio Occorsio, conducted a two-year investigation into the atrocity, finally bringing charges against a lieutenant within Massagrande's Ordine Nuovo.

Apparently Occorsio also uncovered the links of Ordine Nuovo to other terrorist formations in Spain and Greece. On June 14, 1976, as he was driving his old Fiat sedan through the congested streets of Rome, Occorsio was murdered with thirteen bullets from an Ingram M10 machine pistol.

After that, things got hot for Massagrande. One of Occorsio's murderers turned informant and disclosed details of the inner workings of Ordine Nuovo. Police discovered Massagrande's bank deposit box in Spain, containing currency and gold bars from a 1976 twenty-five-million-dollar bank robbery in Nice, France. It was time for Massagrande to run; he ran to the safety of General Stroessner's Paraguay. At the time he attended the 1979 League conference, he was high on Interpol's list of wanted fugitives.

*　　　*　　　*

The 1979 conference was the high point of Roger Pearson's involvement with the League. He had helped introduce the European neo-Nazis to their Latin American counterparts, forging links that would be helpful in the immediate future. While neither Pearson nor the World Anti-Communist League can take total "credit" for the succession of "dirty wars" that were to haunt Central America in the following years, the Asunción League conference certainly played a vital role. After 1979, Latin American rightists could increasingly turn to other conduits for money, arms and technical expertise in unconventional warfare, and political backing for death squad operations against their opposition.

But Roger Pearson would not be there to see it. The Asians finally became alarmed at the overt extremism of his associates, and the less-radical European chapters were ready to leave the League en masse; Pearson's stardom rapidly faded after the Asunción conference. At an executive board meeting in 1980, he was asked to resign.

He was to leave one last fleeting legacy, however, by passing the American leadership mantle on to Elmore D. Greaves. Greaves was the sort of original thinker and man of action that Pearson could admire; as the organizer of the segregationist Citizens Council of Mississippi in the 1960s, Greaves had once urged that state to secede from the Union.

Today, having twice failed to unite the European ultra-right, and with his World Anti-Communist League adventure behind him, Roger Pearson has returned to conservative respectability. This transformation has been substantially aided by the mainstream academics and politicians who publish articles in his magazines. He still operates the Council on American Affairs and is an officer of a new outfit, University Professors for Academic Order, based in Corvallis, Oregon.

Pearson has a decidedly different version of his involvement with the League. In an interview with one of the authors, he claimed he left the League because it was becoming anti-Semitic and "I want to get away from those people."

The problem was exacerbated by the South American group. They were anti-communists, but also believed the communists were Jews. . . . These Latins tried to swing all of WACL over to their side. They put out some books and there was some truth in what they wrote—everyone knows some communists have been Jews—but ridiculous, really, saying *all* communists are Jewish.

As for the story of his helping Josef "Angel of Death" Mengele escape, Pearson denied even having heard the name, but in the next breath he said of his visit to Paraguay in 1979, "When I was there, I heard a couple of people had been nosing around for him and their bodies had been fished out of the river."[10]

I hope that your efforts continue to receive broad interest and support and wish you every success in your future endeavors.

Sincerely, Ronald Reagan

NINE

Victory over communism first. World peace second.
                                            Juanita Castro,
                                            1970 WACL conference

AT THE 1979 World Anti-Communist League conference in
Asunción, the international ultra-right finally completed its global
journey. Through the League, all the disparate elements from every
corner of the earth were united, joined for the stated purpose of
opposing Marxism in all its forms. While they differed on the form
of the threat facing them, they all profited from the association.

For many members of the League, its conferences were nothing
more than junkets, a way to escape the heat of Manila or the rainy
season in Ghana, to stay in a luxurious hotel and to get their names
mentioned in the local paper upon returning. But for others, participation in the League had tangible benefits. Above all else, by 1979
the League had become a means by which governments or private
groups could maintain links or coordinate actions with others that,
for political or ideological reasons, could not be maintained or coordinated in an official, public capacity.

By 1979, at least eight major power groups could be identified
within the World Anti-Communist League. Some were the traditional leaders who had formed the League to begin with, but new
power blocs had also emerged.

TAIWAN

By the late 1970s, as one nation after another dropped recognition of the Republic of China on Taiwan in favor of the People's Republic of China on the mainland, the members of the Kuomintang found themselves with a vastly diminished circle of friends. They could no longer pick and choose their allies; they had to accept whoever would accept them. And they accepted them in the apartheid regimes of South Africa and Rhodesia, in the right-wing dictatorships of Latin America, and in the Nazi collaborator bands of Western Europe and the United States.

The World Anti-Communist League had become one of the last major instruments of foreign policy for the Kuomintang, and they could not afford to let it languish. For them, the stated aim of the League—international anti-communism—had quite suddenly become secondary to the greater cause of simply retaining relations with whatever nations or groups they could.

KOREA

Although it was a military dictatorship at least as repressive as that of Taiwan, South Korea did not share Taiwan's international loss of diplomatic recognition. What it did have by 1979 was a faltering economy in a world that no longer saw it as an indispensable bastion against communism. Although the League served as an excellent podium for the regime to continue its denunciation of North Korean intrigues, another benefit, a commercial one, had emerged.

Through relationships struck at League conferences, South Korea became one of the principal arms suppliers to South and Central America. The man who led this campaign was retired South Korean Air Force Colonel Shin Chan. Shin Chan, who attended several League conferences, was also the executive director of the South Korean Association for Promotion of War Industry.

THE UNIFICATION CHURCH

Theoretically, the Unification Church left the League in 1975 when the Reverend Sun Myung Moon denounced it as a "fascist" organization. Nevertheless, the Japanese Unification Church, the Church's largest and most powerful branch, continued to be the Japanese World Anti-Communist League chapter, and the Church and the League cooperated in many joint operations throughout the world.

Just as Reverend Moon's operations were myriad, so, too, were the payoffs he received from his involvement in the League. His organization apparently has three major functions: as a church, as a money laundry, and as an agent for the South Korean government. It was able to facilitate each of these activities through its League affiliation.

Relationships nurtured with right-wing Latin Americans in the League led to acceptance of the Church's political and propaganda operations throughout Latin America. From the theological-political standpoint, Latin America is the Moonies' "Promised Land"; the more the Latin right denounces Catholicism as being riddled with Marxism, the more attractive the nationalistic anti-communist dogma of the Unification Church appears to be. No doubt Moon dreams about the influence—and money—that would come from millions of Latin Americans turning their backs on Catholicism in favor of Unificationism.

As an international money laundry, through the World Anti-Communist League and its own operations, the Church tapped into the capital flight havens of Latin America. Escaping the scrutiny of American and European investigators, the Church could now funnel money into banks in Honduras, Uruguay, and Brazil, where official oversight was lax or nonexistent.

In pursuit of its function as an agent of influence for the South Korean government, the Church has done well in Latin America. Between 1977 and 1979 the Church quietly channeled over a hundred million dollars into the Uruguayan economy; in 1980, the Uruguayan government signed a huge arms deal with South Korea, part of which went to Tong-il Armaments Company, owned and operated by the Unification Church.

SOUTH AFRICA AND RHODESIA

As did Taiwan, South Africa and Rhodesia (now Zimbabwe) saw the number of their international allies shrink in the 1970s as a result of their racist apartheid policies. One means of maintaining those ties that did remain, and hopefully of establishing new ones, was the League. This scheme operated on several different levels, from continuing links to racist groups in the United States and Western Europe to making arms deals with Latin American governments represented within the League. The League also gave the South Africans and Rhodesians an introduction to potential supporters in the American New Right and in the Unification Church.*

LATIN AMERICA

Probably the most tangible—and deadly—advantages of League involvement were gained by its South and Central American chapters. Through the League, ultra-rightists from "Southern Cone" nations like Paraguay and Argentina were able to link up with their brethren in the Central American countries of Guatemala, Honduras, and El Salvador. Since the membership of these chapters was often drawn from government officials, resolutions agreed upon at League conferences—mutual cooperation and the sharing of information on "subversive" labor leaders, academics, and liberal priests—could be put into practice. League participation also meant that Latin governments were given the opportunity to train their counterinsurgency forces and military intelligence officers in one of the world's most efficient schools, the Political Warfare Cadres Academy in Taiwan.

MEXICO

To the Tecos, the League gave not only access to other anti-Semite and anti-Vatican circles throughout the world but also the prestige to pursue their ambition of taking over the continent's autonomous universities. With their status in the League and with their control of the World Youth Anti-Communist League, the Tecos were able to embark on this program in a concerted way. Their scheme seems to have partially succeeded; in 1985, Dr. Luis Garibay Gutierrez, the head of the Tecos' Autonomous University of Guadalajara, was named president of the International Association of University Presidents.

*It has been reported that the Church's newspaper in Washington, D.C., *The Washington Times,* has been subsidized by the South African government to the amount of $900,000 annually.

NAZIS

For both the Nazi collaborators of World War II and their modern-day torchbearers throughout Europe and the United States, the League was an avenue of contact with kindred spirits in Latin America, southern Africa, and Australia. Through acquaintances made at League conferences, a British Nazi might be invited to attend a fraternal Swedish conclave; an article by an Australian neo-Nazi might be reprinted in a similar publication in Germany; or a former Belgian SS officer might come to the United States as a speaker at a Nazi rally. It could also mean that an impoverished fascist cell in Norway could come to the attention of philanthropic Arab sheiks.

For the "historical" Nazis—the Iron Guard and the Ustasha—League conferences were a cover under which various branches of the same organization could reunite in relative safety to talk about old times and plan joint actions for the future. On his own, it might have been difficult for a wanted war criminal like Stejpan Hefer to have entered the United States to meet with his Ustasha comrades there; under the auspices of the World Anti-Communist League, it was far less likely that he would come to the attention of an observant immigration official.

ARABS

By 1979, one of the most intriguing aspects of the League was its ability to embrace opposing factions simultaneously, proving the adage of politics making strange bedfellows.

As two nations isolated from most others and confronted with implacable enemies close to their borders, Taiwan and Israel have long had close diplomatic relations. Yet this did not prevent Taiwan either from inducting former Nazis into the World Anti-Communist League, or from accepting en masse a group of militantly anti-Israel Arabs at a special League executive session in 1978.

Starting with the 1979 League conference, militant Arabs, under the banner of the Middle East Security Council, became a major force and financial backer of the League. Their chief "anti" was not communism but Israel. This explains why government officials from Arab nations that are closely allied with the Soviet Union, such as Syria, have found a platform in the World Anti-Communist League.

It is quite easy to see the Arabs' interest in the League. Here in one fell swoop they tapped into bitter enemies of Israel in the United

States, Latin America, and Europe. Certainly some of their new allies had different reasons for their anti-Israeli stance—they hated Israel because they hated Jews—but the result was the same: dedicated and unwavering enemies of the "Zionist state." With membership in the League, the Arabs could now play both sides of the fence, subsidizing the far left for its pro-Palestinian sentiments and bankrolling the far right for its anti-Israel ones.

By 1979, the World Anti-Communist League had become a powerful federation spanning six continents and consisting of national chapters from some ninety nations. Its very growth was problematic; in light of their different reasons for joining the League, it stood to reason that there would be some very great political rifts among the various chapters. The supposed communist threat facing, for example, the Southeast Asian nation of Malaysia was far different from that facing the West African nation of Liberia. For the exiled Vietnamese, the chief enemy was the People's Republic of China, while for the Ukrainians it was the ethnic Russians. In Indonesia, the communist threat was personified by the resident Chinese community at large, chief victims of a horrible "anti-communist" pogrom in the 1960s. This racial focus could hardly have found favor with the Kuomintang in Taiwan, who were, after all, ethnic Chinese. In South Africa, the "communist threat" was anti-apartheid blacks; in Sri Lanka it was the Tamils; in Guatemala, the liberal clergy. In short, what League chapters defined as the enemy varied wildly.

But the League did have some unifying beliefs. What all League members had in common by 1979 was their conviction that the United States, under the Carter Administration, was part of the problems they faced. Here again their rhetoric ranged widely, some only feeling Carter was hopelessly naïve, others claiming he was being duped by communists, others accusing him of being an outright traitor and a tool of communism. Whatever their individual grievances, one of the major adhesives holding the entire World Anti-Communist League together in 1979 was a burning resentment of the American president.

Indeed, in three years as president, Carter had managed to enrage virtually ever chapter of the League. His human rights stand and selective trade embargoes on offending nations had not gone over well with Latin American rightists. His recognition of the People's

Republic of China was seen by the Kuomintang in Taiwan as the ultimate betrayal. His plans for an American troop withdrawal from South Korea had caused a panic there. His call for the dismantling of apartheid in South Africa and Rhodesia had made him bitter enemies among those nation's white rulers. His support of Israel drew the wrath of the Arabs. Domestically, his establishment of the Office of Special Investigations in the Justice Department, empowered to investigate and prosecute suspected Nazi war criminals living in the United States, had sent tremors through the Eastern Nazi collaborator contingents.

League attacks on Jimmy Carter were relentless; his name became something of an epithet. At the 1978 League conference in Washington, he was attacked for everything from sanctioning the Sandinistas' fight against the Nicaraguan dictator Anastasio Somoza to causing unrest in South Korea; at the 1977 Belgrade conference, he was attacked for failing to take up the cause of the captive nations.

"I accuse the Carter Administration," Guatemalan Vice-President Mario Sandoval Alarcon thundered at the League conference in Washington in 1978 (he had taken the speaker's podium after Senator James McClure of Idaho), "of meddling and intervening in the internal affairs of other nations, especially in Latin American countries. . . . I accuse the Inter-American Commission on Human Rights [used as a foreign policy instrument of Carter] of being a Marxist instrument that has used the cause of human rights as a tool for slander aimed at the countries that refuse to accept compromises with Marxism. . . . May God save humanity and may He forgive those responsible for such a catastrophe. We, the free men here today, accuse them of treason against the human race."[1]

On their own turf, the Carter-haters could be even more direct. Commenting on the 1978 conference and on the upcoming one in Asunción, the Paraguayan newspaper *Hoy* issued a warning to Carter and his ambassador in Paraguay, Robert White:

> If the peanut farmer from Georgia has the diplomatic strings to exercise pressure, meddle in the internal affairs of other countries and send obdurate envoys [White], then it is necessary to paraphrase the following saying: "The white horse did not understand the offensive lion."[2]

Undeterred, Ambassador White, whom *Hoy* had characterized as "a Bostonian with Marxist feelings," forced an invitation to the 1979 conference from President Alfredo Stroessner. One speaker after another, he recalls, railed against "Carter-Communism."

The League's loathing of Carter was actually only the culmination of resentment that had built up against the United States for many years. In fact, one of the common threads running through most chapters of the World Anti-Communist League was the belief that, at the very least, the United States had consistently failed to pursue options open to it in the anti-communist struggle. Others were convinced that since the American government had "sold out" long ago, that government was now part of the problem, a sentiment best illustrated by the CAL resolution introduced at the 1974 conference seeking the overthrow of the American government and its replacement with a military junta.

This disgruntlement existed for different reasons in every region from which League membership was drawn. In some cases, it extended back forty years: The Romanian Iron Guard and other Eastern European fascists charged that the United States had joined the wrong side in World War II, that it should have joined Germany in its fight against the communist Soviet Union. The Croatian Ustashi were still smarting over the British and American refusal to collaborate with them in 1945 in fighting Tito's partisans. "The great Western powers," Stejpan Hefer charged in 1970, "preferred to fight against the idea of nationalism because of their own selfish reasons."[3]

The Asian League chapters attacked American "timidity" in Asia, dating back to Korea in the 1950s and continuing up to Indochina in the 1970s. The Latin Americans and the Cuban exiles had spent nearly two decades blasting successive administrations for coexisting with Fidel Castro and for cutting off aid to right-wing governments just because they violated human rights.

> The unjust condemnation by free world liberals, particularly those in the U.S.A., of communist-threatened countries like Argentina and Chile under the pretext of "human rights" should be exposed as serving Communist purposes and preventing economic and military help going to these countries.[4]

Then there were, of course, the American and Western European neo-Nazis, who were convinced that the United States was in the pocket of the Zionists, as close relations to Israel and the prominence of American Jews clearly attested.

The League chapters also shared a number of other regional enemies. For the neo-Nazis, Latin Americans, and Arabs, the Jews,
through their "control" of international finance, were subsidizing the
spread of communism through Zionism. For European and American
racists, the diplomatic pressures against the white ruling minorities
in Rhodesia and South Africa were covers for eventual communist
black rule. And all the League chapters shared a concern over the
"clear signs" of Marxist infiltration into the Catholic Church in Latin
America.

The anti-Carter and anti-American sentiments of the World Anti-
Communist League are actually only symptomatic of an even greater
shared belief: that traditional Western institutions and values cannot
combat the Marxist threat. Communism can only be countered by
strong, resolute leadership, without the shortcomings or vacillations
displayed by the United States or Western Europe. "The fact that
the West is, today, in a sad condition," Horia Sima wrote to his Iron
Guardists in 1977, "is due to the lack of great men of State, and of
a political elite, able to understand its great responsibility."[5]
In order to win the international struggle, "anti-communists have
to be as cruel as the communists" (Taiwan), "red terror has to be
fought with black terror" (Italy), "against the red guerrilla, the white
guerrilla" (Mexico). Democracy, in the eyes of the League, is so morally bankrupt and/or infiltrated that it is unable to lead this struggle.
In fact, democracy has become the ultimate tool of subversion employed by the communists and their "fifth columnists," the Zionists.
"Personally, I am convinced that Freemasonery, Judaism and Communism act together to subjugate the world," Hernan Landivar Flores
of the Bolivian League chapter said in 1974. "From this indisputable
truth arises my deep distrust of the so-called democracy through
which you act and which is no other than the ante-room to immo-
rality and Communism."[6]
This repudiation of democracy is the single most broadly accepted
tenet—and the lasting bond—of the World Anti-Communist League.
Whether as willing accomplices or not, in the eyes of the League it
is Western democracies that have steadily bartered away the world
to the communists. For them, democracy has been compromised, is
decaying, and is unable to fight back. "The saddest aspect," Giorgio
Almirante, leader of Italy's fascist MSI, said about that nation's coun-

terterror program, "is the total impotence of the State, which has demonstrated to lack both the capacity and will to adopt suitable measures to combat terrorism. . . . It can be stated with certitude that at this time Italy possesses neither security nor intelligence services worthy of that name."[7]

Given the failure of democracy, what is needed, in the view of League members, is strong nationalist regimes such as the Kuomintang in Taiwan or that of General Pinochet in Chile. In the "correct" nations, one doesn't find the hobbling presence of working parliaments or troublesome human rights activists. These regimes don't show timidity in the face of the Marxist threat, nor do they lack the resolve to engage in the same brutal tactics their enemies employ.

Since they cannot count on the democracies of Western Europe and the United States, League members have appealed to the world's remaining far-right governments while also urging the formation of private groups to carry out the struggle independently. At least as early as 1965, the Asian People's Anti-Communist League had endorsed the formation of an "international brigade of civic-action volunteers" to help out in South Vietnam. The brigade, to be funded by the League, would of course be protected by "appropriate security forces."[8]

"As I suggested two years ago," Stejpan Hefer wrote in 1970, "one should try to form and prepare in any free state, under the protection of NATO, armed units of individual peoples from among the members of their national liberation movements. At the outbreak of rebellions and uprisings in the Communist-occupied countries these units would have the task at the favourable moment to take over the initiative and help their peoples to liquidate tyrannic Communist governments."[9]

It might seem ironic that while the ultra-right in the World Anti-Communist League looks upon democracy with disgust, they frequently voice almost a begrudging respect of their leftist opposition. They study and copy their enemy's methods and train their terrorists in much the same manner as the communists. The Political Warfare Cadres Academy in Taiwan was designed—and still teaches—according to the Soviet model of military instruction, with its commissars and political officers assigned to regular army units. In El Salvador, security forces studied the terror tactics of the guerrillas and reemployed them through "counterterror." American League members, after analyzing leftist programs of indoctrination, assassination, and sabotage, urged that anti-communists employ this same "unconventional warfare" strategy.

There have even been instances, especially in Western Europe, of terrorist cells of the extreme right and left joining together in coordinated actions. The fascist Croatian Ustashi, according to terrorism experts, have received support in their war against socialist Yugoslavia from the Soviet Union and communist Albania. Fabrizio Panzieri, an Italian terrorist belonging to the ultra-left Red Brigade, escaped a prison sentence for murder by using a passport furnished by rightist terrorists. Investigations by the West German government have revealed extensive ties between the Palestine Liberation Organization and a variety of German neo-fascists. The justification for these strange alliances was probably best stated by Mehmet Ali Agca, the would-be assassin of Pope John Paul II. "I am an international terrorist, ready to help other terrorists everywhere. I make no distinction between fascists and communists. My terrorism is not red or black; it is red and black."[10]

For this reason, it is often impossible to determine responsibility for a terrorist attack. A liberal politician in Guatemala might be killed by the right for his "Marxist taint," or he might be killed by the left because he remains part of the "oligarchy." A German businessman might be assassinated by communists for his "parasitic existence," or he might incur the wrath of the fascists for his role in the "Zionist-International Finance Conspiracy."

Such overlapping is not as anomalous as it might appear. The first enemy for both political extremes is the center. Both ultra-leftists and ultra-rightists have the same primary objective: to polarize the country, to implement the breakdown of the governing system, and ultimately to create a situation of chaos where armed conflict will be between the right and the left, the center having been discredited by its failure to prevent it. In the interim, a victory for one side—a governmental collapse in Italy, the murder of an industrialist in Spain, the "disappearance" of a human rights activist in El Salvador—works for the benefit of both.

Little wonder that terrorist after terrorist, and terrorism expert after terrorism expert, have agreed that the purpose of both Red and Black terror is to destroy the open, democratic forms of liberal government, and to replace them with something elitist and totalitarian. Rightist terror seeks "the brutal intervention of repressive forces," Leftist terror seeks the same, believing that only complete repression will bring a self-satisfied, quiet bourgeoisie to a flash point, a revolutionary "critical mass."[11]

If this is the objective of the World Anti-Communist League, then it goes a long way toward explaining the strange alliances it has formed. It is this very pursuit of international polarization and its ability to embrace openly leftist elements in an anti-communist cause that have led many to speculate about the League's true nature. Some have even suggested a secret sponsorship of the League by the Soviet Union or other communist governments, employing it as the ultimate *agent provocateur*.

The idea may not be as absurd as it first sounds. The open antipathy—and, in some cases, hatred—for the United States and Western democracy that can be found in the League are outlooks that could easily be manipulated by the Soviets, if they haven't been already.

Within the League can be found Soviet-supported Arabs who in turn support European and South American rightists in their fight against U.S.-supported Israel. The current British League chapter pushes for the dissolution of the European Economic Community, certainly a proposal that would aid the Soviet Union more than the United States. In his Madrid lair, Horia Sima rails against Western European unification.

> Only a "Europe of Fatherlands" can constitute an efficacious and durable organism. Supranational organizations are unnatural because they violate the laws, based on history, which are confirmed through the existence of nations and national cultures.[12]

Then, of course, there is the intelligence advantage the Soviets would gain in establishing ties with groups of malcontents in virtually every nation in Western Europe, individuals who reject democracy and who in some cases have taken up weapons to fight it. By infiltrating the League, the Soviets or their satellites could have access to the workings of counterinsurgency, "political warfare," "counterterror," and "unconventional warfare" programs, both official and private, throughout the world.

Whatever the real or imagined communist presence in the League, it would certainly appear that no one would be more sorry to see its demise than they. Despite political differences—and on paper they appear to be considerable—communism and fascism, as embodied in the World Anti-Communist League, are comrades in the war against democracy.

INTRODUCTION

ALTHOUGH the 1979 World Anti-Communist League conference in Asunción was significant in completing the global circle of fascism, the following year proved to be far more important. In 1980 a new, more action-oriented and dangerous League began to take shape.

The year 1980 was a landmark for the forces of the international right, for in the immediate past there had been only disaster.

The Nicaraguan dictatorship of Anastasio Somoza Debayle had fallen to the leftist Sandinistas while the United States had stood idly by. Revolutionary fervor had spread into El Salvador and had re-sparked the long-simmering guerrilla insurgency in Guatemala; instead of coming to their aid, the American president complained about those governments' human rights abuses. "White" Rhodesia had become "black" Zimbabwe, with the makings of a communist state. The pro-American despot on the Caribbean island of Grenada had been toppled by pro-Cuban Marxists. The Soviet Union had invaded Afghanistan to prop up a shaky puppet regime; the United States had feebly reacted by boycotting the summer Olympics. The military junta of Argentina had confronted a wave of leftist terrorism and for their trouble, Carter had imposed sanctions on them.

In 1980, there were some rays of hope; chief among them was the defeat of Carter and the election of Ronald Reagan as president of the United States. Here was a man whom anti-communists in general, and the World Anti-Communist League in particular, could depend on, one who would bolster friendly governments and dispense with the naïve human rights policies of his predecessor.

With Reagan, the picture quickly brightened. Military aid sanctions against Guatemala, Chile, and Argentina were soon lifted. There was increased assistance to the Afghan *mujaheddin* resistance forces, who were engaging the Soviets in a fierce and determined guerrilla war. Anti-Sandinista Nicaraguan "contras," organizing on the nation's borders and launching sniping attacks on the new leftist government, began receiving covert CIA funds.

Soon the League would gain an important new leader in the person of retired American Major General John K. Singlaub. As the head of the new American League chapter in 1981, Singlaub's outspoken advocacy of unconventional warfare, which he defined as "low intensity actions, such as sabotage, terrorism, assassination and guerrilla warfare," would dramatically change the function of the League.

By 1980, the site of the anti-communist battlefield of the world had changed. Just as it had been Europe in the 1940s and Asia in the 1960s, so now it was Central America in the 1980s. Throughout the region, rightist governments were besieged by revolutionary movements, some reportedly financed by Cuba and/or the Soviet Union. Leftists were assassinating prominent businessmen and government officials on the streets, radicalizing labor unions, and organizing rebellion in the countryside.

It was here that the World Anti-Communist League would make its stand. They had "lost" Eastern Europe, then China, then Southeast Asia; they would not lose the Western hemisphere.

By 1980, they had a role model for this new theater of conflict. In a "dirty war" that had taken the lives of an estimated nine thousand people, the Argentine government had effectively crushed the leftist Montonero movement in the late 1970s. Moreover, they had done so without any assistance from the vacillating Americans. "In the Argentine Republic," a 1977 government report states, "the term 'subversive' is used as a synonym for 'terrorist.' "[1]

Operating under this official guideline, Argentine security forces were empowered to arrest any suspect at will. The definition of what constituted subversive activity was extremely broad; the same government report states that a clear sign of potential terrorism is the lobbying of university students for student cafeterias.

The government's victims were almost invariably held incommunicado, tortured, and then executed. Bodies were dumped into the

Rió de la Plata from helicopters, buried in secret cemeteries, or thrown out onto roadsides. All institutions—the courts, schools, labor unions, even churches—were seen as likely sources for subversion; they were systematically infiltrated, and anyone found to have "subversive tendencies" quickly "disappeared." By 1980, leftist terrorism in Argentina had practically ceased to exist.

This vicious form of warfare was now ready for export to other Latin American regimes that felt similarly threatened. A primary vehicle for this export operation was the World Anti-Communist League. At a 1980 League conclave, an agreement was made in which Argentine counterterror and torture specialists would be dispatched to El Salvador to assist in the anti-communist struggle there.

In the battle for Latin America, the World Anti-Communist League did not relegate itself to a mere intermediary role. Four major elements within the League—the Taiwanese, the Unification Church, the Latin American Anti-Communist Confederation (CAL), and the American New Right—actively turned their attention to the region. Collectively, they initiated all forms of warfare necessary to fight communism—organizational, political, unconventional, even theological. They operated throughout the continent, financing, training, supplying, preaching. They would be an unseen and unaccountable force behind the scenes: the force "Lobo" called the White Hand.

TEN

The more democratic a society is, the more serious the collapse of its traditional value system appears to be. This shows that democracy is failing to provide solutions to the problems currently facing our societies and the world.

The Reverend Sun Myung Moon
December 1983

THE UNITED STATES Congressional "Koreagate" hearings in 1976–78 focused on the South Korean government's campaign of influence-peddling by giving American congressmen and senators gifts, all-expense-paid trips, and even bribes.

It was not only the Korean government that was involved in the scheme; the Kuomintang government of Chiang Kai-shek in Taiwan had also been engaged in a quieter and more subtle public relations offensive for years. For both countries, the World Anti-Communist League had acted as an important instrument in establishing and maintaining close ties with influential American anti-communists, although it was an instrument that wasn't itself closely scrutinized by Congress. Prominent Americans were invited to attend its conferences; their expenses were picked up by the League and, by extension, by the Korean and Taiwanese governments.

"In the last two years," *New York Times* reporter Richard Lyons wrote in November 1976, "at least 64 senators and representatives have visited Seoul. . . . The costs of many of these excursions have been met, wholly or in part, by such groups as the Pacific Cultural

Foundation, the World Anti-Communist League and the Korea-United States Economic Council."

The Taiwanese and Koreans spared no expense with their American visitors at League functions. They were fêted at banquets, paraded before American-flag-waving schoolchildren, given awards, and put up in lavish hotel suites.

In 1970, for example, Richard Walker, a conservative political science professor at the University of South Carolina, was contacted by Sung il Cho, a young Korean colonel with KCIA affiliations. Walker was invited to go to Korea to advise and observe the upcoming WACL conference in Japan, all expenses paid. The money came from a secret account in the Korean Embassy in Washington, D.C. While there may have been no impropriety involved since the professor was not an American official, it is interesting to note that Richard Walker is presently the American ambassador to Korea.

In the Koreagate investigations, Representative Donald Fraser's House Subcommittee on International Organizations exposed the ties between the Unification Church and the Korean CIA and concluded that the Church often acted as a virtual foreign policy extension of the Korean government. Moon, with his loyal cadres and financial resources, was able to initiate operations that the Park regime could never have attempted. One such example was the "young ladies" campaign.

"If you fulfill your mission in America," Moon told his disciples, "you can restore America and at the same time help Korea to be restored. So now we have to make bases in fifty states. We also have to restore Senators. So Master will assign three young ladies to each Senator. The Senators are archangels, so restoration will have to be done through Eve. So we need 300 young ladies. To restore the Senators you must first make the aides your friends, particularly secretaries. . . . By doing this you can save America."

This Moonie infiltration program was put into effect in the mid-1970s. The female disciples were "directed to 'hang around' the offices and volunteer to take on extra work. When the workload became especially heavy, their offers would be accepted. Employment would then follow, either with the office or through a well-placed recommendation. The favored offices, of course, would be those who dealt in legislation that could touch Moon, either in an investigatory or regulatory way. The objects would be leaks, and influence."[1]

Although the "young ladies" operation never achieved the level Moon had hoped for, his followers were able to ingratiate themselves into several congressional staffs, including those of House Speaker Carl Albert (D–Arkansas), Les AuCoin (D–Oregon), and John Hammerschmidt (R–Arkansas).

As these revelations and those of other Moonie operations were disclosed, the Unification Church went on the offensive. Bo Hi Pak, Moon's chief lieutenant, made tearful appearances before the subcommittee both to defend the Church and to attack its chairman, Donald Fraser.

"I cannot help but believe," he charged, "that you are being used as an instrument of the devil. Yes, 'instrument of the devil,' I said it. Who else would want to destroy a man of God?"

In the end, the Church exacted its revenge on the chairman. With the aid of an ultra-right "journalist," they charged that the liberal Fraser was an agent of the KGB, and he was narrowly defeated in the Minnesota senatorial contest in 1978. Afterward, the Moonies could crow, "Mr. Fraser's defeat was due to more than political fortune. It was an act of God."[2]

As the world has seen, the Reverend Sun Myung Moon has not disappeared from the scene, both as a result of his involvement with the Japanese *yakuza* warlords and of the Koreagate revelations. He remained active even while he was behind bars for income tax evasion in a New York penitentiary in 1984 and 1985. His disciples are still being trained in government-sponsored "anti-communist training centers" scattered throughout South Korea. His advisers, chief among them Bo Hi Pak, the former Korean CIA agent, have spread his empire throughout Asia, Europe, and the Americas by funneling money through corporations and organizations that are supposedly independent of the Church.

One group from which the Church has publicly disassociated itself is the World Anti-Communist League; in 1975, Moon announced that he would no longer be associated with this "fascist" organization. His umbrage is perhaps just so much more of his "Heavenly Deception."

In his quest for a global anti-communist movement that he could use for his own financial and political ends and that would legitimize his claim of being the world's new Messiah, Moon apparently had seen the League as a ready-made outfit to take over, saving him the bother and expense of creating one independently. It seems that this bid for power had been aborted, giving rise to his angry outburst and "withdrawal" in 1975.

But the Church is actually still very much a part of the League. Even after Moon's denunciation, it was represented at League conferences by Paul Werner, the head of the Church in West Germany. The Japanese League chapter is still controlled by Shokyo Rengo, the political arm of the Unification Church in that nation. The head of Japanese delegations to the World Anti-Communist League and one member of its executive board is Osami Kuboki, head of Japan's Unification Church, one of Yoshio Kodama's *yakuza* lieutenants, and one of the original Shokyo Rengo founders of 1967.

The Moon-controlled Japanese League chapter has kept close to its *yakuza* origins. When Yoshikazu Soejima, a trusted Church lieutenant and editor of its newspaper in Japan, *Sekai Nippo* ("World Daily News"), resisted overt Church takeover in 1983, Shokyo Rengo was called in.

> On the first of October, about 100 people—including about 30 in special karate training groups—barged into the paper's office. . . . They broke into desks, stole papers and beat up some of the employees. . . . On June 2 of this year [1984], Soejima was attacked outside his home in Tokyo and stabbed repeatedly, according to police reports. When the attack occurred, he was preparing an article critical of Moon.[3]

One means by which the Church continues its involvement with the League is its new political arm, the Confederation of Associations for the Unity of the Societies of America (CAUSA).[4] Founded in 1980 by Bo Hi Pak and Kim Sang In, the former Korean CIA station chief in Mexico City, CAUSA's executive director was Warren Richardson, formerly the general counsel to the historical revisionist and anti-Semitic Liberty Lobby. In 1981, CAUSA and the Paraguayan chapter of the League held a joint anti-communist seminar in Asunción.

In addition to its CAUSA operations, the Unification Church pursues a public relations offensive through the International Conference for the Unity of the Sciences, the World Media Conference, and a host of other front groups. According to *The Washington Tribune,* the Church was operating over a hundred such fronts in 1982.

Clearly, the Unification Church of the Reverend Sun Myung Moon remains very active in spreading its brand of anti-communism, theological patriotism, and fealty to the "Heavenly Father." Ever since its vocal defense of President Nixon during Watergate, it has gained respectability through its alliances with conservative American professors, journalists, policymakers, and former intelligence agents. Most disquieting is the Church's close and extensive ties with American New Right leaders, present and former high-ranking military officers, and officials of the Reagan Administration.

The U.S. Global Strategy Council, an organization that former CIA Deputy Director Ray Cline helped create, purports to advise the Reagan Administration on foreign policy matters. On the council is Arnaud de Borchgrave, a fellow senior associate with Cline at the Georgetown Center for Strategic and International Studies and editor of the Moon-owned *Washington Times.* The council's executive director is retired General E. David Woellner, president of CAUSA World Services.[5]

The retired head of the Defense Intelligence Agency, Major General Daniel O. Graham, is on CAUSA USA's board of directors. Lynn Bouchey, president of the Council for Inter-American Security, organized two CAUSA conferences. Joseph Churba, former senior policy adviser to the Arms Control and Disarmament Agency and director of the Center for International Security, spoke at a CAUSA symposium in January 1985. Retired Lieutenant General Gordon Sumner, former chairman of the Inter-American Defense Board, was the cochairman of a conference of the International Security Council, a CAUSA project, in Paris in February 1985. General George Keegan, former chief of Air Force Intelligence, paneled a CAUSA seminar in September 1984. Miles Costick, president of the Institute on Strategic Trade; Terry Dolan, executive director of the National Conservative Political Action Committee (NCPAC); and Jay Parker, president of the Lincoln Institute and head of the NCPAC-funded Blacks for Reagan 1984—all have attended CAUSA conferences.

The Church also conducts its elaborate public relations campaign with New Right newspapers and magazines. Donald Holdgriewe, associate editor of the Moonie *Rising Tide,* is also the managing editor of *The Washington Inquirer,* the weekly of the conservative Council for

the Defense of Freedom. The communications director for Reed Irvine's Accuracy in Media, Bernard Yoh, is a regular contributor to
Rising Tide and a strong defender of both Moon and the South Korean
regime.

This public relations campaign got a tremendous boost when the
Church launched *The Washington Times* in 1982. With endorsements
from the Moral Majority's Jerry Falwell, and Senators John East (R–
North Carolina), Paul Laxalt (R–Nevada), Jesse Helms (R–North
Carolina), and Orrin Hatch (R–Utah), Bo Hi Pak, Moon's righthand
man and publisher of the *Times,* was able to line up an impressive
array of conservatives, former intelligence operatives, and Reagan
insiders to work for this "alternative" newspaper. Proof of the mar-
riage of the Moonies with the New Right and the Reagan Administration requires nothing more than examining the *Times* masthead.

Roger Fontaine, formerly a Latin American specialist on the National Security Council, now works for *The Washington Times,* as does
Jeremiah O'Leary, former National Security Adviser William Clark's
special assistant. The list also includes John McLowery, an unsuccessful senatorial candidate from Vermont who served on Reagan's
transition team; and Cord Meyer, a former top CIA official spe-
cializing in clandestine operations.

The newspaper firmly supports the Reagan Administration in
practically all issues, while also producing "puff pieces" on the South
Korean government. What the *Times* has come to resemble in its four
years of operation is the closest thing to a government-sponsored
newspaper the United States has seen in modern times.

One question that all journalists and investigators studying the
Unification Church eventually ask themselves is where the money
comes from. It is a question that is extremely difficult to answer.

What is known is that the Unification Church is operating commercial fishing fleets at massive losses throughout the United States.
It lost an estimated $150,000 in the first two years of its publication
of *The Washington Times* and many millions more through its New
York–based *The News World,* the Spanish-language *Noticias del Mundo,*
and *The Middle East Times* in Cyprus.

At the same time, its membership has declined dramatically. Although the Church claims 500,000 Korean, 300,000 Japanese, and
30,000 American followers, most independent observers place the

figures at 15,000, 8,000 and 4,000, respectively. *The Washington Times* once claimed to have a circulation of 126,000; actual circulation hovers around 70,000. This figure was independently verified only in April 1985; until then, the *Times* had repeatedly canceled outside auditing, a process that sets advertising rates and that most newspapers initiate regularly.

And yet the Church has quietly channeled over $100,000,000 into the South American nation of Uruguay, buying up its biggest hotel, its third-largest newspaper, and a printing company, and depositing at least $50,000,000 in one of its banks. It has also underwritten half-million-dollar Asian junkets for American journalists (among them Reed Irvine, chairman of Accuracy in Media, and William Rusher, publisher of *National Review*) through the World Media Conference and has picked up the costs for international meetings of CAUSA and the International Conference of the Unity of the Sciences.

It also spends $1,500,000 a year on a conservative Washington think tank; has sunk $15,000,000 into national distribution for the unsuccessful *Washington Times*; has given a half-million dollars to the National Conservative Political Action Committee (NCPAC); and still has money left over to scour northern Virginia for a suitable location to build a new radio station.

According to Mike Murphy, a former NCPAC official who was hired by Bo Hi Pak to advise on that particular project, "We drove all over northern Virginia in limousines looking at empty lots on high ground. When I asked them how soon they were thinking of starting [the radio station], one of them opened up a suitcase and smiled. It was full of dollars."[6]

It is clear that the Unification Church is applying its "Heavenly Deception" dogma—that lying is necessary when doing God's work and that truth is what Moon, as the son of God, says it is—to its financial matters. For a church of dwindling congregation and of annual profits from its industrial holdings in Korea estimated at considerably less than $10,000,000, to lose $150,000,000 on a newspaper in the United States, to operate unprofitable fishing fleets in Massachusetts and Louisiana, to spend untold millions for conferences throughout the world, and simultaneously to deposit $100,000,000 into a South American country, leaves a financial discrepancy that cannot easily be filled by the earnings of pallid disciples selling flowers in airports, however fervent they may be.

Two former high officials of the Unification Church in Japan have disclosed that as much as $800,000,000 was funneled into the United States from Japan over a nine-year period, often by disciples carrying cash in their luggage. They attribute this enormous cash flow to the success of Happy World Inc., a Church subsidiary in Japan that markets religious icons; yet it seems doubtful that such an amount could be generated through the selling of miniature pagodas and marble vases.

Suspicions about the origin of some of the money run a wide gamut; some Moonie-watchers even believe that some of the business enterprises are actually covers for drug-trafficking.[7] Others feel that, despite the disclosures of Koreagate, the Church has simply continued to do the Korean government's international bidding and is receiving official funds to do so. Perhaps the most realistic hypothesis, put forth by a former high official of the South Korean government, is that much of the money is "flight capital" from wealthy Koreans and the same Japanese racketeers, Sasakawa and Kodama, that Moon formed an alliance with in the 1960s.

Whatever the origin of its money, the Reverend Moon's Church, with its connections into the Reagan Administration, the American New Right, and the global anti-communist movement, remains a powerful and ominous force on the world scene. Its impact can perhaps best be seen in CAUSA's operations in Latin America.

With offices throughout the region, CAUSA preaches its brand of active anti-communism to the masses and helps "freedom fighters" with basic supplies, cash, and emergency relief. This has resulted in the somewhat jarring sight, witnessed by one of the authors, of seeing gun-toting guerrillas in Honduras clad in red CAUSA T-shirts.

In this effort, the Church often works jointly with various chapters of the World Anti-Communist League, reflecting the new emphasis of both organizations on bolstering the governments of El Salvador and Guatemala and on aiding the contras in their guerrilla war against the leftist government of Nicaragua. CAUSA and Refugee Relief International, an affiliate of the current American chapter of the World Anti-Communist League, both ferried supplies to the same contra camps in 1984.

CAUSA's stated goal is to have conservative leaders from throughout North and South America join forces under a single ideological banner to fight communism. That ideological banner would of course be Unificationism. It has pursued this goal by extending invitations to CAUSA seminars to businessmen, political leaders, scientists, and journalists, all expenses paid. It also organizes "fact-finding" trips to Asia and the United States and carries the message of theological anti-communism into the hinterlands of Latin America through radio stations and newspapers in eighteen countries.

What has emerged, then, is a pattern of Moon joining forces with prominent American conservatives, former military and intelligence officials, and Reagan Administration appointees to jointly pursue a Latin America policy independent of the will of any government and of the dictates of any congress. This alliance has in fact been secured to such an extent that the disclosures of Koreagate might pale in comparison. It is perhaps for that reason that an analyst for the Institute of Defense Analysis, a Pentagon-funded think tank, warned of the possible effects that exposure of the Administration's ties to the Church might have on the 1984 elections.

> Current Moonie involvement with government officials, contractors and grantees . . . could create a major scandal. If their activities and role become public knowledge, it will unite both the left and the right in attacking the Administration.
>
> Moonie involvement leaves the government open to charges that can only be called mind-boggling. . . . If efforts are not taken to stop their growing influence and weed out current Moonie involvement in government, the President stands a good chance of being portrayed in the media as a poor, naive incompetent.

Lest the point be missed, the writer concludes, "Any thought that this festering problem will go away if ignored is foolish. There have been comments in the media about Moonie activities and the likely-hood [*sic*] of a reporter or a democratic staff member piecing the total picture together is too great to be neglected."

ELEVEN

The [China-WACL] International Publicity Committee held a special work group meeting on April 15 [1970] to discuss accelerated overseas distribution of anti-communist data and publications. . . . The United States shall be the major target area. . . . Major objectives shall be to correct the fallacious views of appeasers, expose the true face and weak points of communists, check the spread of the communist evil and promote the ideals of WACL and APACL.

WACL China chapter,
May 1970

IN 1978, the vice-president of a Central American republic had dinner with an old school friend, a newly promoted lieutenant colonel in the nation's armed forces. The officer had just returned from two months in Taiwan. "It is such a pretty island," the officer told his friend, "with mountains and gorges and beaches. And the women! They are so beautiful and friendly."

Throughout dinner, the officer talked of the cuisine, the hospitality of the people and the scenery of the island. He never mentioned what his true mission in Taiwan had been. "I realized then," the former vice-president told one of the authors, "that he was one of the brotherhood."

Political change has been slow to come to Taiwan since the Kuomintang took over and created Nationalist China. By intimidating overseas Chinese, by blanket censorship in Taiwan, and by the extravagant hospitality shown American visitors, the Nationalist regime has successfully kept quiet the story of what one American official of a religious human rights group calls the most repressive country he has visited in Asia.

Although the tiny island nation has experienced an economic boom, giving it one of the highest standards of living in Asia, it is still ruled by a nepotistic dictatorship of aging Kuomintang generals and industrialists; the native Formosans, ninety percent of the population, are largely shut out of the system. Permanent martial law is in effect, and dissidents are routinely arrested, tortured, banished to the prison on Green Island, or executed. The police and military leadership positions are almost exclusively the domain of mainlanders or their children. Opposition candidates are allowed to vie for only fifteen percent of the seats in the National Assembly; the rest are constitutionally reserved for the Kuomintang, who were elected on the mainland in the 1940s.

The regime has a curious rationale for this system: since they cannot return to their native Chinese provinces to stand for elections, the Kuomintang legislators in Taiwan have no choice but to remain in the leadership roles to which they were elected in the 1940s. Likewise, all security measures, including the arbitrary arrests, surveillances, "disappearances," and kangaroo courts, are justified as necessary hardships that must be tolerated in order to recover the mainland.

The Kuomintang has also pursued a program of repression in its activities throughout the world. A principal conduit for this "organizational warfare" is the World Anti-Communist League.

The Kuomintang "undertook to use organizational principles to counter and compete with the Communist talent for subversion through front groups. . . . In a strategic sense, the principles of organizational warfare were realized by membership in the United Nations and anti-communist alliances. All types of international organizations were seen as appropriate targets to be influenced from within by being a member and lobbying from that vantage point. Special emphasis was also given to infiltrating overseas Chinese populations and the interest groups that exist within them. International conferences, diplomacy and unofficial international contacts and channels were considered excellent means to spread anti-communist influence."[1]

Consequently, it is not only Taiwanese residents or citizens who must accept the dictates of the Kuomintang. Taiwanese students in the United States live in a state of fear due to the presence of "professional students," KMT agents sent to watch over the Chinese community and to report on any deviant (pro–mainland China or pro–Formosa independence) behavior or activities. The Kuomintang's informants even have standardized index cards ("total number of students who are patriotic," "total number of students who are pro-Communist," "information about the enemies") that they fill out and send to Taiwan every month. Students in the United States who fail to follow the KMT line have had their exit visas revoked, have received death threats, or have been warned of the dire effect that further political activity might have on the student's family remaining in Taiwan.

Taiwanese professors living in the United States are no safer. In 1981, Wen-Chen Chen, an assistant professor at Carnegie-Mellon University who had criticized the Kuomintang government, visited his family in Taiwan. He was picked up by the secret police and interrogated for thirteen hours; then he reportedly committed suicide when "overcome with remorse" for his anti-state pronouncements.

In 1984, David Liu, a journalist living in California who had written a book critical of the Kuomintang, was shot in the face and chest by two men on bicycles outside his home. The FBI investigation of the murder implicated high Taiwanese government officials, including the director and the deputy director of the intelligence bureau of the ministry of national defense.

One of the most ardent critics of Taiwan's foreign surveillance and harassment campaign is Representative James Leach (R–Iowa), who led a Subcommittee on Asian and Pacific Affairs investigation of KMT activities in the United States in 1981. "In the activities documented by our subcommittee," he wrote Attorney General William French Smith, "it would appear that the Taiwan government has massively violated the Foreign Agents Registration Act. In addition, there is a strong possibility that it has stretched or violated tax, mail, and immigration laws and conventions, as well as our privacy statutes. . . . It is clear that many Taiwanese are directly and indirectly prevented from exercising the rights of free speech, privacy, and association guaranteed by the Constitution."[2]

The Kuomintang program against dissidents in the United States is just one aspect of the regime's campaign of political and unconventional warfare against those it considers its enemies. This warfare has become far more prevalent—and deadly—since the opening of mainland China to the outside world in the early 1970s.

As nations began dropping recognition of Nationalist China in favor of the People's Republic of China, organizations like the World Anti-Communist League and the Asian People's Anti-Communist League took on far more significance for the Kuomintang government. With their embassies relegated to the status of missions or abolished altogether, the Taiwanese sought to maintain their foreign ties by whatever channels were still left open to them, namely "independent" international associations such as the League.

So quick and total was the diplomatic about-face by Taiwan's primary allies in Western Europe and the United States that the Kuomintang had to scramble to consolidate their last great bastion of support—Latin America. They established large diplomatic missions that were totally disproportionate to the level of economic or political ties in such countries as Paraguay and Guatemala; through them, the Nationalist Chinese appealed to the anti-communist sentiments of Latin leaders to ensure continued support for Taiwan.

To achieve unity with anti-communist countries, "the General Political Warfare Department enlisted cultural, educational, social and economic organizations in this campaign. Virtually all individual and governmental activities, domestic and international, were expected to proceed from an ideological perspective."[3] To this end, the Nationalists expanded the League throughout Latin America, creating the regional affiliate, the Latin American Anti-Communist Confederation (CAL) in 1972. The Kuomintang did not view such organizations as mere public relations forums but rather as the "organizational warfare" aspect of their global political warfare scheme.

In their search for new allies and in their effort to retain old ones, the Nationalists in Taiwan were willing to do much more than simply orate about the need for a common anti-communist strategy at League conferences. They also used their League connections to render a mutually beneficial service to their right-wing allies in South and Central America. Through the offices of the World Anti-Communist League, they offered to train the police, military, and security forces of the region in unconventional warfare, interrogation, and counterterror tactics at their Political Warfare Cadres Academy in Peitou.[4]

In the past decade, most Latin American nations have accepted the Taiwanese offer; this has created a continental fraternity of thousands of high-ranking officers who are united by their anti-communist convictions and the Kuomintang-taught creed, "you have to be as cruel as the enemy" to win. This is the "brotherhood" that the Central American vice-president referred to.

During his tenure in office, the vice-president met other members of the fraternity, graduates of the Political Warfare Cadres Academy. "All of them were the same. They would talk about the food, the girls, but about the training, never! It was eerie, as if there was some sort of pact of silence. I was the Vice President and even I had no idea of what went on there."

Although the civilian vice-president didn't realize it, there was a very good reason why he did not know what transpired at the academy. Through their political warfare training program, the Kuomintang were erecting in Latin America carbon copies of what they had created in Taiwan: a politicized military whose first loyalty was to the party, then to the military, and finally to the nation. "You have to create a political structure to support your own military." Brian Jenkins, a counterinsurgency expert for the Rand Corporation, explained the Taiwan system to *Los Angeles Times* reporter Laurie Becklund in 1983. "That gives it a flow of intelligence. In a sense, you wind up with a political party, with the military being the armed component of that party."[5]

Through this quiet program, Taiwan was attempting to mold anti-communist and pro-Kuomintang Latin officers in every branch of the military in South and Central America.

Although officials of nearly all Latin nations have participated in the Peitou program at one time or another, it has not been regarded with universal approval by their leaders. Some have reportedly acquiesced because of the Kuomintang's insistent demands and veiled threats of economic retaliation. One leader caught in this bind was General Omar Torrijos, the late strongman of Panama. "I don't trust the Taiwanese," he once told a visiting dignitary, "and I don't trust my men when they came back. They brainwash them. I have to prepare them before they go."[6]

Torrijos prepared them by telling them what to expect at the academy and warning them not to succumb to the relentless "cruelty as a necessity" and anti–Communist China rhetoric of the instructors. The Panamanian leader was so suspicious of the Taiwanese methods and of their effect on his men that upon their return he submitted them to "geographical debriefing," stationing them in jungle outposts with only four or five men under their command.

This Kuomintang scheme is conducted through one of their "organizational warfare" arms, the World Anti-Communist League. This Taiwanese version of *The Invasion of the Body Snatchers* in Latin America is developed in two stages, each coordinated through the offices of the League. This plan has already been pursued and accomplished in countries such as El Salvador and Guatemala.

First, through its liaisons in the League, the Kuomintang identifies the political party in a Latin country that is the most militantly anti-communist. The political party chosen to be represented in the League is invariably the one that has already actively proven its anti-communist mettle or else displays the ability and will to do so. Following the Kuomintang model, the chosen party establishes a nationwide intelligence and counterterror network. These paramilitary groups are then gradually incorporated into the nation's armed forces. This is usually accomplished when, in a moment of national crisis, the army turns to these civilian bands for support, or when it is too impotent to curb them.

In so doing, the paramilitary "party" effectively takes over those branches of the military with which it operates, just as the Kuomintang did in prerevolutionary China.

This first phase of the Kuomintang model is well illustrated in Guatemala and El Salvador. In each, the death squad apparatus that became institutionalized in the military was first created by a pseudopolitical party. In Guatemala, this party was the National Liberation Movement (MLN) of Mario Sandoval Alarcon; in El Salvador, it was first the National Conciliation Party (PCN) and later the Nationalist Republican Alliance (ARENA) of Roberto D'Aubuisson. It is not coincidence that the World Anti-Communist League chapters from Guatemala and El Salvador have predominantly been composed of officials from these parties. Nor is it coincidence that El Salvador's ARENA, the so-called "death squad party," has a structure remarkably similar to the Kuomintang.

"ARENA," former U.S. Ambassador to El Salvador Robert White reported in 1984, "has a politico-military organization which embraces not only a civilian party structure but also a military arm obedient to the party."[7]

The second phase of the exported Kuomintang model is the one that most directly benefits Nationalist China. Once its power base is established in the military, the Latin political party is used as a conduit to relay Taiwan's invitation to the nation's armed forces to train select officers at the Peitou academy. These offers are often extended through the party officials who attend the World Anti-Communist League conferences. Because the political party has infiltrated its cadres into the decision-making offices of the military, those selected to go to Taiwan are naturally party loyalists or sympathizers. When the officers return, they are promoted and scattered throughout the various military branches. Consequently, the Latin political party gains supporters—and Taiwan gains allies—in prominent positions at all levels of the armed forces.

The Latin American cadres who travel to Taiwan to be trained return to their native countries, where they in turn instruct their comrades in the "Taiwanese method." This method of "total war" includes aspects of unconventional warfare, or counterterror. Although the Taiwanese may not actually urge the formation of death squads, some of their Latin pupils have incorporated aspects of their instruction to these ends. Among those who have received training at the Political Warfare Cadres Academy is Roberto D'Aubuisson of El Salvador. D'Aubuisson is widely believed to be the mastermind behind his nation's death squads.

TWELVE

These people aren't Jew-haters; they're killers. This anti-Semitism is bullshit; it's a smokescreen to throw people off the track of what they're really doing. And what they're really doing is killing people.

Former Salvadoran government official referring to CAL, March 1985

HAVING BEEN GIVEN free rein by the World Anti-Communist League leadership, the Tecos of Mexico established League chapters throughout South and Central America in the early 1970s. As could have been predicted, their initiates into the Latin American Anti-Communist Confederation (CAL) were drawn from fanatic circles throughout the region.

The Tecos had a well-established network of "men of action" from which to choose: secret police officials, military officers, and wealthy landowners and industrialists who were ready to defend their fortunes at any price. For the Tecos were well known in the region by the 1970s; in the name of anti-communism, they were reportedly in the business of eliminating whoever needed eliminating for whoever would pay for the job.*

---

*Some observers suspect that the Tecos recently eliminated at least one well-known person for personal reasons. In April 1984, Manuel Buendia, Mexico's foremost investigative journalist, wrote a three-part series exposing "Los Tecos," their secret code of honor, and their control of the Autonomous University of Guadalajara. A month later, leaving his Mexico City office, Buendia was assassinated with four close-range shots to the back. His murder has not been solved.

"I've dealt with these people [the Tecos]," Colonel Roberto Eulalio Santivañez, the former counterespionage chief of El Salvador, told one of the authors. "They came to me when I was in the military and offered us their services. To show they meant business, they bragged that they had a death list of people in the States, people they wanted to get rid of. They were trying to work out the logistics then; I don't know if they ever got anyone. But in Salvador, they didn't see any problem. They said they could get anyone I wanted. They offered to provide everything—the guns, the people—but they wanted money up front. I threw them out; so they went to the civilians, the oligarchs."[1]

Apparently spurned by the Salvadoran military and possibly by others, the Tecos pursued their program with civilian groups. It was in establishing CAL that the Tecos' true mission was revealed. What they were attempting to create was not an "Anti-Semitic International," as American League member Stefan Possony had feared, but a "Death Squad International."

The World Anti-Communist League provided a perfect cover for this recruitment operation and within a short time, some of the most notorious killers, sadists, drug traffickers, and terrorists in Latin America could be found under the CAL umbrella.

Mario Sandoval Alarcón, the founder of Guatemala's National Liberation Movement (MLN), is a heavyset man in his mid-sixties. Since 1972, he has headed the Guatemalan chapter of the World Anti-Communist League. Due to throat cancer, he speaks in a rasp aided by an electronic amplifier.

When Sandoval eventually dies from his cancer, his end will come too late for the tens of thousands of Guatemalans who have been kidnapped, tortured, executed, and dumped onto roadsides by the death squads that this former vice-president has helped control for the past twenty years. Sandoval attended the 1985 League conference in Dallas and President Reagan's Inaugural Ball in 1981.

In drawing Sandoval into the League, the Mexican Tecos acquired a high-profile personality who was a member of one of Guatemala's ruling families. In the 1970s he achieved mentor status among Latin rightists and became the guiding force of the Latin American Anti-Communist Confederation. By giving material assistance and advice to other death squad parties, Sandoval established a regional network

of terror and earned himself the title "Godfather." Although the Tecos and the Argentine Tacuaras of Julio Meinveille may have been
CAL's spiritual leaders, Sandoval, "the biggest anti-communist leader
in the world, now that Chiang Kai-shek is dead," according to one
right-wing Salvadoran admirer, was to be the "on-site" manager who
would put their plans into action in Central America.

In the 1970s, Carlos Barbieri Filho was practically unknown in
his native Brazil. An ultra-rightist in his thirties, Barbieri Filho's politics—and his habit of carrying a pistol on his hip—were too extreme
for most of his countrymen. His call for violent confrontation with
the forces of communism seemed a little out of step in a nation that
had not experienced the horrors of an all-out civil war and that did
not see the need to "kill or be killed." Nor could Barbieri find much
support among the rightist military, which, although ruling Brazil,
was rather benign compared to the neighboring juntas of Argentina,
Bolivia, and Uruguay. Even the arch-conservative Brazilian organization Tradition, Family and Property (TFP), with its goal to return
Brazil to a kind of medieval Catholic feudalism, considered him
something of a volatile madman.

The Tecos, scouting for a Brazilian branch of CAL, did not share
that view. Barbieri was duly anointed chairman of the chapter representing the largest and most powerful nation in Latin America.

Barbieri has played a much greater role in the World Anti-Communist League than merely attending conferences. He is reportedly
an important agent in the Taiwanese government's campaign to gain
influence in South America.

According to a TFP official, Barbieri Filho operates out of a front
company in Paraguay. His Financiera Urundey office reportedly ar-
ranges the rosters of the officers to be sent to Taiwan and handles
the logistics of their travel. Traveling frequently to Taiwan himself,
Barbieri is the object of lavish praise from his Kuomintang paymas-
ters.

One night in 1981, a man was murdered in his home in San
Salvador. The man killed that night was a wealthy businessman, a
former member of the National Assembly, and the chairman of the
Salvadoran chapter of the World Anti-Communist League. He was
also a compulsive murderer, sadist, and drunk who had once acci-

dentally killed a servant boy while shooting at a "friend" during a cocktail party argument. Former Salvadoran army officers also remember him as a man who used to appear at interrogation centers and beg for permission to torture the prisoners.

"The man had a dual personality," former Salvadoran Colonel Santivañez recalls, "drunk and sober. When he was sober, he was a torturer and killer; when he was drunk, he was worse."

With the death of Adolfo Cuellar, the League lost an anti-communist "man of action" but gained a martyr.

Pastor Coronel was not one to complain about the repressive rule of General Alfredo Stroessner in the South American nation of Paraguay. The litany of accusations made against the government—that it was the smuggling center for Latin America, a haven for Nazi war criminals, a place where the indigenous Ache Indians were hunted down and killed for sport, where eight-year-old girls were "bought" for $1.25 and used for the sexual depravity of government officials—could not have found any sympathy from Pastor Coronel. Then again, no one who participated in the 1977 Latin American Anti-Communist Confederation conference in Asunción, Paraguay, would have voiced such criticisms to Coronel, their fellow attendee. They probably would have agreed with Bo Hi Pak when he said of Stroessner, "I believe he's a special man, chosen by God to run his country."[2]

Coronel was among the few Paraguayans who had benefited from the cruel reign of the general and his Colorado political party. As chief of the Investigative Police, the country's secret police, Coronel had become an extremely wealthy man. In the early 1970s, according to a classified CIA document, he had been smuggling partners with Auguste Ricorde, a Corsican drug kingpin. Together, with the assistance of many of the nation's highest-ranking generals, they had turned Paraguay into the "Heroin Crossroads of South America," channeling the contraband on its way to the United States. Ricorde was finally extradited to the United States in 1973; Coronel was left unscathed.

Simultaneously amassing his personal fortune and seeing to Paraguay's internal security had made Coronel a busy man. Under a state-of-siege decree that has existed since 1954, the chief of the Investigative Police is empowered to arrest and interrogate anyone at any time. Survivors from Paraguayan prisons tell of Coronel's personal involvement in the "interrogations," submitting his victims to beatings and electric shocks, hanging them by their wrists, and holding their heads in tubs of excrement.

Coronel did not focus his attention solely on Paraguay, however. As secret police chief, he knew that Paraguayan subversives sometimes escaped across borders to voice their opposition in exile. At the same time, subversives from other nations occasionally came into Paraguay for safety.* In the 1970s, a clandestine regional program, Operation Condor, was devised to meet this threat, with Pastor Coronel directing its Paraguayan operations.

What united all these disparate "anti-communists" and drew them into the World Anti-Communist League was a school of thought that had taken hold in right-wing circles throughout Latin America by the 1970s; Operation Condor was just one manifestation of this philosophy put into practice.

Paraphrased, it is based on four principles: 1. all dissidents and opponents of the state are communists; 2. all communists are taking orders from the same source in the pursuit of communist control of the world; 3. since their orders come from the same source, the opposition in one nation is the same as the opposition in another; and 4. for the nations of Latin America to fight a united enemy, they too must unite. This implies that one nation has the right, in fact the duty, to silence not only the opposition to one's own regime but also the opposition to any neighboring regime.

The brainchild of the Chilean secret police (DINA), Operation Condor was created in 1976 to coordinate the security forces of Latin American right-wing governments, enabling them to track and hunt down their enemies. Through joint intelligence-gathering and -sharing, a leftist who had fled Brazil, for example, could be located in Argentina. Then "Phase Three" could be initiated.

Phase Three, according to a top-secret 1979 report of the Senate Foreign Relations Committee that was obtained by columnist Jack Anderson, "involves the formation of special teams from member

---

*The assassination of the deposed Nicaraguan dictator Anastasio Somoza in Asunción in September 1980 was carried out by Argentine leftists who had slipped into Paraguay.

countries assigned to travel anywhere in the world to non-member countries to carry out 'sanctions'—including assassination—against Condor enemies."

According to Anderson, "One 'Phase Three' team is charged with drawing up the Condor 'hit list' in a particular country. Then a second team is dispatched to locate the targeted victims and conduct surveillance on them. Finally, a third team, drawn from one or more member police agencies, is sent to carry out the 'sanction' decided upon."[3]

It now seems likely that the car-bomb killing of Chilean dissident Orlando Letelier in Washington in 1976 (orchestrated by an American contract agent of the Chilean secret police and conducted by anti-Castro Cuban exiles) and the attempted murder of Bernardo Leighton (shot by an Italian fascist on orders from Chile, with the "credit" taken by Cuban exiles) are examples of the work of Condor. There are other cases throughout Latin America with the Condor imprint, from liberal Uruguayan politicians murdered in Argentina to Chilean dissidents killed in Bolivia.

Officially, Operation Condor was dismantled after American authorities became aware of it and exerted strong pressure on the dictators responsible. In reality, it has simply changed form; Latin American governments continued to carry out "trans-national terror," now often contracting out its assignments to private groups. One of those private groups was the World Anti-Communist League, specifically its Latin American affiliate, the CAL.

At the 1977 Confederation conference, Pastor Coronel, the Paraguayan secret police chief and his nation's Operation Condor coordinator, was in the company of other ultra-rightists and officers from right-wing governments from around the hemisphere. Together they formulated a new, more violent role for the League.

Since the 1960s, the opposition to the right-wing governments in South and Central America had steadily grown until, by the late 1970s, it had reached perilous proportions. Dissent could now be found over a very wide and expanding spectrum and was far too extensive to be dealt with by the sort of "surgical strikes" that were Operation Condor's specialty. After decades of practice, security forces could deal with labor leaders, liberal politicians, and agrarian reformers, but a much more serious and powerful movement was growing, one that could not be dealt with in the same manner: the Vatican Church.

During the 1960s, many Catholic priests in South and Central America rejected the Vatican tradition of allying with the ruling militaries and oligarchies and had shown new concern for the plight of the majority, who were poor, uneducated, and malnourished. Priests, including many from Europe and the United States, became spokesmen for the rights of the disenfranchised, whether they were striking workers or landless peasants or families inquiring into the fate of a family member picked up and taken away by the security forces. By the 1970s, as conflict spread throughout the region and the ruling regimes reacted with even greater repression, many of the Catholic clergy became radicalized along with the general population, voicing a doctrine termed "liberation theology." Priests became some of the most vocal and visible opponents of the right-wing juntas, in some cases to the point of taking up arms. To the League, rather than representing legitimate concerns, liberation theology was just one more insidious form of communism.

"I accuse," Sandoval Alarcón charged, "and at the same time denounce, the fact that the Catholic Church is the victim of an intense Marxist penetration. . . . This comes from revolutionary priests . . . [and is] one more trick of Communism and its infiltrated accomplices strongly acting within the highest echelons of the Catholic hierarchy."[4]

This anti-Vatican stance was of course mirrored in the vicious attacks of the Mexican Tecos on Pope Paul VI ("a Jew and a drug addict"), but it also touched a responsive chord in non-Latin League members, including the Romanian Iron Guard. "When the powers of darkness threaten the very existence of Christianity," Horia Sima told his followers, "there is no other solution but the recourse to arms. The 'peaceful co-existence' with Communism, adopted by many Christians of today, is nothing but an expression of cowardice. It is a 'running away' from sacrifice and responsibility. The Church has been abandoned to the anti-Christ."[5]

What the juntas needed was a new regional network to spot, track, and silence, through murder, deportation, or jail sentences, liberal priests. This new form of transnational terror, just one more variation on the unconventional warfare theme, was delineated in 1975 in the "Banzer Plan" (named after the Bolivian dictator of the time, Hugo Banzer Juarez) and would be achieved through the offices of the Latin American Anti-Communist Confederation.

"The backbone of this strategy was a central depository of intelligence containing dossiers on all progressive laity, clergy and bishops, with which to 'monitor and denounce Marxist infiltration in the Church.' . . . The three main thrusts of the campaign were to sharpen internal divisions within the Church, to smear and harass progressive . . . Church leaders, and to arrest or expel foreign priests and nuns."[6]

This plan was first discussed at the CAL conference in Asunción in 1977 by the Bolivian chapter and was accepted by nine other Latin American countries. In 1978, the Paraguayan delegation introduced a priest-tracking resolution to the entire assembly of the World Anti-Communist League, repeating almost word for word the tenets of the Banzer Plan.

> Since a few years back, the Catholic Apostolic Roman Church, as well as some other Christian denominations, have worked together or parallelly [sic], in an institutional form or through groups of individuals having as an aim attempted changes in the total structure of society, especially in underdeveloped countries.
>
> All this has originated actions scientifically motivated by the Marxist ideology, and politically directed by international communism, directly disturbing order and harmony in the political field. In underdeveloped countries, priests or nuns of foreign nationality, whose personal background and ideological attitude are difficult to know at the moment of their entrance into the country are frequently present.
>
> Therefore, based upon the reasons above, the 11th. Anticommunist Conference resolves: to recommend the settlement of an office which specializes on religious affairs, organized on a regional basis, and especially devoted to maintain up-to-date information about the ideological orientation of the main religious institutions, as well as to elaborate a file containing the names of priests and nuns along with their personal background, to be annually revised.[7]

The resolution passed overwhelmingly.

Whether this priest-watching network ever reached the sophisticated level the Paraguayan chapter called for in 1978 is not clear. What is clear is that during the two years after CAL adopted the Banzer Plan, at least twenty-eight bishops, priests, and lay persons were killed in Latin America; most of their murders were attributed to government security forces or rightist death squads. That number multiplied after 1980 as civil war spread through Guatemala and El Salvador.

Although they were used by right-wing governments to combat the "communist threat" within the Church, the Latin chapters of the World Anti-Communist League did not confine themselves to this mission. In 1980, they served as the major liaison in exporting death squads, sophisticated surveillance, torture, and infiltration techniques from South America to Central America.

In 1980, Argentina was just beginning to recover from a bloody civil war that had claimed thousands of lives and that had helped leave that nation, once the wealthiest in South America, bankrupt and reliant on foreign aid to pay its bills.

The enemies of the state in Argentina had been the Montoneros, a small leftist guerrilla band that throughout the 1970s had waged a campaign of kidnapping, selective assassination, and bank robbery. When the civilian government had proved unable to eliminate the Montoneros, the army had stepped in and established a military junta. What occurred then is known as the "dirty war."

Journalists, students, Jewish leaders, liberal priests, and anyone suspected of being anti-state or pro-Montonero were rounded up, tortured, and killed by the Argentine security forces. In the spirit of Operation Condor, prominent exiles residing in Argentina were eliminated as a favor to the right-wing governments of Uruguay and Chile. Thousands were buried in secret cemeteries; others were thrown into the Río de la Plata or dropped from helicopters into the Atlantic Ocean. By 1980, an estimated nine thousand people, only a small fraction of them actual Montoneros, had been murdered. Despite the death toll, the military government accomplished what it had set out to do: the Montoneros had practically ceased to exist.

The "dirty war" caused the Argentine junta to be viewed with repugnance throughout the world but not by the military regimes of its neighbors or by the ultra-rightists in the World Anti-Communist League. "Argentina," Teco Professor Rafael Rodríguez told the 1980 League conference, "along with Chile and Uruguay, are the only countries in the world who overthrew and rid themselves of the Marxist revolutionary guerrilla. Argentina has no reason to give explanations to international committees which show up to interrogate about events which happened in war actions and in which the men on both sides were armed and had the same chances of living or dying."[8]

Rather, in destroying the Montoneros and all other opposition, Argentina served as an example to the League rightists of just what was necessary to combat the international communist threat.

> The [leftist] violations of human rights endured by Argentine society in the last decade and which, in particular, became more pronounced during the period of a full democratic government, must be known by the organisms of American nations. These nations should be prepared to take joint measures against a danger that has no boundaries.[9]

The Argentine interrogators who had tortured information out of their victims went on to teach their methods to their counterparts in other Latin countries. The security agents who had transported truckloads of bodies to dumping grounds under the cover of darkness would have to show their fellow anti-communists elsewhere how to dispose of their corpses efficiently. For the promotion of this "educational process," the Latin American Anti-Communist Confederation once again served as the key coordinator.[10]

In September 1980, the annual CAL conference was held in Buenos Aires, capital of Argentina. Presiding over the meeting was General Carlos Guillermo Suárez Mason, commander of the Argentine First Army Corps; he was responsible for executing much of the "dirty war" in the capital. There were several celebrities among the audience, including John Carbaugh, an aide to North Carolina Senator Jesse Helms, and Stefano delle Chiaie, an Italian terrorist wanted for countless murders and bombings throughout Europe. He had made the journey from his asylum in Bolivia, where he was allegedly in a cocaine-smuggling partnership with Klaus Barbie, a notorious Nazi war criminal known as "the Butcher of Lyon."* Also at the meeting was Mario Sandoval Alarcón, the Guatemalan "Godfather." He had brought along a cashiered Salvadoran major who was both a friend and a protégé, Roberto D'Aubuisson.

---

*Klaus Barbie was deported to France to stand trial for war crimes in 1982, after a democratic government was elected in Bolivia. In 1982, Italian commandos staged a raid in Bolivia to capture Stefano delle Chiaie and a cohort, Pierluigi Pagliai. Pagliai was mortally wounded; delle Chiaie escaped and his current whereabouts are unknown.

D'Aubuisson had already made a name for himself by carting off hundreds of files from the Salvadoran National Security Agency, where he had been deputy chief until late 1979. A few weeks later, he had appeared on national television, files in hand, to denounce those he called "subversives" in the government, military, Church, universities, and labor unions; many of them later turned up dead.

In 1980, the civil strife in El Salvador was expanding. What was needed were not select assassinations of opponents but an all-out anti-communist campaign along the lines of the Argentine "dirty war." For that, though, the rightists in El Salvador needed help. Like a college graduate "networking" for a job, D'Aubuisson was in Buenos Aires to make the necessary contacts.

Sandoval Alarcón introduced him to the right people. Within two months, at least fifty Argentine unconventional-warfare advisers were dispatched into El Salvador to assist their anti-communist compatriots. They helped their students perfect their counterterror tactics so well that the extent of the "dirty war" in Argentina would be dwarfed by that in El Salvador.

In 1983, according to the chairman of the World Anti-Communist League, retired U.S. Major General John K. Singlaub, there was a major purge of the violent elements in the Latin chapters of the League. "We got rid of all those types," he asserts. "We've been trying to get rid of them since we joined [1981]. The people in WACL from Latin American now are good, respectable anti-communists."[11]

In reaction to the Jack Anderson articles that exposed CAL in January 1984, Singlaub turned to a prominent friend in the New Right for help. His January 30, 1984, letter to Reed Irvine, of Accuracy in Media, concludes: "Any help that you can give us in obtaining a retraction from Jack Anderson for that part of his articles which link WACL with the death squad activity will be greatly appreciated. If a retraction is not possible, I would appreciate your assistance in neutralizing the negative impact of these articles."

No retraction was made, for nothing had really changed in the League. Those that were purged in 1984 (not in 1983, as Singlaub asserts) were the Mexican Tecos. The others, the Bolivians who first

announced the Banzer Plan, the Guatemalans who esta
nation's death squads, and the Brazilians who coordinate the
warfare training program for Taiwan are still there and still wi
their deadly influence.

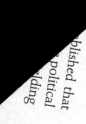

THIRTEEN

The term "unconventional warfare" includes, in addition to terrorism, subversion and guerrilla warfare, such covert and non-military activities as sabotage, economic warfare, support to resistance groups, black and gray psychological operations, disinformation activities, and political warfare. . . .

We find ourselves forced into inactivity because we lack the capability and the will to exercise [this] third option for our own defense, to take pressure off of an ally, or to exploit to our advantage the many vulnerabilities that now exist in the Soviet Empire.

What is needed as a matter of urgency is a national strategy which recognizes the whole spectrum of potential conflict and most especially the current unrecognized conflict at the unconventional warfare end of the scale.

Retired Major General John K. Singlaub
Phoenix, 1982

ON NOVEMBER 22, 1981, a meeting was held at the Mountain Shadow Resort Inn in Phoenix, Arizona. At the conclave were some of the top luminaries of the American ultra-right. The purpose of the meeting at the Mountain Shadow, which had been called by retired Major General John K. Singlaub, was to create a new American chapter of the World Anti-Communist League.

During his thirty-five-year career in the military, Singlaub had continually been involved in an official capacity in the sort of unconventional warfare that the World Anti-Communist League was now pursuing unofficially.

As an officer in the Office of Strategic Services (OSS), he had parachuted behind Nazi lines in France in 1944 to organize Resistance forces in advance of D-Day. He was then transferred to the Pacific theater, where he commanded an OSS team that instructed the Chinese in guerrilla warfare against the occupying Japanese. In 1946, he was assigned to be chief of the U.S. military liaison mission to Mukden, Manchuria, then served as the China desk officer for the CIA in 1949. After being involved in the establishment of the Ranger Training Center at Fort Benning, Georgia, he became CIA deputy chief in South Korea during the Korean War and served as a combat battalion commander.

His two-year stint in Vietnam in the mid-1960s is probably the most controversial period of his career. As commander of the Joint Unconventional Warfare Task Force, known as MACSOG, Singlaub was one of the on-site commanders of Operation Phoenix, the American-directed assassination and counterterror program.[1]

As a specialist in unconventional warfare and covert operations, Singlaub necessarily kept a low profile. That ended in 1978, when, as chief of staff of the United Nations Command in South Korea, he publicly denounced President Carter's plans to scale back American troop involvement there. Rebuked, Singlaub was forced to retire.

No one can dispute Singlaub's heroism: he is one of the most decorated officers in modern American history—the Distinguished Service Medal with Oak Leaf Cluster, the French Croix de Guerre, and the Silver Star Medal are just some of the dozens of military decorations he has received—but one can certainly wonder about his participation in the World Anti-Communist League.

In the two years before the Mountain Shadow meeting, Singlaub had become increasingly interested in the international federation. In 1980, he had been a speaker at the Asian People's Anti-Communist League conference in Taipei. Already in 1981 he had been an observer at the World League conference in Taipei. There he had been beseeched by League leaders to become more active in his support of the organization.

"They were concerned that after the [Roger] Pearson disaster," Singlaub recalls, "they no longer had an American chapter. They asked me if I would be interested in establishing a new one. After thinking about it and talking to different people, I agreed."[2]

Singlaub's new American chapter was not to be on the fringe of American conservatism, as had been Roger Pearson's. "I called a group together, mostly people who were interested in, or had been involved with, national security and foreign policy."

The new American League chapter, the United States Council for World Freedom (USCWF), was born, facilitated by a loan of nearly twenty thousand dollars from Taiwan.

What Singlaub was able to create was a body of powerful and respected American conservatives the likes of which the League had never seen. As the USCWF grew, this new League chapter came to include high-ranking former officers of the American military and intelligence community. Lieutenant General Daniel O. Graham, former director of the Defense Intelligence Agency, became its vice-chairman, while a retired Air Force lieutenant colonel, Albert Koen, was treasurer. On the advisory board was General Lewis Walt, former commander of Marine Corps forces in Vietnam, and Ray Sleeper, a retired Air Force colonel.

With Singlaub's status as a darling among conservatives—they compared his political outlook and the circumstances of his military downfall with those of General Douglas MacArthur—the United States Council for World Freedom could also reach leaders in New Right political and academic circles.

Today, John Fisher, president of the American Security Council (who first became involved with the League in the 1970s through the American Council for World Freedom) has returned to the League by serving on the USCWF's advisory board. He is joined there by such notables as Howard Phillips, chairman of the Conservative Caucus, and Andy Messing, formerly the caucus's executive director and now head of the National Defense Council. On the board of directors are Anthony Bouscaren, a professor of political science at Le Moyne University; Anthony Kubek, professor and curator of the General Claire Chennault Library at Troy University in Alabama; and Fred Schlafly, a constitutional lawyer and the husband of Phyllis Schlafly of anti-ERA fame. Also on the board of directors is Robert Morris, former chief counsel for the U.S. Senate Internal Security Subcommittee and current chairman of the National Committee to Restore Internal Security and president of Plano University in New Jersey.

Is it possible that in 1981 the members of this new American League chapter were somehow ignorant of the notoriety of the organization they had joined?

No, it is not possible, for joining the USCWF were at least four officers of the old American Council for World Freedom. The recollections of Stefan Possony, Lev Dobriansky, Jay Parker, and Fred Schlafly should have been sufficient for the new American chapter to learn all it needed to know about the anti-Semitic, fascist, and neo-Nazi elements that populated the World Anti-Communist League. If that were not enough, there was also the curious presence in the USCWF of David Rowe, professor of political science at Yale University. In 1970, as an executive member of the American Council for World Freedom, Rowe had written a scathing attack on the chairman of the World Anti-Communist League, Ku Cheng-kang, and had resigned when the council had joined the League over his objections. His contempt for Ku did not, however, dissuade him from joining the new American chapter of a League that Ku still headed. The presence of former ACWF officers is probably the most incriminating evidence against the new USCWF. As has been illustrated, by the early 1970s, the ACWF knew perhaps better than anyone else of the presence of unsavory elements within the League. It seems inconceivable that they wouldn't have passed this information on to their fellow officers in the new USCWF.

It certainly wasn't because the World Anti-Communist League had changed. In 1981, the Eastern European Nazis were still a major power bloc. The Tecos in Mexico were still a dominant force. The Unification Church still controlled the Japanese chapter. All that had really changed was that, through the admission of the Saudi-dominated Middle East Security Council, the League had become even more anti-Semitic and anti-Israeli, and that the Latin American chapters were now killing people with their death squads, whereas they has been mostly only talking about it before.

The USCWF's tolerance isn't that surprising, for along with respectable conservatives and former military and intelligence officers, it could count among its members some who quietly supported neo-fascism. Anthony Bouscaren, for example, in the 1960s had worked for Wycliffe Draper's Pioneer Fund, which sought to prove that blacks are genetically inferior to whites, and was still publishing articles in Roger Pearson's *Journal for Social, Political and Economic Studies* in 1982, four years after *The Washington Post* had exposed Pearson's background. In 1977, Lieutenant General Graham had been a guest speaker at a meeting of the League's executive committee at the invitation of Pearson.

Then there were the USCWF's Canadian brethren in the North American Regional World Anti-Communist League (NARWACL). The Canadian League chapter, the Freedom Council of Canada, is controlled by Ron Gostick and Patrick Walsh, both officers of the anti-Semitic (nongovernmental) Canadian Intelligence Service, with Walsh doubling as the Canadian correspondent for the historical revisionist Liberty Lobby in the United States. Whatever repugnance the officers of the United States Council for World Freedom may feel for the Canadian chapter's activities, it has not been sufficient to dissuade their meeting with them in annual NARWACL conferences. Nor did the rabid anti-Semitism of Mexican Teco Professor Rafael Rodríguez prevent their inviting him to be a main speaker at the second NARWACL conference in 1982.

Officers of the United States Council for World Freedom have also actively supported the organizations of the Eastern European Nazi collaborators independently of their joint participation in the World Anti-Communist League. General Singlaub was a guest speaker at an Anti-Bolshevik Bloc of Nations conference in London in 1982 and visited its headquarters in Munich. Lev Dobriansky, Reagan's ambassador to the Bahamas, wrote a laudatory—and totally inaccurate— history of the Ukrainian Insurgent Army that was published by *ABN Correspondence* in October 1982. Albert Koen and Jay Parker spoke at an ABN-sponsored seminar in Canada in 1983, and in 1984, retired General Daniel O. Graham held a joint seminar with the ABN in Canada on "The High Frontier [Star Wars] and a New Strategy for the West." In 1985, they also joined various Eastern European emigré groups in attacking the Office of Special Investigations of the Justice Department, the branch engaged in prosecuting alleged Nazi war criminals residing in the United States. In a telephone conversation with one of the authors, General Singlaub warned that much of the OSI's information came from the Soviet Union, "and I don't think we should take much stock in material supplied by the KGB."[3]

One might draw from this that the new American chapter shares the goals and sentiments of their notorious fellow League members, but this would probably be wrong. Rather, the USCWF sees the League as a vehicle to further implement its own international agenda. If there are anti-Semites, war criminals, and death squad leaders within the association, such unpleasantries have to be overlooked for the greater goal.

For the World Anti-Communist League, the new American chapter was a boon, revitalizing a federation plagued by deep schisms, jealousies, and unfavorable press coverage throughout the world. Starting in 1981, the League could look forward to new vigor. Under the tutelage of General Singlaub, it was no longer to be an organization that would "eat, meet and retreat"; it could now put its plans into concrete action. At the meeting at Mountain Shadow, the World Anti-Communist League had reached into the heart of American conservatism and found a group of powerful American leaders who wanted action. If their memberships in other New Right organizations are taken together, the officers of the United States Council for World Freedom gave the World Anti-Communist League a voice in all the major coalitions of the American New Right movement. Most of these other New Right organizations would go on to assist the USCWF, and by extension the League, in joint operations in Central America. They would also act as unofficial envoys of the Reagan Administration in establishing links with ultra-rightists in Guatemala, El Salvador, and Honduras.

WESTERN GOALS
Operating out of a quaint townhouse in Alexandria, Virginia's colonial Old Town, Western Goals seeks to keep track of "subversives" in the United States. It was the brainchild of Representative John P. McDonald, the late chairman of the John Birch Society, who once described Martin Luther King, Jr., as a man "wedded to violence." Until his death aboard Korean Air Lines flight 007 in September 1983, McDonald watched Western Goals grow dramatically. Today, Western Goals carries on its business; the martyred McDonald's office within the townhouse is preserved as something of a shrine. To his fellow ultra-rightists, McDonald was "the first victim of World War Three."

Established in 1979, Western Goals brought together a whole range of rightists who lamented the passing of domestic surveillance of "subversives." Among its primary sponsors are Nelson Bunker Hunt, the Texas billionaire who made an unsuccessful bid to corner the international silver market in 1982. On the advisory board are General Singlaub and another member of the United States Council for World Freedom, Anthony Kubek. In Western Goals they are in the company of conservative congressmen (Bob Stump, R–Arizona, and Philip Crane, R–Illinois), retired high-ranking military officers (Admiral Thomas Moorer, General Raymond Davis, General Lewis Walt, and General George S. Patton III), and such McCarthy-era luminaries as redbaiting lawyer Roy Cohn.

Western Goals is open about its mission: it seeks a return to the internal surveillance practices of the 1950s. One of its "documentary" films, *The Subversion Factor,* details the internal security problems that in their view have beset the United States since the late 1950s. It also operates a weekly radio program that is carried by over seventy stations throughout the country and publishes a newsletter and such monographs as *D'Aubuisson on Democracy* and *The War Called Peace,* "a startling account of those who are actually financing the nuclear freeze movement."

Not content to merely pine for the past and lament the present, Western Goals has a plan and the means to implement it.

> In the field of Marxists, terrorism and subversion, Western Goals has the most experienced advisors and staff in the United States. Acting on the advice of these nationally known professionals, the Foundation has begun the computerization of thousands of documents relating to the internal security of our country and the protection of government and institutions from Communist-controlled penetration and subversion.[4]

Such a programme hit a responsive chord among the New Right; from a modest budget in 1980, revenues increased over 500 percent the following year. According to the Goals's own records, 29 percent of this came from foundations, with another 14 percent from corporations. By 1983, it had an operating budget of nearly a half-million dollars.

COUNCIL FOR THE DEFENSE OF FREEDOM

Begun during the Korean War as the Council Against Communist Aggression, the Council for the Defense of Freedom (CDF) is a non-profit, tax-exempt organization based in Washington that is dedicated to the dissemination of information about the communist

Horia Sima (front row, fourth from right) with Chirila Ciuntu on his right, at fascist shrine in Spain, 1970.

Chirila Ciuntu (second from right) with other North American Iron Guard leaders beside grave of deceased Guardist, 1972. The tombstone is emblazoned with the Iron Guard Symbol.

ABOVE LEFT *German troops enter Lvov, Ukraine, on June 30, 1941. Stetsko becomes Ukrainian Premier on the same day.*

ABOVE *Before the break: Romanian Iron Guard leader Horia Sima (front left) alongside General Antonescu at memorial service for Codreancu, 1940.*

LEFT *Ukrainian Jews being rounded up for execution by German troops and Ukrainian collaborators, June 1941. Original German caption read: "A bullet is too good for these savage-like Jews . . ."*

FAR LEFT   Yaroslav Stetsko, President of the Anti-Bolshevik Bloc of Nations and major leader of WACL.

NEAR LEFT   Stejpan Hefer, Ustashi Governor General, President of Croatian Liberation Movement.

BELOW LEFT   Ante Pavelic (left), Poglavnik of Croatian Ustashis, with Hitler, 1942.

BELOW   Before the bloodbath: Ustashi troops in Sarajevo, Yugoslavia, 1941.

National Archives

Library of Congress

ABOVE LEFT   *Chiang Kai-shek exhorting the troops during Sino-Japanese War.*

BELOW LEFT   *Chiang Kai-shek reviewing Kuomintang cadres, 1935.*

ABOVE   *Chiang Kai-shek opens the first WACL conference, 1967.*

BELOW   *The partners: Chiang Kai-shek and South Korean President Park Chung Hee, 1966. Within months, WACL would be formed.*

Library of Congress

RIGHT Taiwan's ruling
elite: Premier Chiang
Chin-Kuo (far left);
WACL's Ku Cheng-kang
(far right).

BELOW Ku Cheng-kang
in a more somber mood,
with Brazilian fascist
leader Carlos Barbieri
Filho (center) and WACL
Secretary General Woo Jae
Seung (right).

BELOW *Ku Cheng-kang*
with General Alfredo
Stroessner, dictator of
Paraguay.

ABOVE RIGHT   *Ku Cheng-kang with former CIA Deputy Director Ray Cline.*

BELOW RIGHT   *Senator Jesse Helms of North Carolina and Ku Cheng-kang.*

BELOW   *Ku Cheng-kang with Ronald Reagan, 1977.*

ABOVE *Swearing-in ceremony for new officers of the Tecos, a Mexican secret society.*

RIGHT *Former Major General John K. Singlaub (second from left) with the Nicaraguan contras in a Honduran base camp, 1985.*

BELOW *Stefan Possony addressing WACL conference.*

Jean-Marie Simon, Visions, 1981: Guatemala

LEFT *Mario Sandoval Alarcón,
Guatemala's death-squad godfather,
with his poodle Suki.*

*Honduran strongman General
Gustavo Alvarez Martinez after his
downfall, 1984.*

Time Inc.

*Salvadoran Lieutenant Colonel
Domingo Monteirosa, conducting
Taiwan-style political warfare in
countryside shortly before his death in
1984.*

Charles Bonnay, JB Pictures

Former National Guard Major Roberto D'Aubuisson, El Salvador's ultra-rightist leader campaigning for the presidency, 1984.

The death squads cross frontiers. Graffiti of D'Aubuisson's Broad National Front (FAN) seen in Honduras.

threat. Among its officers are members of the old American League chapter, the ACWF (Fred Schwarz, Reed Irvine, Walter Judd, Marx Lewis, and Lev Dobriansky), as well as of the new USCWF in the person of the ubiquitous Stefan Possony. In 1982, the CDF created "country committees" on nations taken over by communists or waging war with Soviet troops. They selected six countries—Afghanistan, Angola, Cambodia, El Salvador, Nicaragua, and Vietnam—and turned to other New Right leaders to serve on the respective boards of directors. For Angola, for example, they chose M. Stanton Evans (head of National Journalism Center, radio broadcaster for Western Goals, and author of books attacking alleged Marxist infiltration of the Catholic Church), Andy Messing (former executive director of the Conservative Caucus and now a member of the advisory board of the United States Council for World Freedom), and Helen White (member of the advisory board of Western Goals). The purpose of the CDF country committees was intended to be largely educational; this would soon be overshadowed by the USCWF's own far more aggressive international campaign.

AMERICAN SECURITY COUNCIL

Begun and originally financed by industrialists wanting background checks done on employees, the American Security Council has grown to become one of the most powerful New Right private groups. Under its affiliate, the Coalition for Peace Through Strength (CPTS), it has drawn together some of the most influential elected officials and former military officers in the nation. Serving as CPTS cochairmen are the two top former military officers who head the United States Council for World Freedom, Singlaub and Graham, as well as retired Joint Chiefs of Staff Chairman Admiral Thomas Moorer of Western Goals. Among the organizations belonging to CPTS are, in addition to the United States Council for World Freedom, such groups as the Bulgarian National Front, Inc. (created by Ivan Docheff, a Bulgarian fascist sentenced to death in absentia for war crimes), the Byelorussian American Committee (headed by John Kosiak, the SS engineer in Minsk during World War II who is wanted for war crimes in the Soviet Union), and the Slovak World Congress (cofounded by Josef Mikus, who is wanted for war crimes in Czechoslovakia). All of these groups are also members of the World Anti-Communist League.

COUNCIL FOR INTER-AMERICAN SECURITY

Both Singlaub and Anthony Bouscaren serve as advisers to the Council for Inter-American Security (CIS). Its chairman is Lieutenant General Gordon Sumner, Jr., former chairman of the Inter-American Defense Board and a special assistant to the secretary of state for Latin American affairs. The council, whose main recent function has been to refute charges of death squad involvement by the ultra-right in El Salvador and Guatemala, was founded in 1976 by Ronald Docksai, another former member of the American Council for World Freedom. Its executive vice-president is Lynn Bouchey, an active organizer of the Unification Church's CAUSA operations in South and Central America. In the CIS, the World Anti-Communist League—especially its Latin American affiliates—gained a powerful friend in Washington; in 1980, Singlaub and Sumner traveled to Guatemala to tell the ultra-right government that help was on the way in the form of Ronald Reagan.

CONSERVATIVE CAUCUS

Created in 1975 by Howard Phillips and Richard Viguerie, the Conservative Caucus is another New Right organization having an interlocking directorate with the American chapter of the World Anti-Communist League. Both Phillips, the caucus chairman, and Andy Messing, its former executive director, are on the advisory board of the USCWF. John Singlaub has been active in caucus activities, including participating in a caucus defense strategy seminar in April 1983. The caucus acts as an umbrella for "pro-life, pro-family" causes; officials of the Conservative Caucus were instrumental in the campaign to make the "death squad parties" of Central America palatable to the American public in the early 1980s. Most recently, Messing was a key middleman in the New Right campaign to channel private aid to the contras fighting the leftist Nicaraguan government.

Although confusing, there is nothing untoward, and certainly nothing illegal, about this overlapping of directorates among the New Right organizations. Indeed, much the same thing occurs among liberal organizations. Affixing the names of prominent people to a letterhead aids fund raising and gives readers the impression that the organization is in close contact with influential people. Often, when a prominent personality agrees to be an honorary chairman or serve on the advisory board of a particular organization, this agreement is the extent of the relationship. He or she may participate in its annual meetings or give a speech at a seminar, but day-to-day involvement is likely to be nonexistent. That is not the case, however, with the individuals discussed here.

Likewise, despite the grandiose names and the optimism of their stated goals, many politically oriented organizations spend most of their time dealing with the mundane matters of issuing press releases (which are ignored by the media), inserting articles into the back section of the *Congressional Record* (which no one reads), or organizing seminars (which no one attends). It can be safely assumed that an organization like Western Goals, with its mission "to rebuild and strengthen the political, economic and social structure of the United States and Western Civilization," effects far less legislation than, say, the American Association of Hot-Dip Galvanizers.

But if one looks at the American legislative process for the effect of these ultra-right organizations, one is simply looking in the wrong place. These are people who have given up on the American system. They feel the democratic form of government is weighted against them. Congress is filled with obstructionists; the media is controlled by liberals; the government is dominated by leftists; and President Reagan isn't a "true conservative." It is time to act on their own; if they can't take over the government, they will create their own government, carry out their own foreign policy, and make their own allies throughout the world. Along with this, they will supply "freedom fighters" abroad and compile dossiers on "subversives" at home.

This New Right policy of pursuing its own agenda independent of any governmental constraints has expanded dramatically during the Reagan Administration, leading some to charge that it is being done with the president's approval. Certainly, the Reagan Administration has found it useful to use such groups at various times, but the alliance is a shaky one. In fact, probably the chief motivation for building the "New Right Government" was widespread dissatisfaction with Reagan among ultra-rightists and the realization that if they couldn't rely on Reagan, the most conservative president in the past fifty years, to pursue a foreign policy based on anti-communism, then they could rely on no one. Despite his 1980 campaign promises to "get tough" with the Soviets, he still made trade deals with them, still tolerated the existence of Castro's Cuba, and still kept aid to anti-communist guerrillas in Afghanistan and Nicaragua at grossly inadequate levels.

Reagan was the ultra-right's last, best hope; after him, there is no one else who stands a reasonable chance of election who would pursue their policies. Consequently, if Reagan has "sold out," it is time to go it alone.

This they have done. Despite the United States' scaled-back diplomatic relations with Taiwan, the American Council for World Freedom and its New Right allies see to it that the Kuomintang maintains and exerts its influence. Despite the cutoff of U.S. government military aid to the Nicaraguan contras fighting the Sandinista regime, the guerrillas are still receiving considerable amounts of supplies from private American conservative groups. Despite the growing anti-apartheid sentiment among the American people and politicians of both parties, South Africa can still rely on New Right journalists, evangelists, and foundations to come to its defense. And despite curbs placed on the FBI that constrain it from routinely placing leftists under surveillance, and despite the dismantling of such government agencies as the House Un-American Activities Committee, the ultra-right keeps tabs on its "subversive" domestic opposition through private bodies like Western Goals.

In all these causes, the United States Council for World Freedom has played a key role. Under its credo of the need for unconventional warfare, the new American League chapter has united frustrated rightists in the "total war" against communism, independent of the policies or limitations of the U.S. government.

This "New Right Government" has not had completely smooth sailing. In 1984, the American Civil Liberties Union (ACLU) was in the process of suing the Los Angeles Police Department's Public Disorder Intelligence Division (PDID), which had maintained files on such possible "enemies of the state" as the First Unitarian Church and the National Lawyers Guild, when the ACLU discovered that some PDID officers had removed files from their offices. One in particular, Jay Paul, was discovered to have had a garage full of PDID reports, which he had computerized and sent to Western Goals in Alexandria, Virginia. The foundation's executive director finally turned most of the documents over to a California grand jury after negotiating immunity from prosecution.[5]

*   *   *

With its connections into the "New Right Government," the new American chapter of the World Anti-Communist League was able to play its own vital role in the growing challenge in Central America. In Guatemala, El Salvador, and Honduras, General Singlaub's United States Council for World Freedom called for and initiated unconventional warfare on a level that the American government was unwilling or unable to do itself.

FOURTEEN

I admit that the MLN is the party of organized violence. Organized violence is vigor, just like organized color is scenery and organized sound is harmony. There is nothing wrong with organized violence; it is vigor and the MLN is a vigorous movement, a vigorous party that bravely confronts all those seeking to subvert order in our country in order to throw us into the arms of a masked or unmasked left.

Leonel Sisniega Otero,
MLN Public Relation Director, 1980

"Her name is Suki," the old man rasped, patting the poodle on its head. "This is the newest Suki. When one dies, we get another and name it Suki, too."

Mario Sandoval Alarcón smiled at the little dog, as did the others in the room. It might have been a touching scene if it weren't for the fact that most of the men in the room were cradling snub-nose machine guns and that the old man with the poodle was the mastermind of his nation's death squads, which have killed tens of thousands of people in the past two decades.

The armed men surrounding Sandoval were not his bodyguards—they were either in the yard or on the roof of the fortress home with sharpshooter rifles—but were rather the political advisers of the National Liberation Movement (MLN), the political party that Sandoval took over in the 1950s and continues to head.

Called "Mico" ("Monkey") by his friends and followers, Sandoval is still a stout and burly man and a commanding presence on the Guatemalan political scene. He recently campaigned for yet another try at the presidency. "Mico is the future of Guatemala," a misty-eyed supporter says.*

He is also the past. As head of the MLN, Sandoval is a principal architect of his nation's twenty-year reign of terror. Under his guidance, the MLN and its death squads are accused of murdering thousands of fellow Guatemalans, including hundreds of Christian Democrat politicians, dozens of liberal priests, and even a Miss Guatemala beauty queen.

Mario Sandoval Alarcón is known by a number of labels. By his comrades in the World Anti-Communist League, he is called one of the world's pre-eminent anti-communist fighters. Others call him a fascist. "I could perhaps accept the label of Fascist," Sandoval told a French reporter in 1981, "in the historical sense of the word were it not for the fact that it refers to a type of socialism, albeit national socialism."[1]

To his detractors in Guatemala, he is known as "Darth Vader," due to the throat cancer that necessitates that he speak in a robotic tone with the aid of an electronic box. It is another nickname, however, that most reveals the pivotal role the old man has played in the bloody history of Central America.

For Sandoval has not been content to carry out his murderous campaigns solely in Guatemala; in the early 1980s he helped erect the same lethal apparatus in El Salvador and Honduras. Sandoval's assistance to others in the international "anti-communist" struggle and his concrete plan of action have won him the awed respect and admiration from death squad leaders throughout Central America. To them he is "The Godfather."

Guatemala is the most exotic of the Central American republics. A tropical land of jungles, shimmering mountain lakes, and high volcanoes, it is a place where unexcavated Mayan ruins jut up from the jungle floor and where the indigenous Indians have retained much of their pre-Columbian culture. In their bright dress, they still pray to their ancient animist gods along with the "new" Jesus Christ.

*Sandoval lost the November 1985 election and the current Guatemalan president is Christian Democrat Vinicio Cerezo.

If it is a land of dreams, Guatemala is also a land of nightmares. No other country in the Western hemisphere approaches the level of brutality that is a way of life here. One might compare it with Idi Amin's Uganda or Pol Pot's Cambodia, except that the pogroms in Guatemala have gone on for far longer. It is a place of total war, where a scorched-earth policy has been pursued for so long that, of all Central America's war-torn republics, it is the one that evokes the most horror and disbelief in observers, from the foreign press, from the diplomatic community, and from the Guatemalans themselves.*

Guatemala is a land that appears to be caught in a series of time warps. For the Indian peasants, tilling their tiny plots of land and living in hamlets without electricity or running water, time has stood still, perhaps even regressed, since the time of their Mayan ancestors. Economically, Guatemala exists in a system akin to medieval feudalism; the middle class is embryonic, and the masses, living in abject poverty, work to provide fantastic wealth for a handful of families. Politically, it is a land where the large landowners live much as their thirteenth-century European predecessors did, complete with private armies and a partnership with the military to protect their hold on the nation. They keep the peasants under their control through terror, organize them into vigilante bands, and mobilize them to support their *patrones* in elections.

"The problem," a conservative former Guatemalan general explains, "is the whole structure of the government. It doesn't much matter whether the government is civilian or military because the power always is with the military and the military supports the oligarchs. There are no legal channels of expression and, thus, no consensus of what democracy means. To the *finqueros* [large coffee plantation owners] it means free enterprise, a continuation of the oligarchy, not the right to vote or form labor unions. These people live in a different era, maybe of a 100 or 150 years ago."

Asked how this system could be changed, the ex-general reflected. "The only way," he finally replied, "is to stage a coup. Then you call together all the generals, all the oligarchs, the three hundred men who really run the country, by telling them this is going to be a

---

*It has also given rise to a certain perverse kind of humor. Guatemalans of all political stripes still tell—and laugh about—the story of the landowner who awoke one morning to find twenty-six bodies dumped on his farm. When he called the police, he was cited for operating a private cemetery without a license.

truly anti-communist government. When you have them all in one room, you kill them. If you want change in Guatemala, you must kill those 300 people."

There are many seemingly innocent things a Guatemalan might do that will cause him or her to come to the attention of a soldier, police officer, or informant, and then a death squad. Enrolling in a night class, digging a well so that a village can have clean drinking water, teaching philosophy—Guatemalans have been murdered for all these "subversive" acts.

"The victims," Allan Nairn, an American reporter, wrote, trying to define some parameters for the killings, "are typically students, priests, labor leaders, journalists, teachers, peasant activists and members and leaders of moderate opposition parties."[2]

"You can't fuck around in Guatemala," a Salvadoran rightist warned one of the authors. "They don't even know what human rights are. You talk social change to these people and they point the finger at you and that's it. And if you want to get rid of someone, all you have to do is go down to the right office of the Armed Forces, the Special Operations Command, and denounce someone. You do that and the job is done. You don't need a lot of proof."

And they are not subtle. On October 18, 1978, the Secret Anti-Communist Army (ESA) issued a death list to the press of Guatemala. On the list was Oliverio Castañeda de León, president of the Association of University Students. Three days later, on a busy street in downtown Guatemala City, Castañeda was gunned down by machine-gun fire from a passing car bearing official license plates. As he lay dying on the sidewalk, gunmen in three more cars and on a motorcycle passed by to administer the coups de grâce.

Yet with few exceptions, Guatemala has been able to dodge world attention and condemnation. Little is regularly heard outside Guatemala about the continuing slaughter. One reason may be the lack of an overt American presence, which is apparently a necessity to interest U.S. readers. Or perhaps it is in part due to a guilty conscience, for much of Guatemala's current strife is directly traceable to American involvement there in the 1950s. In fact, most of those responsible, including Mario Sandoval Alarcón and his MLN, were nurtured and first given prominence by the CIA.

In the early 1950s, left-leaning Guatemalan President Jacobo Arbenz Guzman became a target of the Eisenhower Administration, which accused the government of being pro-communist. These charges reached a fever pitch when the Arbenz regime nationalized the railroads and an Atlantic coast port, both of which belonged to the powerful American United Fruit Company, the largest landowner in Guatemala. Much as it assists the Nicaraguan contras today, the CIA organized a ragtag Guatemalan exile force in Honduras. The final spark came when Guatemala bought arms from the Soviet satellite Czechoslovakia, "proof" that Arbenz* had joined the communist camp.

The CIA-sponsored paramilitary force invaded, calling itself "the Army of Liberation," with cashiered Colonel Carlos Castillo Armas playing the part of "liberator." After marching into Guatemala and forcing out Arbenz, Castillo Armas organized his followers in what became the official government party, the Nationalist Democratic Movement (MDN).

The 1954 invasion was the event which launched Mario Sandoval Alarcón into the political arena. An active Castillo Armas supporter, Sandoval was awarded for his efforts following the coup with a post as the liberator's personal secretary. It was the beginning of his ascendancy as the nation's premier anti-communist.

On July 12, 1954, which was proclaimed "Anti-communism Day," Castillo Armas exhorted his countrymen to militancy.

Communism . . . has been completely destroyed by the force of arms. But communism still remains in the conscience of some bad sons of our Guatemala. . . . The battle has begun, the hard battle that requires us to demand each citizen to be a soldier of anti-communism. . . . To eradicate communism does not signify to persecute the worker and the honest peasant who in every case merits the protection of the government. . . . Workers and peasants have in me their best friend. . . . My unshakeable spirit of justice will be their greatest guarantee.[3]

*Evidence suggests that Arbenz wasn't the democratic martyr many liberals have tried to portray him as being. He won the presidency in 1952 after his principal opponent was assassinated. Among those implicated in the murder were close Arbenz associates, including the chauffeur of Arbenz's wife. If the assassination was conducted without Arbenz's approval, it was certainly done for his benefit.

Castillo Armas's guarantees aside, 1954 marked the end of Guatemala's democracy and the beginning of its long descent into government-sanctioned terror.

When Castillo Armas was assassinated in his palace in 1957, the radical right faction of his followers formed the MLN. Sandoval emerged as the new party's strongman. Leonel Sisniega Otero, who had been one of Castillo Armas's propagandists in his clandestine preinvasion radio broadcasts and who would later give the MLN the label "the party of organized violence," became Sandoval's righthand man. In keeping with its political outlook, the MLN adopted a symbol from the Middle Ages—the sword and the cross.

With the MLN, Sandoval and Sisniega carried on the anti-communist battle that Castillo Armas had demanded; they soon got the chance to put their campaign into action.

In 1960, some junior army officers, disgruntled over governmental corruption, staged a mutiny. When it failed, the rebels took to the hills of the eastern Zacapa farmlands to continue the fight. It was the beginning of the Guatemalan guerrilla war that is still being waged today.

In 1966, Colonel Carlos Arana Osorio was put in charge of suppressing the insurgency in Zacapa. Although the fledgling guerrilla "army" was estimated to consist of only a few hundred men, they were hard to track in the hills. Arana turned to someone he knew could help.

By the time of the Zacapa rebellion, Sandoval had begun to create a political paramilitary network in Guatemala in emulation of the Kuomintang model in Taiwan. To Colonel Arana, it was just what was needed in Zacapa.

With support from the military, the MLN appointed party members and recruited former soldiers who were loyal to MLN aims as *jefes politicos* (political chiefs) in villages throughout the country. The *jefes* kept track of anyone who had "subversive" tendencies. Those tendencies could be manifested in a variety of ways, from genuine support for the guerrillas to holding anti-MLN views, or they could simply stem from a personal dispute with the *jefes*. Whatever the reason, the result was almost always the same: those who ran afoul of the *jefes* were brought to "justice" either by the MLN's paramilitary groups or by the army or both; their deaths were attributed to the mysterious La Mano Blanca (The White Hand).

The existence of this network was admitted to in 1985 by an American diplomat stationed in Guatemala.

> The MLN has always been fervently, violently anti-communist. A lot of the supporters of the MLN were probably members of those [1960s paramilitary] groups. These are the historical origins of the death squads that you hear of.[4]

In the late 1960s the MLN expanded into urban areas, directing its attacks at students, teachers, and anyone associated with the Arbenz government who had foolishly remained in the country. One operation attributed to the MLN was the abduction of conservative Guatemalan Archbishop Mario Casariegos. The archbishop was eventually released, and he identified his captors as top MLN officials. The apparent motive for his abduction was a scheme to blame the kidnapping on leftist guerrillas to justify an increased MLN role in the government's campaign of suppression of dissidents.

The embarrassing incident with the archbishop taught the MLN an important lesson: don't release victims. From that time on, only a handful of those picked up by La Mano Blanca would ever be seen alive again.

The archbishop episode didn't do much damage to Sandoval, for he came under the protective embrace of a rising military officer. With the help of Sandoval's vigilante bands and with the secret assistance of U.S. Special Forces pilots and Green Beret advisers, Colonel Arana Osorio had crushed the insurgency in Zacapa. In the process, he had killed between three and ten thousand and had won the nickname "The Butcher of Zacapa." While the label might have had an adverse reaction upon an officer's career elsewhere, this wasn't the case in Guatemala; promoted to general and hailed as a war hero, Arana ran for president in 1970 and won.

In gratitude to the man who had helped launch him to prominence and whose MLN party had backed his presidential bid, Arana named Sandoval president of the National Congress.

With Arana's ascension to the presidency and Sandoval's political legitimacy in Congress, the Taiwan model had been recreated in Guatemala. The political party with its intelligence network and its death squads had helped out the military in a moment of crisis. Out of that initial alliance, the party, or at least the paramilitary functions of it, had become institutionalized into the military. And since the military also ran the country, it meant that the death squads were now sanctioned by the government and were in fact a branch of it.

"People ask if the death squads are controlled by the Army." A Guatemalan political analyst smiled grimly. "They are the army. Look, in 1982, Ríos Montt [then president of Guatemala] said he was committed to ending the paramilitary killing. He gave the word to the Army and, literally overnight, the killing stopped. How do you think that happened? Do you think the death squads received flyers in the mail? No, the death squads stayed in their barracks."

"My personal experience," a former Guatemalan general said, "was that when the Army said no, there were no paramilitary groups. All the groups were run by the same people. I think the regular Army, the junior officers, were against these groups, but the higher officers were in control of them so nothing could be done."

The economist agreed to talk only after receiving an assurance of anonymity; Guatemala City was still a very dangerous place to speak out in 1985. In the week of the interview, two university professors had been murdered on the street by gunmen in passing cars. Several human rights advocates had also been kidnapped, tortured, and mutilated. The economist, himself a miraculous survivor of the violence that has claimed the lives of dozens of his friends and colleagues over the past twenty years, said that it was in 1970, during Sandoval's tenure as president of the National Congress, when the rightist death squads began operating openly and with impunity. High MLN officials not only orchestrated their "hits" but participated in them. "Oliveiro Castañeda, the vice-president of Congress under Sandoval, was also a top MLN leader. He personally led some of the [Guatemala] City death squads."

The economist knew two of Castañeda's victims. After their abductions, he obtained testimony from their wives, and they identified Castañeda as the leader of the gangs that had abducted the men. One was killed; the other was saved when a relative in the army heard of his capture and obtained his release. That victim now lives in exile in Mexico and has identified Castañeda as one of his "interrogators."

Elections held in 1974 brought "Mico" to even greater heights of power. Although the Christian Democrat candidate, General Efraín

Ríos Montt, won, Sandoval mobilized his vigilantes to prevent the victory.

"We won it," said Luis Martínez Montt, a Christian Democrat official, "but we made the mistake of choosing Ríos Montt as our candidate. When Sandoval organized his army of thirty-five thousand peasants, who threatened to march on the city and set off dynamite, Ríos Montt went to an exile post in Spain instead of standing up against the military. We should have known he [Montt] wouldn't go against his own institution."

Instead, Colonel Kjell Laugerud Schell, the handpicked candidate of outgoing President Arana, took power. Sandoval Alarcón was named his vice-president. " 'Mico' is a violent man," Luis Martinez continued, "who believes in . . . force to shut those up who don't share his points of view."[5]

It was a brave statement for the Christian Democrat to make; over 350 of his party's officials have been murdered in the past decade; most of them they blame on Sandoval's MLN.

During the Laugerud-Sandoval administration from 1974 to 1978, the right-wing death squads ran rampant. "Great clandestine cemeteries began appearing in the country, mass common graves," an opposition politician who is still in Guatemala said. "The government said it was the work of the guerrillas. It wasn't the guerrillas' work. This was the work of Sandoval," he spat, stressing each syllable of the MLN leader's name.

It was also during Sandoval's tenure as vice-president that closer ties to Taiwan were forged. "Sandoval went to Taiwan while he was vice-president," a former government minister said, "and he brought them in. If you want to trace the Taiwanese presence here, you can begin in 1974 [when Sandoval was vice-president]."

Through his leadership role in the Latin American Anti-Communist Confederation and in the World Anti-Communist League, Sandoval made numerous trips to Taiwan, where he was fêted by the Kuomintang leaders. Quietly, Guatemalan officers, an estimated fifty to seventy, were sent to Taiwan to receive training in political warfare.

The courses at Peitou, which were taught in Spanish, met Guatemalan educational requirements for military advancement; majors that went to Taiwan returned as lieutenant colonels. Even as their Guatemalan armed forces salaries continued, Taiwan picked up most if not all of their air fare and living expenses while they were in Taiwan.

The Peitou training also benefited Sandoval politically. Although those sent were drawn from all branches of the military, final approval for their selection was made by G-2, or military intelligence. Since this was a branch of the military largely operated by MLN members or Sandoval followers, it ensured that those sent were men who approved of the "party of organized violence." Upon their return and promotion, Sandoval was able to build support throughout the military.

The key Guatemalan officer in this Taiwanese-Sandoval influence operation in the early 1970s was Colonel Elias Ramírez. In charge of security for the Guatemala City region, Ramírez was the liaison to the Nationalist Chinese Embassy personnel in Guatemala who organized the officers' groups going to Taiwan. He was also one of the commanders of the capital's death squads, which apparently is why the guerrillas killed him in 1976.

For the Kuomintang, the program was a positive one in that it predisposed the Guatemalan military to conform to its wishes. Francisco Villagran-Kramer, Guatemala's vice-president in the late 1970s, recalls trying to forge greater ties with the People's Republic of China through trade deals:

> Negotiations were going well. We had a commitment from the [mainland] Chinese on the particulars of the trade deal and then, all of a sudden, it was killed. I checked around why and I found out that a lot of the generals had voiced disapproval about it. They did not want to do anything that might offend the Taiwanese.[6]

The "Guatemalan Kuomintang" had exerted its quiet influence.

The reign of Laugerud and Sandoval was a time of terror in Guatemala. It became commonplace to see plainclothesmen with machine guns cruising the streets in Jeeps bearing no license plates. "The Chamber of Commerce," a Guatemalan exile charged, "would ask its members for a list of those it wanted to hit. The leaders would send the list on to the G-2 or to the police chief [Chupina Barahona]."

The exile holds a special resentment for the Chamber of Commerce death squad; he believes it was they who murdered his politically active and prominent brother.

It was the Chamber of Commerce that ordered it. At the meeting were [Police Chief Colonel] Chupina and [Army Chief of Staff General] Cancinos [Barrios]. Afterwards, they all sent condolences and flowers to the funeral. One of them told me, "It is really too bad about [name deleted]. It was a difficult decision for us to make, but he had become a subversive." That is how I know they did it.

The mass killings in Guatemala were viewed with repugnance by the new American president, Jimmy Carter. He immediately began criticizing the Laugerud government for its gross human rights violations and warned of trade sanctions if they continued.

But the Guatemalan government would not be cowed; in 1977, the Laugerud regime beat Carter to the punch and canceled all its military assistance programs from the United States. With other allies, like Taiwan, and other arms suppliers, like Israel, Laugerud was no longer beholden to the United States.

The Guatemalan vice-president shared this smug appraisal. "We don't have any problem with Carter," an associate recalls Sandoval saying. "Our problem is to kill two hundred communists a week."

Despite his bravado, Sandoval's power went through a temporary setback in 1978; he had to temporarily divert his attention from killing "communists" to keeping his MLN afloat. "While he was in the Congress and then vice-president, Mico had no shortage of money to finance his private army," one source said, "but in the 1978 elections, he lost out by backing the wrong candidate. He went against the will of the armed forces. Their candidate was General [Romeo] Lucas García."

In the Guatemalan tradition, election results were manipulated so that Lucas García "won." Now in the opposition, Sandoval turned to Mafialike tactics to get financing. "He authorized the leaders of his bands to obtain funds by robbery and kidnappings," says a wealthy Guatemalan politician who knows the MLN chief well. "He would send death threats, supposedly from the guerrillas, to the rich *finqueros* [coffee growers] and the next day, either Leonel [Sisniega] or Raul [Midence Pivaral, Sandoval's brother-in-law] would collect the money.

"It was a joke for a while at the sporting club I and a lot of these farmers belonged to. They used to say to each other; 'Have you solved your problem with the guerrillas yet?' and the answer would be, 'Yes, Sisniega paid me a visit.' "

Through this campaign, directed at the same wealthy landowners who were the MLN's source of strength, Sandoval alienated many of his potential backers within the ruling elite. His monolithic MLN broke into smaller parties; these splits at least partly resulted from the dissension over the party's new targets of violence.

Sandoval fought this dissolution in a way familiar to him. The same politician recalled a conversation with the right-wing patriarch: "One day, 'Mico' told me that the problem with the liberal parties is that they can't control their followers. He then said, 'I do. I either buy them or I kill them. They know it and that's why they obey me.' "

And kill them he did. According to several Guatemalan analysts, Sandoval's efforts to remain the top ultra-right leader in the nation led to the deaths of many MLN leaders at the hands of their former comrades. Among the murders cited were those of Oliverio Castañeda, Sandoval's former second-in-command in the National Congress, and Raul Lorenzo, one of the party leaders implicated in Archbishop Casariegos' abduction.

Sandoval also turned his attention outward. Blocked from attaining power in his own country after his vice-presidential term was over, he attempted to strengthen his power base by "internationalizing" the MLN through a network that one Guatemalan politician called "the international anti-communist union."

"In the [late] 1970s," a conservative Guatemalan journalist recalls, "Sandoval sought help from abroad. He got it, too, principally from Taiwan. The MLN's leaders go there with frequency, where they get advice in psychological warfare and money. Right-wing groups in the United States and Europe do the same." What the journalist was referring to was the World Anti-Communist League network.

As head of the Guatemalan chapter, Sandoval had stacked his nation's delegations to League functions with MLN officials, including Carlos Midence Pivaral, his nephew, and Hector Andrade, his secretary. As one of the Latin American Anti-Communist Confederation's leaders, Sandoval had forged close ties with like-minded military governments and with rightist groups abroad. Chief among them were the military regimes in Taiwan, Paraguay, Argentina, and Chile, and New Right groups in the United States.

These allies continued to serve Sandoval and the MLN after 1978. It was through his affiliations with the World Anti-Communist

League that Sandoval helped create a "death squad party" in El Salvador—a mirror image of the MLN—and remained the undisputed *capo di capos* in the Latin American netherworld of the ultra-right.

It was also these allies, especially the American New Right, that "rehabilitated" Guatemala in general, and Sandoval in particular, in 1979.

By 1979, the Guatemalan death squads were claiming ever-greater numbers of victims. Actions were directed by the army and by Police Chief Colonel German Chupina Barahona, under orders from President Lucas García, Interior Minister Colonel Donald Alvarez Ruiz,* and a group of top-ranking generals. Private businessmen met regularly to compile lists of those they wanted dead and passed the rosters on to the government. In return, the businessmen provided part of the payroll.

Despite this campaign of institutionalized murder, conservative groups in the United States, sensing a Ronald Reagan victory in 1980, rose to defend the Guatemalan government. "The policy of the Carter Administration," retired General Gordon Sumner told reporter Allan Nairn, "is to destabilize the Lucas government and there's no excuse for it. That is a government that was elected by the people."[7]

In December 1979, a delegation from the American Security Council went to Guatemala. At the head of the delegation were retired generals John Singlaub and Daniel Graham, both of whom would soon become the top officials of the American chapter of the World Anti-Communist League. There was no ambiguity in their message; in an audience with President Lucas García, Graham promised that he would urge Reagan, once elected, to resume military ties with Guatemala.

The ASC trip helped confirm the Guatemalan ultra-right's darkest suspicions about the Carter Administration. The editor of the Guatemala City daily, *El Imparcial*, "reported in his column that the Singlaub-Graham delegation from the ASC 'is convinced that the State Department and White House are infiltrated with elements abetting subversion in this part of the world, and probably in others as well.' "

But it also gave them hope. "One high Guatemalan official who

---

*Ruiz now lives in Miami and runs a taxi company.

met with Singlaub and Graham, and who later discussed the impli-
cations of the visit with his government and military colleagues, said
that the message was clear. First, 'Mr. Reagan recognizes that a good
deal of dirty work has to be done.' . . . The Reagan aides' advice and
supportive comments were the talk of official Guatemala for days
after their visit."[8] Within days after the Singlaub-Graham visit, the
level of death squad actions in Guatemala increased dramatically.

In a telephone interview with Allan Nairn, Singlaub defended his
Guatemalan trip. "Singlaub said that he was 'terribly impressed' at
how the Lucas regime was 'desperately trying to promote human
rights' and lamented the fact that 'as the [Guatemalan] government
loses support from the United States, it gives the impression to the
people that there's something wrong with their government.' Singlaub urged sympathetic understanding of the death squads, arguing
that the Carter Administration's unwillingness to back the Lucas regime in its elimination of its enemies 'is prompting those who are
dedicated to retaining the free enterprise system and to continuing
progress toward political and economic development to take matters
in their own hands.' "[9]

The Singlaub-Graham expedition was followed by many more in
1980. Dozens of American New Right leaders—including officials
from Young Americans for Freedom, the Heritage Foundation, and
the Moral Majority, and such New Right activists as Howard Phillips
of the Conservative Caucus—went to Guatemala on "fact-finding"
missions. Roger Fontaine, the director of Latin American studies at
the Center for Strategic and International Studies at Georgetown University, made at least two 1980 trips to Guatemala. "It's pretty clear,"
he told *The Miami Herald* in July 1980, "that [after a Reagan victory]
Guatemalans will be given what aid they need in order to defend
themselves against an armed minority which is aided and abetted by
Cubans."

On the Guatemalan end, the public relations campaign was led by
Roberto Alejos Arzu, a wealthy ultra-rightist who had made one of
his plantations available to the CIA as a staging ground for the ill-
fated Bay of Pigs invasion of Cuba in 1961; he was a principal leader
of his nation's "Reagan for President" bandwagon.[10] Funds were
made available for the Reagan presidential bid both from Americans
in Guatemala and from the Guatemalan oligarchy. Although the contributions from foreign nationals were never disclosed by the Reagan

it was an open secret in Guatemala. "Sure," a Guatemalan
one of the authors, "everyone was giving money to Rea-
yone was bragging about how much they gave."
re overt source of funding for the Republican presidential
camp_ gn came through Amigos del Pais (Friends of the Country). A
lobbying group established by wealthy Guatemalans, Amigos del Pais
retained a public relations firm for eleven thousand dollars a month
to carry their cause in the United States. It was probably not coin-
cidental that the firm they chose was Deaver and Hannaford, the
heads of which would both occupy high governmental posts after
Reagan's victory in November.

Amigos del Pais also hosted a visit of U.S. congressional staffers
to Guatemala. One of the participants was Belden Bell, coordinator
of Reagan's foreign policy advisory committee, who concluded that
"it is in the best interests of the United States, as well as Guatemala,
to throw our national support behind this beleaguered country."

It appeared there might be a hitch in this campaign when Elias
Barahona, the former press secretary to the Guatemalan interior minister, held a press conference from his Panamanian exile in September
1980. Revealing he actually had been a guerrilla "mole," Barahona
laid bare the extent to which the Lucas government ran the death
squads; he even named the fourth floor of the National Palace annex
as the operations center and furnished the addresses of government
safehouses and interrogation centers where prisoners were tortured
and killed. Barahona further claimed that Sandoval had worked for
the CIA and that Colonel Alvarez Ruiz, the interior minister, was
in contact with CIA agents in Guatemala and Mexico.

The exile's charges against Sandoval were interesting since at that
moment the MLN leader was acting as the liaison in a covert program to bring Argentine advisers and Argentine-trained Nicaraguan
rightists into Guatemala to prepare for war against the Sandinista
government in Nicaragua. Hector Frances, one of the Argentine advisers involved, corroborated this aspect of Barahona's charges after
his "defection" in 1982. "All this begins in late 1980," Frances explained, speaking in the present tense, "when some fifty ex-Somo-
cista [Nicaraguan] guards are in Argentina [being trained] in guerrilla
activity and to train others. These men leave from Argentina and go
to Costa Rica, Panama, Guatemala, Honduras, and Miami, where

other companions of theirs are trained in the same way in paramilitary [anti-Castro] Cuban–North American camps. At that time in
Guatemala, the coming together of the counterrevolutionary [contra]
groups begins to be orchestrated in Guatemala under the Argentines
. . . and the paramilitary groups there, with close ties to the Guatemalan fascist group of Mario Sandoval Alarcon."[11]

The Argentine advisers also instructed the Guatemalans. "The Argentines were a great help to the death squads [in Guatemala]," a
Salvadoran rightist told reporter Craig Pyes. "Before, they used to
kill right away. The Argentines taught them to wait until after the
interrogation."

Barahona's testimony, "tainted" by his admission of being a guerrilla, was ignored by the New Right, and the "Guatemala as beleaguered country" campaign continued.

Ronald Reagan's 1980 Inaugural Ball was a regal affair, with
women swathed in furs and diamonds and men resplendent in tux-
edos. Among those invited to this most prestigious of the inaugural
events were two Guatemalans. One was former President Arana
Osorio, the man who had vowed to turn his nation into a cemetery
to stop communism. The other was Mario Sandoval Alarcón.

While Sandoval danced and chatted with the elite of Reagan's
inner circle, his minions back home were busy; the Secret Anti-Communist Army (ESA), which was believed to be an extension of Sandoval's MLN, had just threatened to exterminate the entire Jesuit
order in Guatemala.

The election of Reagan coincided with the bloodiest outbreak of
Guatemalan death squad actions in history. Almost five hundred
deaths a month, almost all attributed to the right, were being reported by the American Embassy, but even that figure was considered low by most other monitoring groups. Piles of mutilated bodies
were being discovered every morning throughout the country, and a
concerted campaign to eliminate the centrist parties was under way
in Guatemala City. From July 1980 to June 1981, seventy-six leaders
of the Christian Democratic Party and ten officials of the Social Democratic United Revolutionary Front were assassinated. Most were
murdered by gunfire from passing cars, the trademark of the MLN.

The violence notwithstanding, the Reagan Administration set about to make good its campaign promises of selling military hardware to Guatemala. There was one hitch: a law barred military sales to "governments engaged in gross violations of human rights," and Congress was not about to certify Guatemala as exempt from this clause.

The new Administration sidestepped the problem, simply taking the requested items off the restricted list; in June 1981, the $3.2 million sale of fifty military trucks and one hundred Jeeps to Guatemala was approved.

The wave of rightist killings in 1980–81 did not end the Guatemalan guerrilla war, but attention was now diverted to El Salvador, where fighting had broken out into fullscale civil war. True to his programme to internationalize the MLN and in keeping with his role as the region's "Godfather," Sandoval turned his energies to aiding his comrades in Guatemala's neighboring republic. He reorganized the death squads in El Salvador, gave them financial and technical assistance, and even instructed them on how to operate under the banner of a political party, in emulation of his own MLN. Subsequently the death toll in El Salvador climbed, and ARENA, the "death squad party" of Sandoval's Salvadoran protégé, Roberto D'Aubuisson, achieved political legitimacy. This transference of expertise and money was made possible largely by Sandoval's status within the World Anti-Communist League and with the international contacts he had established through it.

"Paraguay's government was very influential in this effort by Sandoval," a right-wing Salvadoran businessmen who had once supported D'Aubuisson said. "The ARENA party was a result of this effort.

" 'Mico' helped mostly economically. He's even helping them now [April 1985]. These Guatemalans are rich. They have cold cash."

The businessman, who talked to one of the authors in a nondescript San Salvador restaurant, spoke of another aspect of the Guatemalan-Salvadoran ultra-right relationship: the exchange of intelligence. "The right there in Guatemala has a death list of names, which they send to the right here. And the right here has a list it sends to the ones there."

The former ARENA backer said he had a friend whose name appeared on one of the lists sent to Guatemala. "He had to go to Guatemala to tell those people that his was an identical name to the

one they had on their list, but that it was a different person. He had
to do that so the ones here wouldn't kill him."

After his success in organizing the right in El Salvador, Sandoval
ran for the presidency in 1982. But his ambition for supreme power
was frustrated once again when the handpicked successor to General
Lucas García, Colonel Hanibal Guevara, was declared the winner.
Once again, Sandoval and his MLN ally, Leonel Sisniega, went into
action. Hanibal Guevara was quickly overthrown by a junior officers'
coup that was largely engineered and led by Leonel Sisniega, who
briefly served as its spokesman. "Many of the military officers involved reputedly held strong pro-MLN sympathies, in line with their
fierce anti-communism. Working through them, the MLN hoped to
grab key posts in the newly formed interim government, and expected to win new elections that originally were planned for 60 days
after the coup, according to sources."[12]

In a case of poetic justice, the MLN's hopes were dashed when
the junior officers pulled a coup within a coup and invited the retired
General Ríos Montt to be president, the same man whom Laugerud
and Sandoval had cheated out of the presidency in 1974.

Ríos Montt was a strange man; the words Guatemalans most
frequently use in describing him are "emotionally disturbed." A
member of the evangelical Church of the Word, based in California,
Ríos Montt had earlier been director of studies at the Inter-American
Defense College in Washington and had been trained by the United
States at Fort Bragg and in Panama. When he took over Guatemala,
he declared a state of siege, suspended constitutional guarantees, and
imposed strict press censorship. He also quickly isolated his initial
partners in the military junta and declared to the nation that "God
had chosen" him to lead the country.

Whatever overwhelmingly Catholic Guatemala thought of Ríos
Montt, he was a man that the Protestant and evangelical New Right
in the United States could embrace as one of their own. Suddenly,
appeals for donations to fund projects in Guatemala became regular
fixtures on American religious radio and television shows. Evangelist
Pat Robertson went so far as to lobby for "mercy helicopters" to be
sent to Guatemala.

While U.S. evangelicals did not raise the $1 billion which Rios Montt
said he expected from them, they did play an important public rela-

tions role for the general. Courted both by the Guatemalan government—which hosted numerous visits by U.S. evangelicals—and by the White House—which set up a Spring 1982 meeting between Ríos Montt's chief adviser, Francisco Bianchi, and Jerry Falwell, Pat Robertson and James Watt—a number of U.S. churches promoted the new Guatemalan model in their publications and church bulletin inserts and through their prayers and sermons.[13]

Immediately after coming to power, Ríos Montt declared he would put an end to the urban death squads, and for the most part he did so. This sudden end to the daily killings and disappearances in Guatemala City amounted to tangible evidence that the death squads were controlled by—and operated from within—the armed forces. It didn't end entirely, as one of the authors can attest.[14]

Although most of the violence stopped in the cities, the civil war with the guerrillas, who had shown renewed strength during the Lucas regime, continued in the rural hinterlands. In response, Ríos Montt unleashed a highly successful counterinsurgency program. Although regions were pacified, the operations also resulted in many large-scale massacres of Indians suspected of supporting the guerrillas.

Counterinsurgency was complemented by a civic action campaign. "Beans and Bullets" (beans for those who submit, bullets for those who don't) was aimed at winning the hearts and minds of the civilians, no matter what it took.

Ríos Montt didn't fit into the cloak of human rights defender that American conservatives and evangelicals tried to wrap about him. At the same time as the "Beans and Bullets" program was going on, he established secret army tribunals to try and to execute "subversives," defending the executions on the basis of an amnesty he had offered the rebels: "Why should we kill people without legal backing? The amnesty gives us the judicial framework for killing. Anyone who refuses to surrender will be shot."[15]

In 1982, one of the authors questioned Ríos Montt about four suspected guerrillas who had just been executed by firing squads.

"When all the bodies appeared on the roads riddled with bullets," the president rambled, "they said that here was the law of the jungle without any legal validity. These firing squads are legal—judicially established and everything. And the executions were done—but, as I did four, I could have done four hundred. But no, the law is the law."[16]

Ríos Montt's evangelical zeal also had appeal for the Unification Church of the Reverend Sun Myung Moon. In 1982, CAUSA established an office in Guatemala and the following year organized a "World Media Conference" in Guatemala City. The conference included some two hundred participants from forty-five countries. From their base in Guatemala, the press attendees traveled to Honduras, Costa Rica, and El Salvador. "The writers met with military and business leaders in each country, hearing from [Bo Hi] Pak and also from then-President Efrain Ríos Montt of Guatemala."[17]

While Ríos Montt waged war in the country and attempted to convert his countrymen to his version of the "word" of God in bizarre Sunday-night television sermons, elements of the Guatemalan ultra-right were yet again plotting their return to power.

By coincidence, one of the authors was in Guatemala in the company of a former CIA contract agent and mercenary leader, Mitchell Livingstone WerBell III, in October and November 1982. WerBell, it turned out, was there to help Leonel Sisniega launch a new coup, this time against Ríos Montt.

WerBell, a short man who sported a great bushy moustache, was called "the Dwarf" by his employees. To others, he was known as "the Whispering Wizard of Death." He was a master at revising history, exaggerating or omitting his own covert involvement according to the circumstances, while chain-smoking and consuming vast quantities of Scotch. He died of cancer a year after his last Guatemalan caper (which never came off, he later claimed, due to State Department interference), and many of his secrets went with him.[18]

WerBell ran a counterterrorist training camp in Powder Springs, Georgia, called SIONICS. An original member of the OSS chapter in China during World War II—along with Richard Helms, Ray Cline, and John Singlaub*—the old "spook" also ran a flourishing black-market arms trade, which had constantly brought him under the scrutiny of American government investigators. Several years before,

---

*General Singlaub went to Powder Springs in 1982 to lecture WerBell's cadets. At the time, many of the SIONICS trainees were followers of Lyndon La-Rouche, a perennial presidential candidate who believes that most of the political leadership of the United States, the international Jewish financiers, the Soviet KGB, the Queen of England, and Henry Kissinger are all working for British Intelligence in a secret plan to take over the world.

he had bought the patent to the Ingram submachine gun and had developed a special silencer for it.*

During the month the coauthor spent in Guatemala, WerBell stayed in hermitlike isolation in his suite in the Hotel Cortijo Reforma, one of Guatemala City's better hotels. A retinue of Guatemalan colonels, businessmen, and a member of the U.S. military advisory group to Guatemala attached to the American Embassy regularly visited him, usually at night. "Just visiting old friends," WerBell would grin to the author when questioned about the constant parade.

Ríos Montt was finally toppled, but the man that came out on top was not Sisniega of the MLN but General Oscar Humberto Mejía Victores, a portly man with a tendency toward excessive perspiration. Despite the energetic lobbying efforts of the New Right and the Reagan Administration, which constantly tried to certify the nation as an "improved" human rights violator, Congress did not see fit to follow suit, and under Mejía Victores Guatemala remained something of a pariah state.

Meanwhile, the killing went on. "*El Grafico,*" Loren Jenkins reported on one day's victims in December 1984, "told of three bodies, including that of a 15-year old boy, found chopped to death with machetes. . . . All three had their hands tied behind their backs. The daily said the body of Cesar Augusto Martínez, 60, described simply as a 'political activist' because a union card was in his pocket, was found decomposing after neighbors had seen buzzards circling and informed authorities. The cause of death could not be established immediately, according to the local magistrate, because dogs had mangled the corpse.

"*La Prensa Libre* had more detailed accounts of at least seven other killings around the country. As usual, corpses appeared bearing signs of strangulation, knife wounds, gunshots or in some cases all three."[19]

If the U.S. Congress couldn't stomach the "anti-communist" struggle, Guatemala had allies who could. Today the Taiwanese Embassy in Guatemala is second in size only to that of the United

---

*Ingrams were used in the killing of two American labor advisers and the head of Salvadoran land reform, Rodolfo Viera, in the Sheraton Hotel of San Salvador in 1981. Hans Christ was implicated in the killings. The previous year, Christ had been an employee of WerBell's at SIONICS.

States. When the Guatemalan government bought two million dollars' worth of helicopter spare parts from the United States in 1984, it was Taiwanese, not Guatemalan, mechanics who installed them.

The Taiwanese have agricultural projects throughout the country, including a model village where they are teaching displaced Indians how to grow soybeans. Their political warfare training has reached an advanced stage; there are now Taiwanese advisers training officers and soldiers in political warfare throughout Guatemala. "You can't go very far [in Guatemala]," one State Department official said, "without seeing one of their political warfare manuals. They're everywhere."

Under Mejía Victores, Guatemala had other allies, including some old friends in the United States. Among the American New Right groups assisting the government's efforts were General Singlaub's Refugee Relief International and Andy Messing's National Defense Council. The National Defense Council's military adviser is General Harry "Heine" C. Aderholt, who by coincidence also works with Refugee Relief International. Messing is a member of Singlaub's American chapter of the World Anti-Communist League, the USCWF, while Aderholt attended the Singlaub-hosted 1984 League conference.

Another group involved in Guatemala was the Knights of Malta through their "Americares" arm. Most of the Knights' aid was channeled through the army to go to the "model villages," the cornerstone of the "rural pacification" program. Their representative in Guatemala was none other than Roberto Alejos, the same man who had led the Guatemalan–New Right "rehabilitation" public relations campaign in 1980.

The Unification Church also kept its hand in Guatemala. In May 1984, staff members for four Republican senators went to Central America. There they met with government officials and American Embassy personnel in Honduras and Guatemala and served as observers to the elections in El Salvador. Their expenses were picked up by the Freedom Leadership Foundation, the United States front group for the Unification Church.

Through his involvement with the World Anti-Communist-League, Mario Sandoval Alarcón continues to be a leader of the international ultra-right, status that helps to maintain his power base at home. In 1985, he was still the head of the Guatemalan chapter of the League.

Despite his New Right friends' attempts to portray him as a mainstream conservative, Sandoval's true colors can't help but emerge. "If I have to get rid of half of Guatemala so the other half can live in peace," he told a reporter during his unsuccessful presidential bid in 1985, "I'll do it."

Although the MLN is now an opposition party and is distrusted by some officers in the military, the alienation is primarily due to a dispute over power, not over ideology. The MLN remains a key ally to the army in its ongoing suppression of the left. MLN followers still make up the backbone of the nationwide network of salaried government *jefes politicos*. These informers continue to serve as *orejas* (ears) for the armed forces. "They are omnipotent," Martínez Montt, the Christian Democrat official, said of the *jefes,* whom he blames for the deaths and disappearances of hundreds of his party's leaders and followers. "They denounce people and then the army gets them. It's the same system as in a communist or fascist state."

Sandoval also claims to have a private army of three thousand and to be able to put a hundred thousand paramilitary troops in the field in twenty-four hours. His power remains unchecked, as do the actions of his paramilitary squads. And he still has the power to make apologists of Western diplomats. "Sandoval has had to pull in his horns," an American diplomat stressed to one of the authors in April 1985 during Guatemala's presidential campaign. "If, in fact, he controls the death squads or has people eliminated by security forces, he's had to clean up his act. After all, he's running for president."

Several months before, Sandoval had denounced the coauthor by name (in Guatemala, tantamount to a death sentence), and a judge had issued an "order for capture" for him. On this matter, the diplomat was hesitant: "Well, I wouldn't provoke him, at least not while you're in the country. I don't mean he'd order anything, but some of his people . . . well, you know what I mean, they're capable of anything."

This diplomat, one of the Reagan Administration's point men in the campaign to cleanse Guatemala's tarnished image, had a pat answer for any reporter's question. He cited the body count compiled by the Embassy (disputed by human rights groups) as proof that the death squads were on the decline, from a high of 483 a month in

1981 to 90 a month in 1984. Asked about the estimated thirty-five thousand "disappeared" in Guatemala, the diplomat responded: "Some part of those who disappear are probably picked up by the security forces, but we also know that some people 'self-disappear'— go underground."

Just as he did when he lost power after the 1978 elections, Sandoval has now turned to methods that are not necessarily "anti-communist" in nature to keep the MLN funded. Much of Guatemala's organized crime, including drug trafficking, robberies, and kidnappings for ransom, is attributed to the far-right parties. A wave of perverse gang-rapes/robberies in several Guatemala City nightclubs in the fall of 1984 are widely believed to have been the work of the "dogs" belonging to the MLN.

In part, these tactics led to the public falling-out of Sandoval and his longtime protégé Leonel Sisniega. Sisniega now heads his own party, the Unified Anti-Communist Party (PUA), also known as "the Spike." Still, insiders insist that the two continue to plan paramilitary operations together. A Salvadoran who knows Sandoval well says that the two former MLN leaders continue to meet regularly with other rightists in a back room of a Guatemala City boutique. "It's a contact place where they all meet. They control the death squads. It's where they exchange information."

Asked about this, the American diplomat explained that investigation of the death squads was not a top priority. "We try to get the whole human rights picture."

That picture remains grim. In March 1985, Mejía Victores stated that the Mutual Support Group, an organization composed of the wives, children, and relatives of the "disappeared," was "a pressure group, managed and directed by subversion, who are causing problems for Guatemala" and warned that "if they continue exerting pressures and trying to subvert order, we will be forced to apply legal norms."

A few days later, the body of the leader of the Mutual Support Group was found on a roadside, his head crushed and his tongue pulled out. Four days later, another leader was found dead on a roadside along with her two-year-old son and her brother. On April 8, the U.S. State Department "energetically deplored" the killings and stated "the need for further improvements in human rights" in Guatemala.

Those improvements were on the way, according to the Guatemalan regime. "The violence," Ramon Zelada Carillo, press spokesman for the Mejía government, announced in 1985, "is due to the Ides of March. The heat of summer is what causes the violence. Soon, the rains will come to placate the passions."

FIFTEEN

Who ever said that what the peasants of El Salvador wanted was land? Maybe all they wanted was . . . some chocolate.
   Orlando de Sola, Salvadoran landowner,
   March 1984

*I*T WAS THE DAWN on an April morning in San Vicente province. It was already warm, and in a few hours the dew clinging to the leaves and grass would be burned off and the valley would be obscured by a thick humid haze.

In a stubbled field just outside the village of Tecoluca, an army helicopter rose above the treeline, sending a whirlpool of red dust over the gathered peasants. In the chopper were two wounded soldiers and one dead one.

After the helicopter was gone, attention returned to activities on the field, where an army truck had just thrown six bodies off into a ditch. As a cluster of National Guardsmen supervised, civilians of Tecoluca dragged the bodies over to a mango tree, where an elderly *campesino* was digging a big hole. One little boy, valiantly struggling with the body designated to him, kept losing his grip and falling. Women with babies cradled in their arms came out of the surrounding huts to watch.

All six of the dead men were in civilian peasant clothes. None of them was wearing military clothing or boots. They had had weapons, one of the authors was assured, but they had already been taken away.

One of the dead was very young. He could have been nine or he could have been fifteen; the bullet wound just under his left eye had destroyed enough of his face to make an exact determination impossible.

It was the head wound that all the dead had in common. Some had bullet wounds in other parts of the body, but all their heads had been destroyed by point-blank shots.

As the villagers threw the bodies into the pit under the mango tree, the National Guardsmen kicked the corpses or poked at them with sticks. They especially made fun of the dead boy. He was thrown in last. He went in head first, and his head flopped grotesquely when it hit; the National Guardsmen laughed.

Amid the laughter, a shot rang out just behind the coauthor. A bluebird in the mango tree fell in a flutter of wrenched feathers and plopped into the hole. The National Guardsman who had shot the bird laughed again, this time at the way the coauthor had flinched at the gunshot.

A little boy went to the edge of the pit and jumped in. Clambering over the bodies, he retrieved the bird, climbed from the hole, and took it to the base of the mango tree. He was still there examining it when the villagers began throwing dirt over the dead. It was another morning in El Salvador.

Few investigations have ever been made into the estimated fifty thousand murders that have occurred in El Salvador since 1979. When three National Guardsmen and their commanding officer were sentenced for the slaying of four American churchwomen in 1984, it marked the first political murder trial in El Salvador in five years.

It hasn't been necessary to conduct trials to know who is responsible for the slaughter, however. All observers agree that most—some say over ninety percent—of the victims were killed by right-wing death squads. The guilty, many of whom are well known, remain free, their crimes unpunished. The most prominent of their leaders frequently travel to the United States, where they meet with their New Right allies and conservative congressmen and senators.

Sometimes the hit teams are soldiers or police carrying out orders from their superior officers. Others are composed of civilians or cashiered soldiers hired for specific assassinations; their fees are paid by rich businessmen who, for their own political or economic self-interest, organize and fund the paramilitary network in coordination with friends in the military hierarchy.

A U.S. Embassy official in San Salvador attributes the country's death squad "phenomenon" to "a generalized lack of faith in the corrupted judicial system," which has resulted in traditional "vigilante-style justice." "When a country like El Salvador sees itself traumatized [by leftist guerrilla violence], and its constitutional authorities unable to deal with it, they're going to do something about it."[1]

Raul García Prieto, a ranking member of El Salvador's ultra-rightist ARENA party, has a different explanation. "Maybe we, as Latins, just get hotter quicker, and in the U.S. the differences are settled in a more paused fashion."

In the office of his candy factory, Hugo Barrera, a former ARENA vice-presidential candidate, told one of the authors his own theory: "Violence," he said, "is part of our national folklore."

Folklore aside, El Salvador's history is important in explaining the civil strife currently searing this tiny Central American republic of five million people, most of whom are illiterate rural peasants. Many argue that it was the corrupt system of government—held in place since the 1930s by a succession of iron-fisted military rulers, a ruthless National Guard and police force, and a small elite class of fantastically wealthy landowners who exercised feudal control over the country's primary sources of income—that led to the leftist guerrilla insurgency in the 1970s.

For years, the strongman who held El Salvador's "system" in place was General José Alberto "Chele" (Blondie) Medrano, the commander of the National Guard. In the 1960s, Medrano rose to power in El Salvador with the assistance of an American government alarmed by the rise of communism after Castro's takeover in Cuba. Under the aegis of President Kennedy's Alliance for Progress program, which stressed regional defense coordination against subversion, Medrano created and directed ORDEN and ANSESAL. These state agencies were established at the behest of the United States and reported to the CIA, as did counterpart agencies in Guatemala and Nicaragua. All became the core groups for ruthless counterterror campaigns in these countries when the political struggle intensified during the 1970s. In El Salvador, ORDEN and AN-

SESAL later became the breeding grounds for El Salvador's government-run death squads.

In a March 1985 interview with one of the authors on the breezy veranda of his San Salvador home, Medrano remembered the heady days of "the Alliance," when he was at the height of his power.

> To counterarrest the actions of the international communism, the heads of Central America met in San José [Costa Rica] with President Kennedy and signed the Act of San José.
>
> Afterwards, many things were coordinated regionally, in the economy and so on. We also had to unite in military defense. That's when CONDECA [a short-lived regional defense committee uniting Central America's armies in 1964] was formed.

ORDEN ("Order") was the acronym for the Democratic Nationalist Organization, a rural paramilitary army of some eighty thousand anti-communist informers and vigilantes. "ORDEN was an ideological school we had created to organize the peasants," Medrano said. "We formed ORDEN by calling up ex-policemen, Guardsmen, and military officers. We organized courses which taught [the] representative democratic system, the advantages of belonging to the free world, and the disadvantages of the socialist world. When the struggle against communism began, ORDEN was used to help the military."

"The problem with ORDEN," explained Francisco José "Chachi" Guerrero, a former National Conciliation Party (PCN) chief and presidential candidate and now El Salvador's Supreme Court chief justice, "was that it was a paramilitary group. It began as a support group to help the PCN. They were organized to be PCN activists. General Medrano gave it legality and lent it to fight communism in the rural areas.

"Then there were problems because PCN was a political party and ORDEN was paramilitary. ORDEN wanted to supplant the PCN."

If this sounds remarkably like the "Taiwan model"—a political party establishing a paramilitary network and "lending" it to the army—it is apparently not a coincidence. Salvadoran officers frequently mention the role of a Taiwanese officer, Colonel Chu, who was stationed in El Salvador during the 1960s. According to these military officials, Chu was a key adviser and consultant to Medrano during the formation of ORDEN.

When ORDEN collected intelligence data on "subversives," it turned the data over to the Salvadoran National Security Agency (ANSESAL). Both agencies were headquartered in the Presidential Palace, where Medrano was presidential chief of staff at the same time that he was National Guard chief and on the payroll of the CIA.

> For defense, one needed his eyes open to see the enemy. That's how ANSESAL was born. We created one in each country in Central America; like the CIA, we had reunions to interchange intelligence on the communists. That is when the concept of indoctrinating the Central American peasants on the village level was born. But the communists beat us to it.

When the threat from leftist insurgents finally became visible, Medrano said, the armed forces had a problem. "The law doesn't permit us to use terrorism. We have to use countersabotage and counterterrorism. So when we captured [a communist], we applied the law to them."

But the law applied was not one found in any law books. "All the guerrillas are traitors to the Fatherland, because they fight in the service of a foreign power [the Soviet Union]. And the law against that is the death penalty. So we applied that law against them."

The old general, his blue eyes bright, admitted that his creations had "gone bad" and become the core groups for the death squads, but he blamed it on the men who took over after him.

Medrano's account conflicts with reality. Although he lost his post as National Guard chief after a 1970 coup plot against the incumbent president, Medrano launched an unsuccessful bid for the presidency in 1972 using ORDEN as a power base. Even in the 1980s, he was generally believed to exercise enormous influence as a kind of patriarch in the political machinations of the far right, aided by the protégés he had left behind, Roberto D'Aubuisson, Adolfo Cuellar, and Raul Molina. These men, all of whom also joined the Latin American branch of the World Anti-Communist League, rose to positions of power in ORDEN, ANSESAL, and the National Guard.

During the interview, Medrano distanced himself from his pupils.

"When I left, the military chiefs put delinquents in charge," he said with disgust. "They sold the ORDEN cards. They gave them out so they could commit abuses."

It was these "abusive" men, he claimed, that formed the death squads. "The people are mistaken when they say the death squads came out of ORDEN. It is the richest, the cupola [oligarchy] who distinguish in this. They don't want to give up their land. They are criminoids. They have to be crazy for what they do, like raping the dead, putting the head in the belly. . . .

"I defended the masses. I never defended the cupola."

It was the general's last interview. Shortly before noon the next day, as he dropped off his maid at her housing project, four young men, apparently leftist guerrillas, walked up to the general's blue van and pumped five bullets into him. Medrano didn't even have time to reach for the .45 he always carried or for the hand grenades that reportedly filled his glove compartment.

The coauthor arrived at the scene shortly afterward and found the old man still in the blue slacks and long-sleeved blue shirt he had worn during the previous night's three-hour interview. Now his clothes were covered with shattered window glass and blood. A bullet had made a small, neat hole above Medrano's left eye, and the godfather of El Salvador's White Hand was clearly dead.

One of the "criminals" put in charge of ORDEN after Medrano's official discharge in 1970 was Adolfo Cuellar. "Cuellar was one of the abusive ones," Medrano had said. "He was part of the cupola when they formed the death squads."

Cuellar was a member of the National Assembly for the National Conciliation Party (PCN), which since 1961 had been the party vehicle that the nation's military rulers used to provide themselves with a democratic facade. Cuellar was also a founding member of the Latin American Anti-Communist Confederation. Throughout the 1970s, the Salvadoran representatives to World Anti-Communist League conferences were mostly Cuellar friends, ranking members of ORDEN, ANSESAL, and the PCN.

One man that remembers the less-public side of Cuellar is Colonel Roberto Eulalio Santivañez, the former chief of El Salvador's military intelligence and the last head of ANSESAL; he now lives in exile. "You must understand the structure of the death squads," Santivañez explained as he sipped apple juice in a Washington restaurant. "At the top are the brains, the military officers and businessmen. At the bottom are the guns, the ones who actually do the killing. In between are the *perros,* the dogs. That is what they call them. The dogs take the orders and supervise the operation. If a victim is to be interrogated and tortured first, the dogs will do this.[2]

"And Cuellar," Santivañez said, stabbing at the list of Salvadoran WACL members shown him, "was one of the worst dogs." From one of El Salvador's wealthy families, Cuellar was no ordinary member of the oligarchy, nor even a normal death squad "dog." He was a man who delighted in sadism and murder. In periodic drunken binges, he was known to saunter into military interrogation centers and plead to be allowed to "interrogate" any prisoners they might be holding.

Cuellar is openly discussed by his former allies because he is dead; he was murdered in his San Salvador home in 1981. The rightists say the guerrillas did it. "Cuellar was a raging anti-communist," Chief Justice Guerrero recalls, "until he was finally killed by the left. They got him because, as one of the top people of ORDEN, he got intelligence on them, which was passed on to ANSESAL. ANSESAL then turned the information over to the security forces, where it was acted upon."

In fact, the murder could have been by any number of people; by 1981, Adolfo Cuellar had made plenty of enemies.

Another of Medrano's protégés, Roberto D'Aubuisson, made a bigger name for himself. While Cuellar was in command of ORDEN, D'Aubuisson was rising through the ranks of the National Guard. Eventually he became the deputy chief of ANSESAL under Santivañez. The post was ideally suited for the future mastermind of El Salvador's death squads, since ANSESAL's files were the intelligence bank of the ORDEN network.

During the 1970s, D'Aubuisson, a chain-smoking, boyishly handsome member of El Salvador's oligarchy of wealthy families, was trained at some of the world's most proficient unconventional warfare finishing schools: in Uruguay; at the now-banned International Police Academy run by the State Department's Office of Public Safety in Washington, D.C.; and, of course, at the Political Warfare Cadres Academy in Taiwan.

In an interview with a French reporter in 1985, D'Aubuisson said that the course he took in Peitou in 1977 was "the best class I ever studied."

> Those lessons were what I applied when I organized, we started organizing, civic groups. Political war is different from military war. It is different in its space; a political war is defined as 360 degrees. The military war is a war in space, but there is one military front, one theater of operation. In the military war, the young people could participate, the young men especially. In political warfare, everybody participates.[3]

Political warfare, D'Aubuisson said, "is psychological warfare against the enemy. I started psychological warfare against the communists. I denounced their program, their treasons, their infiltrations into the government.

"The political warfare is a complement to the armed fight."

Immediately following his Taiwan experience and his training in Washington, D'Aubuisson returned to El Salvador to join the National Guard's intelligence branch, then became deputy chief of ANSESAL. He also wrote a report on the alleged ties between moderate reformists and the communist guerrillas that was distributed to the various intelligence agencies. Whether those links existed in real terms or not didn't matter to D'Aubuisson. "You can be a Communist," he told reporter Laurie Becklund in 1983, "even if you personally don't believe you are a Communist."[4]

D'Aubuisson's report would serve as the basis for the coming war against El Salvador's political center, in which he was already becoming involved; by 1978, he was widely believed to be the driving force behind the White Warriors' Union (UGB).[5]

The death sentence came in the fall of 1979 and was delivered to the home in a small, yellow manila envelope: "For betraying democracy and the Constitution, you are condemned to death. You will receive the merited punishment at any moment."

The communiqué was signed by the *Union Guerrero Blanco*, the White Warriors' Union.

The lawyer, a quiet, spare man in his late fifties with a receding hairline and intense brown eyes, told his story in a calm, paced manner, betraying no emotion. A former judge, he spoke to one of the authors in San Salvador recently.

At the time when the envelope came, he was active in one of El Salvador's moderately leftist political parties, now underground. True to their word, the killers came for him, pulling up to the house in a van one day in December 1979. Not finding the lawyer, they emptied their weapons on those they did find—his daughter, her year-old baby, and her eight-year-old son—as they stood in the doorway of the home. The eight-year-old was killed in the barrage of bullets. "When it happened," the grandfather said, "the authorities promised to investigate, but nothing has ever been done."

Every year since then, on the same December day, the telephone rings in the suburban San Salvador home. Every year for the last six it has been the same anonymous voice, that of a young, educated male, conveying the same message: "Sorry about the boy's death." Then he hangs up, until next year.

The family has grown accustomed to the annual "condolence" call. Several years ago, however, increasingly distraught over the constant reminder of their tragedy, they sought the advice of a psychologist. The psychologist told them that since the killer calls every year on the same day, the day he murdered their boy, he isn't displaying remorse but sadism. He wants them to suffer.

The White Warriors' Union was one of the first anti-communist death squads to appear in El Salvador in the mid-1970s, having grown out of the Armed Forces of National Liberation—War of Extermination (FALANGE). Many other names were to follow it: the White Hand, the Death Squad, the Salvadoran Anticommunist Brigade, the Secret Anticommunist Army.

According to the few death squad members who have spoken of their work, these titles are just so many names, chosen to instill fear and make the public believe there are many groups in operation. To the contrary, they are usually one and the same, a small group of men operating on the orders of an elite inner council. It is the council that decides who dies.

As for the names, they are freely borrowed and interchanged, even across national boundaries. The name "the White Hand," for example, was taken from the death squads in Guatemala. Actually, this particular choice was not made for purely esthetic reasons. "The

[Salvadoran] death squads were a reflection of the White Hand in Guatemala," according to Roberto Santivañez. As ANSESAL chief from 1977 to 1979, he had intimate knowledge, both of how the death squad system worked and of the role his former deputy, Roberto D'Aubuisson, had in creating it.

> There were many attempts to bring death squads into El Salvador. They were always avoided in the past [before 1979]. People from Guatemala wanted to start death squads in El Salvador, always called the White Hand. When I worked in the administration, death squads were forbidden because of their negative image.[6]

Despite Santivañez's claim, death squads did in fact operate throughout the 1970s, averaging some two hundred victims a year; after 1979, they killed four times that number every month.

In October 1979, El Salvador's president, General Carlos Humberto Romero, was overthrown by reformist junior officers. Installing a progressive civilian-military "revolutionary junta," the new rulers quickly abolished ORDEN and ANSESAL, blaming the organizations for having created and operated death squads. Santivañez, the ANSESAL chief, fled into exile in Guatemala. Major D'Aubuisson, his deputy, remained.*

As Christopher Dickey reported in *The New Republic*:

> When the October 15, 1979, coup ousted the President D'Aubuisson served, the ambitious Major nevertheless knew how to take advantage of the situation. The same morning, D'Aubuisson advised Colonel Jaime Abdul Gutierrez, a conservative and one of the coup's principal organizers, that the ANSESAL files should be removed before they could fall into the hands of the communist rebels, many of whose closest allies were being brought into the government as part of a short-lived attempt at pluralism. Gutierrez told D'Aubuisson to get the files and take them to the headquarters of the armed forces general staff. But Gutierrez apparently did not anticipate that D'Aubuisson would keep the most important dossiers for himself. A few days later, D'Aubuisson asked to be discharged because, he said, he couldn't go along with the left-wing leanings of the new government. Within a matter of weeks, D'Au-

*One who lost his job in the 1979 coup was Colonel Luis Benedicto Rodríguez, a top member of the CAL branch of the World Anti-Communist League. The head of ORDEN, he had, like Medrano, also been chief of staff for the presidency.

buisson was appearing on nationwide television, his time paid for by some of El Salvador's wealthy families, making detailed denunciations of "subversives" inside and outside the government. Several of the people he denounced were killed shortly thereafter by the death squads.[7]

If death squads had been "resisted" before the coup, as Colonel Santivañez claims, because of their potential for bad public relations, following the coup they were embraced with ghoulish zeal by key members of the Salvadoran military. D'Aubuisson was the pointman in this counterterror campaign designed to undermine the new moderate government.

One of the first prominent victims was Mario Zamora, the attorney general of the new junta. In late February 1980, days after he had been denounced by D'Aubuisson on television, armed men in civilian dress broke into Zamora's home. Since a party was in progress, the intruders dragged Zamora into a bathroom, where they shot him in the face at least ten times.

The next month, D'Aubuisson again appeared on television to tell progressive Archbishop Oscar Arnulfo Romero that he "still had time to change his ways." Days later, as Romero was giving mass in a chapel, he was assassinated by a marksman with a single shot through the heart.

Eight months later, U.S. Ambassador to El Salvador Robert White sent a cable to Washington detailing D'Aubuisson's role in the murder. White reported that his information came from an extremely reliable source: one of the Salvadoran military officers who had participated in the assassination planning.

> According to this eyewitness account, Roberto D'Aubuisson summoned a group of about twelve men to a safe house, presided over the meeting, announced the decision to assassinate the Archbishop and supervised the drawing of lots for the "honor" of carrying out the plot. The Salvadoran officer informant was disappointed that the luck of the draw had not favored him. He gave bullets from his gun to the officer selected in order that he might participate vicariously in the murder of the Archbishop.[8]

The officer who "won" was Lieutenant Francisco Amaya Rosa, who in turn chose a sharpshooter, Walter Antonio Alvarez, to do the actual shooting. Later, according to White, D'Aubuisson worried about Alvarez's trustworthiness and had him gunned down while the killer watched a soccer game.

Because of his on-the-air denunciations, D'Aubuisson instantly became the darling of his nation's ultra-right, counting among his allies many police and military officers. Those killed after being denounced by D'Aubuisson were only the most infamous cases; hundreds of other victims were being claimed by D'Aubuisson's supporters throughout El Salvador in early 1980.

An important cornerstone of D'Aubuisson's support was found in the old ORDEN network. Although it had been officially dissolved several months earlier, D'Aubuisson had paid ORDEN's provincial chiefs to maintain the organization, and it continued to operate in the countryside. Now called the Democratic Nationalist Front (FDN), a name thought up by "Chele" Medrano, the people still knew it as ORDEN.

> On Thursday, February 28, 1980, two truckloads of police and National Guardsmen in civilian dress arrived [in Cinquera]. With them were . . . members of ORDEN . . . who were in charge of leading the security forces and the Army to the homes of those people whom they believed belonged to some popular [subversive] organization.

The ORDEN-led detail detained two villagers, a man and a woman.

> They took them away to the National Guard station at Suchitoto, where Aida and Felix were tortured to death. I say they were brutally tortured because Aida's body did not have a single bullet wound, but her nose and her teeth were broken and her lip was missing. . . . She had a hole in her head but I do not know how they did that; it was so large that a hand could fit in easily. They had removed her fingernails; her fingers were shrivelled. Her entire body had been soaked in some kind of acid. She also showed signs of having been raped.[9]

What was not well known in early 1980 was that D'Aubuisson's sudden political clout had been nurtured abroad. The assistance of Mario Sandoval Alarcón in Guatemala, of the right-wing military juntas of South America, and of elements of the American New Right had launched D'Aubuisson on the path to anti-communist stardom.

A former ORDEN organizer and Medrano ally explained to one of the authors how the "international system" worked:

The ultra-right parties here [in El Salvador], in Guatemala, in Argentina, are all the same. They have the same ideology, the same symbols—even the same music. The money the parties use is channeled internationally. It goes to support one another's elections. The [rightist] political parties use the same system as the communists. When they need to eliminate someone, they bring in someone from the outside who is contracted to do the job. This would be directed by a central committee. All the parties have their own shock forces. There are people who hold high offices in these parties who are nothing more than killers. This is how it works.

The first order of business, then, was for the Salvadoran rightists to form a political party. To this end, they had turned to Sandoval.

In December 1983, two investigative journalists, Laurie Becklund of *The Los Angeles Times* and Craig Pyes of *The Albuquerque Journal,* published a remarkable series of articles based on their infiltration of the Central American ultra-right, exposing D'Aubuisson's ties to the Guatemalan MLN chief. According to them, the links were formed in 1979 at a meeting in the MLN headquarters in Guatemala City. Presiding was Mario Sandoval Alarcón.

Sandoval . . . told his audience, a group of young Salvadoran businessmen worried by the leftist direction their country was taking, about the bloody history of the MLN and the sacrifice each of them would have to make to form a party like the MLN in El Salvador.[10]

D'Aubuisson's cohorts were ready to make these sacrifices. The result was the Broad National Front (FAN) and later the Nationalist Republican Alliance (ARENA).

By this time, as Colonel Santivañez recounted in a press conference on March 21, 1985, "Many [Salvadoran] officers were with D'Aubuisson. They were invited to parties, talked into sharing his ideology and getting ready for action. It all centered on the establishment of the FAN that would support the armed forces. That's what they were selling. This organization would later become the death squads."[11]

As the Salvadoran rightists prepared for the unveiling of FAN, their death squads were claiming ever-greater numbers of victims. One reason for their increasing boldness was that their Guatemalan allies were providing them with guns, money, expertise, and temporary asylum.

"From captured documents," Santivañez said, "it's clear that these groups operated between Guatemala and El Salvador. Their sanctuary is Guatemala where they have returned after every action to avoid any reaction from the armed forces or the courts of El Salvador. There, they work closely with Mario Sandoval Alarcón and Leonel Sisniega Otero, heads of the White Hand in Guatemala."

Santivañez was in exile in Guatemala at the time and had occasion to talk with some of the "hit teams" there in between their trips to El Salvador.

> We used to meet with these people. They openly talked about the operations. They were planning a very sensitive murder. On March 24 [1980] they killed Monsignor Romero—after a big meeting of people who were giving money to the FAN and also gave instruction on the action to take place.[11]

Santivañez realized that the Salvadoran ultra-right's international links went far beyond just Sandoval's MLN.

> The D'Aubuisson documents indicate who started the [Salvadoran] death squads. They show that Nicaraguan National Guardsmen from Somoza's time worked with the death squads.

This charge is lent credence by the testimony of Hector Frances, the Argentine military intelligence officer who defected in 1982. He and a team of his countrymen were in Central America at the time, working with anti-communist groups in Honduras, Costa Rica, El Salvador, and Guatemala, as well as organizing exiled National Guardsmen from the defeated Nicaraguan Somoza dictatorship. All this was done in Guatemala in conjunction with Mario Sandoval Alarcón, Leonel Sisniega, and Roberto D'Aubuisson. The Argentines who were sent to El Salvador also helped the rightists perfect their counterterror techniques. They furnished a manual that instructed counterterrorists to "liquidate all those who could bear a grudge against you"; in other words, when killing a subversive, kill his whole family so as not to leave any revenge-seekers behind. Afterward, in an interview with Becklund, D'Aubuisson had nothing but praise for the Argentines: "They were here a very short time, but that time was very helpful [because] they tried to transmit their experiences, tell people and recommend to them, act this way and that, use this system, coordinate information and analyze it this way."[12]

Sandoval also cast his eye south to assist his Salvadoran compatriots. In early 1980, he sent two of his nephews, David Ernesto "Neto" Panama and Carlos Midence Pivaral (the latter a member of the Guatemalan chapter of CAL), to meet with the military leaders of Paraguay, Chile, and Argentina. There they were to be briefed on how best to carry out an unconventional war in Central America. "Sandoval," according to Pyes, "provided them with introductory letters to high officials in the Argentine Army, the Commander-in-Chief in Paraguay, the head of Uruguayan intelligence (where D'Aubuisson had studied), and officials in Chile.

> Panama said they took extensive notes in each of the meetings on methods of psychological war and other anti-guerrilla strategies. Afterward, he said, he wrote a report of about 25 pages for D'Aubuisson, who relayed it "to the right people in the [Salvadoran] Army."[13]

Today, U.S. diplomats in the area profess little knowledge of the interrelationships among Central America's death squads; they blame their ignorance on a pull-back of CIA personnel under President Carter during the crucial period of death squad violence. One diplomat stationed in El Salvador in 1985, however, agreed that such cooperative actions were possible. "I lend some credence to the idea of regional or international affiliations," he said. "There are well-to-do businessmen who have branches in other countries. They travel a lot and intermarry. The contacts were there."

Ten days after the assassination of Archbishop Romero, D'Aubuisson was in Washington, D.C., where he was received by several New Right groups and conservative congressmen and senators. In a meeting room of the House of Representatives, he announced the formation of the Broad National Front (FAN). He also used the platform afforded him by his American sympathizers to launch an attack on the Carter Administration.

> In order to define the State Department policy, we could use this axiom: who is a communist? Those who consciously or unconsciously collaborate with the Soviet cause. We can ascertain that present [U.S.] State Department policy toward Central America has candidly favored communist infiltration.[14]

When the cashiered major returned to El Salvador, he was "on a roll." In May he sent a videotape to the nation's army garrisons attacking the moderate members of the junta as communists. His principal target was the head of the junta, Colonel Arnulfo Majano.

The next week Majano retaliated, arresting D'Aubuisson and a dozen of his followers for conspiring to overthrow the government. Also seized were documents so damaging that it briefly appeared to be the end of "Major Bob."

One item captured was the diary of Rafael Alvaro Saravia, a D'Aubuisson crony. In addition to listing expenses incurred in buying explosives and weapons, in taking trips to Guatemala, and in the "washing of vehicles," the diary listed the conspirator's code names, phone numbers, donations, and leadership positions.*

The diary was so incriminating that U.S. Ambassador Robert White called it "evidence that is compelling, if not 100 percent conclusive," that D'Aubuisson was responsible for the murder of Archbishop Romero the previous month. "In these documents," the ambassador told the Senate Foreign Relations Committee in April 1981, "there are over a hundred names of people who are participating both within the Salvadoran military as active conspirators against the Government, and also the names of people living in the United States and in Guatemala City who are actively funding the death squads."

The move to neutralize D'Aubuisson backfired disastrously; within a week, a military judge released the former major from prison, calling the evidence against him "lacking in merit."

It was the death knell for the progressive junta. The same day, Colonel Majano was removed as its chief, and by year's end he was ousted from power altogether by rightist military officers. During 1980, when an estimated ten thousand people were killed, most of the other junta moderates resigned and left the country, citing their inability to stop either the armed forces' atrocities or the death squads. Most now live in exile or have gone underground to join the leftist guerrilla coalition.

As the influence of the reformers waned in 1980, "the anti-subversive operations began to turn out better," D'Aubuisson told

---

*The entry for March 15, in which the purchase of boxes of ammunition is discussed, is fairly typical: "9 boxes 357 Magnum, 1 box .380, 2 half boxes .45, 20 9 mm. boxes, 21 shotgun boxes."

Craig Pyes in 1983, since the military could now operate them directly.

Pyes and Becklund got confirmation of this "improvement" when they obtained and published excerpts of an internal Salvadoran rightist report.

> On June 17, 1980, nine months after the [reformist] coup, a right-wing intelligence analyst code-named "Alpha" penned a memo expressing satisfaction with the new direction of the war. It read:
>
> "The military operations of the armed forces now are more effective and they are attacking neurological points of the enemy, destroying important sections of their organizational structure. Finally, the Salvadoran Army is making battle outside the scheme of conventional war."[15]

One American diplomat in El Salvador attempted to explain the savagery of the period as something necessary to break the power of the guerrillas. "The 'dirty war' theory certainly had some adherents here in 1979 to 1981," he said. "There were people willing to kill a lot of people to eliminate the supporters of the FMLN [guerrilla faction]. The horror years of '80 and '81 had a lot to do with breaking the FMLN in the city."

But the diplomat disagreed with other observers about the randomness of the death squads. "It wasn't indiscriminate, but it was done with a very fine net."

Having survived his confrontation with Majano, and with El Salvador's unconventional war going full force, D'Aubuisson returned to Washington in July 1980. He was accompanied by Orlando de Sola, an active member of El Salvador's "Fourteen Families" oligarchy who was heavily funding D'Aubuisson. Because of evidence that linked D'Aubuisson to a coup attempt and to death threats against American diplomats, the Carter Administration refused his visa; this necessitated the two Salvadorans' entering the United States illegally. The technicality didn't seem to bother their New Right supporters; both men met with officials of the Heritage Foundation and the Council for Inter-American Security and were honored guests at a Washington conference cohosted by the American Security Council and the American Legion. Attending the conference was Representative Larry McDonald.

Two months later, D'Aubuisson went to Buenos Aires to attend the 1980 conference of the Latin affiliate of the World Anti-Communist League. Presiding over the CAL conference was a former general of the Argentine army, General Suárez Mason. Also in attendance was Bolivian Colonel Luis García Meza, a neo-fascist officer who months before had seized control of his country in a bloody coup, assisted by the Argentine military and bankrolled by his nation's cocaine kingpins. The "distinguished" speakers at the conference were President-for-Life General Alfredo Stroessner of Paraguay; General Jorge Rafael Videla, president of Argentina; and Mario Sandoval Alarcón from Guatemala.*

By the close of the three-day summit, the conference had unanimously passed several resolutions, including a call for "the explusion of the Jesuits [from Latin America] for their being Marxist neo-colonizers" and for "organizing the rural guerrillas under the pretext of evangelizing." They also condemned President Jimmy Carter for "favoring the advance of Marxism in Latin America and the so-called policy of human rights, using it as a political weapon against those governments who combat with efficiency the communist subversion in all its forms." The CAL officers also accused the human rights commissions of the Organization of American States and the United Nations, as well as Amnesty International, for having "Marxist inclinations."[16]

Accompanying D'Aubuisson to the September conference in Buenos Aires was Luis Angel Lagos, a member of the National Assembly for the PCN and a former official of ORDEN. "We are in a permanent struggle," Lagos thundered, "under the motto that the only good Communist that will be left in the country . . . will be a dead Communist."[17]

He then lauded the examples recently set by Latin America's foremost authorities on dealing with subversion through unconventional warfare: Argentina, Bolivia, Chile, and Uruguay.

In his own speech, D'Aubuisson echoed the CAL resolutions, while citing examples of the problems specifically facing El Salvador.

---

*Today Suárez Mason is a fugitive from Argentina, where he is wanted on charges relating to his involvement in the Argentine "dirty war." Colonel García Meza is wanted by American drug-enforcement authorities for his participation in cocaine-trafficking, and General Videla is in a Buenos Aires prison serving a life sentence for ordering illegal detention, torture, and mass murder.

His participation in the CAL meeting in Buenos Aires was an important "career" move for D'Aubuisson; there he met and got to be on personal terms with some of the Latin American rightists who had been helping their Salvadoran comrades for many years.

Francisco José "Chachi" Guerrero, El Salvador's Supreme Court chief justice, is an amiable man who has been involved in his nation's fractious politics for decades. A top PCN leader and an official under successive governments, he was appointed to his present office by President José Napoleon Duarte in 1984 as part of a political payoff in which Duarte was given the PCN votes in the second electoral runoff that would give him a majority in the National Assembly.

Guerrero craves political gossip, which serves ultimately to perpetuate his political strength. He also maintains a strong interest in the work of the World Anti-Communist League.

Before entering his spacious office in the modern Supreme Court building in San Salvador, one passes stacks of Taiwanese propaganda and booklets containing speeches given at League conferences. Asked if there was any significance in the overwhelming predominance of League literature in the lobby, Guerrero just smiles. "No, I haven't attended any of their conferences. I just don't like anti's."

But the Supreme Court justice knows many of those who are in the League. In the 1970s, when Guerrero was minister of the presidency, he was introduced to Rafael Rodríguez, the leader of the Mexican Tecos and its chief emissary. "Rodríguez," he said, "invited me to visit Guadalajara."

Their mutual friend who made the introduction was Luis Angel Lagos, another PCN leader and at that time secretary of information to the presidency. Guerrero described Lagos as "very well-connected" to the Tecos and ultimately to the leadership of the World Anti-Communist League. "It seemed that what they [Tecos] wanted was economic help for an anti-communist publicity campaign," Guerrero recalled. "He [Rodríguez] seemed like a very nice man, but I declined to go.

"They [the League] came here to organize them [Salvadoran anti-communists] and take them to Taiwan, things like that. . . . After they go to Taiwan, they give them I don't know how many dollars to publish things against communism. And they come back with programs for the anti-communist campaign."[18]

Colonel Santivañez had a different impression of the Tecos. While he was still the head of military intelligence, they came to offer him their services.

> They offered to get people for us. They offered everything: guns, intelligence, people to do the killings, but they wanted money in advance. They even offered to get rid of people in the States. They bragged that they had a death list for the United States, but hadn't gotten anyone yet because they still had to work out the logistics.[19]

Santivañez claims the Tecos' services were never contracted; instead, the Mexicans went to the private sector.

It was also at the 1980 CAL conference in Buenos Aires that D'Aubuisson forged closer ties to the American New Right; "observing" the conference were Margo Carlisle, legislative aide to Senator James McClure (R–Idaho) and staff director of the Republican Conference of the U.S. Senate, and John Carbaugh, a former housemate of Roger Pearson and in 1980 an aide to Senator Jesse Helms (R–North Carolina). These two Americans would later play a tremendously important role in "repackaging" the Salvadoran death squad leader.

On the night of Ronald Reagan's election as president in November 1980, the rightists in El Salvador paraded in the streets. Afterward, the bloodbath began. "The most horrifying events in El Salvador," a career American diplomat in San Salvador recalls, "took place between Reagan's election and his inauguration."

In that two-month period, the level of terror in El Salvador soared, with Americans becoming targets for the first time.

In November, five prominent leftist politicians meeting in San Salvador were abducted and murdered; their mutilated bodies were found on the outskirts of the city the next day.

In December, three American nuns and a lay worker were brutally raped and murdered by National Guard soldiers.

In the same month, John Sullivan, a freelance American journalist, disappeared the day after he arrived in El Salvador. His body was finally found in 1983; a forensic specialist determined that he had been killed by a stick of dynamite taped to his stomach.

In January, the head of the Salvadoran agrarian reform agency and two American labor advisers from the American Institute for Free Labor Development (AIFLD) were shot to death in the coffee shop of San Salvador's Sheraton Hotel. Close associates and friends of D'Aubuisson, who were at the scene, were implicated in ordering the killings.

The American diplomat assigns a large portion of the blame for the savagery of that time to junketeering American New Rightists who claimed association with the incoming Reagan Administration.

> [Jesse] Helms and others were coming through here and saying that human rights are not part of Reagan's agenda, that communism has to be stamped out. A lot of people were claiming to speak for the Administration, many of whom did not later get jobs.
>
> There were extensive contacts with D'Aubuisson and Helms' aides, like John Carbaugh, Deborah DeMoss and Chris Manion. I have heard that they were instrumental in forming ARENA's [Nationalist Republican Alliance] gimmickry and sloganry, and the "Republicanizing" in the name.

Helms's involvement with D'Aubuisson was especially offensive to this American diplomat. Some of the American conservatives might have been able to profess ignorance of D'Aubuisson's dark history, but not Helms; as a ranking member of the Senate Foreign Relations Committee, the senator from North Carolina had had access to U.S. Embassy cables that had been detailing D'Aubuisson's involvement in various killings for some time.

Nor could the Reagan Administration claim it was uninformed. "From the first days in office," former Ambassador Robert White testified to the House Subcommittee on Western Hemispheric Affairs in 1984, "the Reagan White House knew—beyond any reasonable doubt—that Roberto D'Aubuisson planned and ordered the assassination of Archbishop Oscar Arnulfo Romero."

> All of the . . . information was reported to Washington.
>
> The Reagan Administration made a major decision, for which it must answer, when it chose not to use embassy reports and other materials to move against the Salvadoran exiles who target victims and fund death squads. The Reagan White House took on a great responsibility when it chose to conceal the identity of Archbishop Romero's murderer and not to use the evidence gathered by the embassy to write finish to the . . . ambitions of Roberto D'Aubuisson.

The former ambassador was characteristically blunt in his conclusion.

> The administration of President Carter classified ex-Major Roberto D'Aubuisson, accurately, as a terrorist, a murderer, and a leader of death squads. As Ambassador, I denied him access to the United States Embassy and succeeded in having him barred from our country.
>
> Shortly after President Reagan took office, this administration overturned this policy and began the process of rehabilitating ex-Major D'Aubuisson. The Reagan Administration granted D'Aubuisson a visa to enter the United States, made him an honored guest at our Embassy and saw to it that he met regularly with high-ranking Administration officials and visiting Senators and Congressmen. The legislators were, of course, unaware of the strength of evidence against D'Aubuisson.*

American conservatives with close links to the intelligence community have offered a simple explanation as to why the evidence was ignored: in the beginning, the Reagan Administration wanted to salvage D'Aubuisson's reputation because he was seen as a counterweight to the liberal inclinations of the Christian Democrat Party. In the new American president's eyes, the Christian Democrats were tainted for having participated in the ill-fated 1979 revolutionary junta, which had seemed to favor the left. The Administration could defend this stand by citing the findings of the so-called White Paper, "Communist Interference in El Salvador," of February 1981, a controversial report based largely on forged documents that D'Aubuisson had furnished.[20]

D'Aubuisson showed his gratitude to his new American benefactors in a strange way. On March 10, 1981, he held a press conference and announced that, after talks with Reagan Administration officials, he had received approval for a coup to install a military government. The United States denied this, and the next day the Embassy was sprayed with gunfire.

"This incident has all the hallmarks of a D'Aubuisson operation . . . ," Frederick Chapin, the American chargé d'affaires, said, refer-

---

*On this last point, Ambassador White appears to be giving Congress a graceful way out. The fact is that by the spring of 1981, D'Aubuisson's involvement with death squads had been repeatedly discussed by the media of all political bents for over a year. The only legislators meeting D'Aubuisson who could have been unaware of the strong evidence against him were those that hadn't read a newspaper since February 1980.

ring to the Embassy attack. "We have no intention of being intimi-dated."

In 1981, D'Aubuisson entered El Salvador's political process with a vengeance, bragging of his "high connections" to the recently sworn-in Reagan Administration. Having done away with his semi-clandestine FAN, he announced the formation of the Nationalist Re-publican Alliance (ARENA) party. That he made the announcement in Guatemala was not an accident.

By all accounts, Mario Sandoval Alarcón was the driving force behind the creation of this new party. It was he who had convinced the Salvadorans to develop a genuine political front party with a base broader than that of the FAN and to branch out from exclusive con-centration on paramilitary or death squad operations. To this end, "Mico" is said to have raised several million dollars in Miami through relatives and contacts there; wealthy Salvadoran exiles in Miami also chipped in. ARENA was the result.

D'Aubuisson's new political vehicle was a virtual carbon copy of Sandoval's MLN. The ARENA slogan, "God, Fatherland and Lib-erty," was an MLN inspiration, as were the red, white, and blue party colors. "It's not new," Sandoval explained to reporter Pyes. "It's a copy of the communists. The parties of the right in Central America have to have a single political organization."

After its creation, Carlos Midence Pivaral, Sandoval's nephew and fellow World Anti-Communist League member, could exclaim to Pyes, "ARENA, that's my baby."*

> Like other MLN members, he [Midence] refers to ARENA as a "copy of the MLN in organization, in ideology and in symbolism."
>
> Said Midence, who advised the Salvadorans on underground tech-niques, 1980 was a year that the Salvadoran rightists spent studying how to get the army to work with them.
>
> "In 1981, they got their diploma."[21]

Although primary responsibility for the creation of ARENA might lie with Sandoval, Becklund and Pyes also fingered an international organization to which the MLN leader belonged: "The inspiration for the spread of militant anti-communist parties worldwide can be

---

*According to Pyes, Midence sports a Nazi medallion that he says was given to him in Argentina by the former private secretary of Joseph Goebbels, Hitler's propaganda minister.

credited in part to the Taiwan-based World Anti-Communist League (WACL)."

If it was the Guatemalans who gave D'Aubuisson the idea for ARENA, it was American conservatives who made it a viable political party. MacKenzie-McCheyne, a Washington advertising firm, took on the task of spreading the word in the United States about this new "anti-communist" party. Judy Bayshore, a MacKenzie-McCheyne employee, shuttled Orlando de Sola around Washington. Margo Carlisle, Senator McClure's legislative aide who had attended the 1980 CAL conference, arranged for Ricardo Valdivieso, an ARENA cofounder, to make the rounds of American New Right organizations. Valdivieso was invited by New Right elections consultant Paul Weyrich to attend his seminar on effective political campaigning in January 1982 and by Senator Helms to testify before the Senate Foreign Relations Committee. Meanwhile, two Helms aides, John Carbaugh and Chris Manion, shuttled between San Salvador and Washington, advising D'Aubuisson on techniques to make ARENA a respectable "democratic" entity.

While the American conservatives scrambled to rehabilitate the former major, the death toll in El Salvador soared to an estimated fifteen thousand in 1981. Most of the murders were the work of the right-wing death squads that D'Aubuisson or his cohosts in the security forces controlled. Nevertheless, by March 1982, D'Aubuisson's new image had been completed. Running in the U.S.-financed elections, "Major Bob" won and so many assembly seats were filled with D'Aubuisson's allies that they controlled the government. ARENA also gained control of the government Institute for Agrarian Transformation, which was in charge of redistributing land from the oligarchies to the peasants. The institute had once been headed by José Rodolfo Viera, the man assassinated, along with the two American labor advisers, in the Sheraton Hotel by D'Aubuisson cronies the year before. After the elections, the land reform program ground to a halt.

Suddenly concerned by the degree of power the ultra-right had gained in the elections, the United States forced in an interim president, a conservative banker and wealthy landowner named Alvaro Magaña, to forestall D'Aubuisson becoming president. "It took the U.S. a long time to realize it had enemies on the right," an American diplomat in San Salvador said. "Before, it wasn't taken too seriously. Then things started to happen."

Reagan Administration reaction to ARENA's successes in 1982 was essentially one of damage control. D'Aubuisson, now president of the National Assembly, and the military officers allied with him gradually came under scrutiny as the public clamor over the atrocities rose. Much of the New Right, however, continued to stand steadfastly by their Central American fellow "anti-communist"; in January 1983, D'Aubuisson received a letter of support signed by Paul Weyrich, the House Republican Study Committee, the Conservative Caucus, and the Moral Majority, among others.

In December 1983, following a resurgence of death squad activity, Vice-President George Bush made a special visit to El Salvador with the message that the death squads had to end. "If these death squad murders continue," he told President Magaña, "you will lose the support of the American people, and that would indeed be a great tragedy."

Although Bush's moral outrage was rather belated, a scaling-down of the killings was the only way the Reagan Administration could certify El Salvador as "improving" its human rights record, which was a necessity for gaining congressional approval for sending aid and military advisers.

Bush handed the Salvadoran president a list of names of officers and civilians that the United States believed to be behind the violence. Within weeks, several of the officers were sent out of the country into diplomatic exile posts, while others were promoted or transferred within the military to neutralize their activity. "When the death squad violence came back in October [1983]," President Magaña told the authors in May 1984, "and we had doubts about certain people, we warned them, and there were no more [violent acts]."[22]

Magaña's casual admission belied the perverse intimacy of the Salvadoran "system." He had, he said, been able to use his contacts to end some of the death squad violence; he didn't, however, have the power to put an end to their organizations or punish those responsible.

*   *   *

"Rafael" is in a profession where "you find out too much for your own good."

A cab driver in the town of Sonsonate in eastern El Salvador, he has been pressed into service on numerous occasions, an unwilling accomplice to some of the violence that has shattered his country.

Twice his cab has been commandeered by guerrillas, once when they killed the mayor of the village of Armenia and again when they attacked the telephone office in Metalio, near Sonsonate. "Rafael" speaks mostly about his military clients, though.

> They never pay, you know. They just come and say, "Let's go." I go; I know not to ask questions.
>
> They direct me to a house and say, "Wait here." I hear the bang-bang-bang, and I know they have just killed someone, but I look away. I don't see anything.
>
> Other times, they'll come back with a person and they tell me to drive and then they kill him somewhere far away. It is for this that my family wants me to stop driving a cab.

When asked by one of the authors if these army killers have given themselves a death squad name, "Rafael" laughed. "They are all Section Two [Intelligence]. There's one in the National Guard, the army; they all have them."

The driver became uneasy when asked about the Metalio commander, Sergeant Rivas.

> "I understand he's very strict."
> "What about his zone? Is there fighting?
> "No. It's very tranquil."
> "How does Rivas keep it tranquil?"
> "If someone fingers you as a guerrilla, Section Two takes you out and shoots you."
> "On orders from Rivas?"
> "I understand he's very strict."

If President Magaña could not completely control the death squads, neither can his successor, José Napoleon Duarte, the liberal Christian Democrat who took over in June 1984. Despite the American-demanded reshuffling of some key commanders believed to be responsible for organizing the death squads, Duarte is impeded from moving too quickly against what he calls the "Nazi fascists" of his country.

The reason is simple: with the assistance of the Guatemalan MLN, the World Anti-Communist League and the American New Right, among others, the "Nazi fascists" are now incorporated under the political banner of ARENA. As ARENA is the chief opposition party, a Duarte move against it would be seen as a partisan attack on what is now a "legitimate" political movement.

Duarte's dilemma is revealed in a 1984 interview he gave *Playboy* magazine:

PLAYBOY: When you speak of Nazi Fascists, are you talking about the political forces of Roberto D'Aubuisson?
DUARTE: Definitely. I have no problem in saying that he has been a key factor in this campaign of destabilization. There is proof of that.
PLAYBOY: But, specifically, are you calling D'Aubuisson a Nazi Fascist?
DUARTE: I am absolutely convinced of that.
PLAYBOY: But if D'Aubuisson and his followers in the ARENA party are Nazi Fascists, and if, as you say, the death squads are linked to them, then certainly these groups could be outlawed if for no other reason than that they are armed.
DUARTE: Not necessarily. ARENA as a political institution is one thing; the armed groups are another.[23]

It would seem that the Reagan Administration would have other reasons to regret its earlier acceptance of D'Aubuisson. In June 1984, after Duarte had been elected president, the former major appeared with Senator Helms, claiming that the CIA had "bought the election" and that the U.S. ambassador, Thomas Pickering, had been "the purchasing agent." Several days later, after D'Aubuisson was accused by American officials of plotting to kill Pickering, Helms was used to placate the hot-headed former major.

The compelling evidence linking him with a conspiracy to murder an American envoy notwithstanding, the Administration soon made its peace with D'Aubuisson. In December 1984 he was given a tourist visa to visit Washington, where he spoke before the Young Americans for Freedom at Georgetown University.

In the past two years, the morale and tactics of the Salvadoran armed forces have greatly improved in the war against the guerrillas. The man many consider pivotal in this turnaround was Lieutenant Colonel Domingo Monterrosa. In an interview with one of the authors in October 1984, Monterrosa gave some of the credit to the Kuomintang government in Taiwan; the bronze plaque on his desk at the Third Infantry Batallion headquarters in San Miguel reported that he had successfully completed the "31st. Political Warfare Course" at the Political Warfare Cadres Academy in Peitou.

Taiwan has great if unreported influence in El Salvador. The Taiwanese ambassador is the dean of the diplomatic corps and sits at the head of every important state function. Since the early 1970s, as in Guatemala, Taiwan has offered select Salvadoran military officers and a number of politicians expense-paid trips to study political and psychological warfare in Taiwan. The course graduates include most of the current top military officers and regional field commanders. Lieutenant Colonel Monterrosa attended the academy from September to November 1978.*

"What we really admired in Taiwan," Monterrosa said, "was the way the government was organized and the control they held over the people. It was like communism of this side.

"If we could have, from then on, organized a unit of political warfare in every field, we could have focused more objectively on the problems of the country and won against the expansion of communism."

Monterrosa complained that, although he and his fellow officers returned from Taiwan "very enthusiastic" about what they had learned, their suggestions weren't listened to by their senior officers.

When he was asked if one of the things he and his comrades had learned was the use of psychological terror against the civilian population, Monterrosa responded with a quick and quiet "yes."†

"In Guatemala," he added, "the Taiwanese did similar work, and the Guatemalans are applying it today. Another thing we were taught was how to project ourselves to the civilian population and win them over.

"We were taught war of the masses."

Several days later, one of the authors traveled with the lieutenant colonel into the rebel-contested hills of Morazán department, near

---

*Monterrosa also attended a Unification Church CAUSA conference in Uruguay in February 1984.

†Monterrosa had already applied that aspect of his training in the field. In December 1981, troops under his command massacred an estimated one thousand civilians in and around the village of Mozóte.

the Honduran border, and had the chance to see Monterrosa put his Taiwan-style warfare into action.

The chopper descended onto a jungle hilltop where, the day before, an advance platoon had flushed the area of guerrillas and organized some two hundred peasants to come to the clearing.

"We know the subversives have infiltrated these people," Monterrosa told the coauthor as the helicopter settled down, "because every time we are attacked in this area, all we find are the peasants."

For several hours, sitting behind a table and using a hand-held microphone, Monterrosa gave the villagers a lesson in consciousness-raising. Beside him was a woman "social worker" and a civilian psychologist, members of a thirty-person unit, mostly women, who had just been trained in psychological warfare and who were slated to begin working out of regional barracks throughout El Salvador.

"We are your true brothers," Monterrosa told the peasants. "We're not the caretakers of the rich. Do you see any rich among us? We give our blood to the soil, but it's up to you to make it fertile."

Those gathered, however, seemed more interested in the soccer balls that were still in their original gray Spaulding cartons and in the boxes of children's clothing that the soldiers had stacked beside the table.

"We are all Indians," the "social worker" shouted when she took the microphone, "the real Salvadorans. We're not going to let foreigners [Cubans and Russians] take our land, are we?"

When she had finished her appeal to nationalism, Monterrosa returned.

"A number of you have come up to me and told me you are having trouble with the *muchachos* [guerrillas]. I know they're here among you. If any have any problems or something to tell us, please come and do it. This is for the good of your villages."

The peasants stirred uneasily.

"Tell me I'm not lying. Isn't it true what I hear, that the guerrillas have been here among you? But even so, I haven't sent the army in here. I haven't called in the air force to bomb you, have I?"

One by one, the people stepped forward. As they did, the soldiers distributed clothing and threw out the soccer balls.

"Is this Taiwanese?" the coauthor asked as Monterrosa wrote down the testimonies of the villagers.

"This is it."

On the day after the coauthor left the field of operations and returned to San Salvador, the forty-four-year-old lieutenant colonel moved on to continue his "war of the masses." As Monterrosa's helicopter sped over the countryside, laden with other high military officers and some civilians, it was blown apart by a bomb. All aboard were killed instantly. Another morning in El Salvador.

SIXTEEN

Were some CAL members linked to the death squads? I believe it's possible. This is a real war taking place in Central America. It's hot; it's not cold.

> Moises Jesus de Ulloa Duarte,
> Head of Honduran CAL chapter,
> Tegucigalpa, March 1985

THE GENERAL looked about the hotel conference room in San José, Costa Rica, and, as if answering all the accusatory questions at once, responded plaintively, "I'll leave my judgment to the judgment of history."

"Did you order the disappearance of political dissidents while you held office?" a reporter in the stuffy room asked.

"I can't answer for every disappeared person in the country," he replied.

Light-skinned and stocky, General Alvarez spoke resolutely and without apology to the assembled journalists, his forehead beading with sweat under his receding hairline. He had called the press conference to explain his fall from power. Three days earlier, he had been commander in chief of the armed forces of Honduras; today, he was just another exile, ousted at gunpoint by fellow officers and put on a plane out of the country.

Out of his uniform, in a tailored gray suit, the once-powerful and feared Honduran military chief seemed physically smaller somehow and not at all fearsome. The man they had begun calling "the new

Somoza" was almost philosophical as he explained the reason for his humiliation. Instead, he called attention to the anti-communist fight.

"My country is in a delicate stage right now, as is all of Central America. We need unity, we need tranquility, and we need stability to confront the mortal enemy. And we all know who that is."

The history of the rise and fall of General Gustavo Alvarez Martínez is the history of modern Honduras. Before him, the nation lived in relative peace, sidestepped by the violence that wracked most of the rest of Central America. With him, Honduras was dragged into the fray and joined the list of nations conducting "dirty war" to deal with its dissidents. After him, the country is paralyzed by internal power struggles and stands on the precipice of war with Nicaragua. To a unique degree in Central America, the "white hand" of just one man, Alvarez Martínez, was everywhere in Honduras, and his meteoric ascension to power, assisted by many elements of the World Anti-Communist League, is the key to explaining the nation's present state of crisis.

Almost singlehandedly Alvarez brought this traditionally peaceful nation into the vortex of Central American strife. The Honduran death squads that took some three hundred lives in four years were his creation. Honduras's current status as a front-line state and the main staging ground for the Reagan Administration's campaign to topple the leftist government in Nicaragua is a direct result of Alvarez's role as the CIA's errand boy.

If the term "banana republic" is an appropriate description of any nation, it is certainly Honduras. Sandwiched between Guatemala, El Salvador, and Nicaragua, it is a mountainous country that lacks natural resources and is populated largely by subsistence farmers. For decades, it was used virtually as a giant plantation by the American multinational corporations Standard Fruit and United Fruit; these companies built most of whatever economic infrastructure exists— the ports, railways, roads, even some of its towns.

It was also these companies that kept Honduras woefully poor, the poorest nation in Central America, only slightly better off than Bolivia and Haiti, the two worst "basket case" nations in the Western hemisphere. The fruit companies ran the country, breaking its labor unions, naming its military presidents in fraudulent elections, and silencing anyone who might disturb their monopoly.

In a perverse way, Honduras's traditional poverty has also been one of its blessings. Because it was too poor to create or support an oligarchy of a few wealthy families, it has escaped much of the turmoil and civil strife that has plagued its neighbors for most of this century. When El Salvador erupted in the 1930s, Guatemala in the 1950s and 1960s, and Nicaragua in the 1970s, Honduras remained comparatively serene.

That ended in the late 1970s when the leftist Sandinistas trying to topple the Somoza dynasty in neighboring Nicaragua used Honduras as a base and staging ground for infiltration of fighters and weapons. The success of the Nicaraguan revolution in 1979 challenged and beat the region's conservative political and military status quo for the first time in modern history. The victory gave fresh sustenance and inspiration to other struggling insurgencies. In the years since, the ramifications have affected all of Central America's political systems.

In the jubilant days following the collapse of Anastasio Somoza's regime, some of the Sandinista's foremost secret collaborators emerged from anonymity, revealing their previously clandestine support networks both in Nicaragua and in other countries, including Honduras. People who had discreetly worked for the revolutionaries while Somoza was still in power suddenly went public as committed revolutionaries. In Guatemala, El Salvador, and Honduras, this reckless "coming out of the closet" was to prove a fatal error, for the ultra-right was mobilizing to exterminate the "communist threat" wherever it existed.

General Alvarez did not invent Honduran paramilitary squads, but he was the man who streamlined them, integrated them into the armed forces, and allowed them to conduct a "dirty war."

In late 1979 and early 1980, three previously unknown groups—the National Front for the Defense of Democracy, the Honduran Anti-Communist Movement (MACHO) and the Anti-Communist Combat Army (ELA)—publicly threatened to assassinate leftist leaders. Although many thought these shadowy organizations were composed of civilian goons bankrolled by some of Honduras's few wealthy, they were actually operating under the orders of the government Public Security Forces (FUSEP).

"Ephron" is a FUSEP agent. Well-dressed and in his late twenties, he exudes a sense of easy self-confidence and has the appearance of an upwardly mobile junior businessman. Only the unusually intense stare of his brown eyes betrays his fear. He has "blood on his hands," is compromised, and knows he can be used again. In the last year, he hasn't received an order to "return to duty" but fears he could at any time.

In several interviews with one of the authors in 1985, "Ephron" described his role in "the war the armed forces can never admit." His testimony is that of a man involved in the Honduran death squads since their inception.

In 1979, he was recruited into the FUSEP anti-communist campaign by a young officer, Alexander Hernández, whom he had known several years earlier during his obligatory stint in the army. His first mission was to spy on an acquaintance whom Hernández believed to be a leftist collaborator. After this relatively innocuous beginning, "Ephron" quickly found himself deeply involved, spending the next five years as an active operative for the captain. It was not until the downfall of Alvarez, Hernández's mentor and protector, that "Ephron" had an excuse to ask for "temporary leave."

"Ephron's" second assignment was a long-term one, the infiltration of the National Autonomous University of Honduras (UNAH), located in the high green hills overlooking the capital, Tegucigalpa.

The Honduran military had long been concerned about leftist control of the university. During the Nicaraguan Revolution, one of the Sandinistas' key support networks operated from Central America's federation of autonomous universities, which are traditional sanctuaries for leftist thinkers, militants, even guerrilla cells. Neither the Sandinistas, the Salvadoran left, nor their Honduran counterparts forsook the legal cover for political organizing offered by the universities. Their activities in Honduras were so open that in 1977 Nicaraguan dictator Anastasio Somoza called the school "a communist sanctuary" and its rector "the principal promoter of subversion and Marxism in the region."

"The problem the government had with the university," "Ephron" explained, "was its autonomy. But we knew that within the university, the communists hid weapons and gave training to others in making booby traps and bombs. They even hid guerrillas there. But since we couldn't enter, the university had to be infiltrated."

After the success of the Sandinista Revolution in 1979, the strident leftist pronouncements and activities emanating from the politicized National Autonomous University of Honduras became a lightning rod for the Marxist-hunting military. The leftist activists were easy to spot. In the monthly university publication *Presencia Universitaria,* editorials denounced Somoza and paid homage to Cuba, Sandinista revolutionaries, and the Marxist government in Angola. The rector, Juan Almendares Bonilla, announced the organization of student brigades sent from his campus to "help with the reconstruction of Nicaragua" and expressed his university's solidarity with the Sandinista revolution.

It was then that the Honduran government responded. "We placed several [Army] officers there as students who were used as bait," "Ephron" recounted. "We sent those who had been intelligence chiefs in the different battalions to act as decoys so the guerrillas would waste their time watching these [men] while others were really watching them."

The real work of surveillance of leftists and recruitment of rightists was undertaken by "Ephron" and fellow FUSEP officers.

> There were five of us in the university. The university was a powder keg, so it was necessary to form paramilitary units. We classified people we figured could work in a shock force. We made up a list of people with everything we could find out about them—their families, details about their personalities and political tendencies. We were looking for impulsive, fanatic people.
>
> Everything was then handed over to Alexander Hernandez. He passed his selections on to the DNI [secret police], and they gave weapons to the chosen people from our lists.

"Ephron" and his four fellow spies chose their "shock forces" well; they recruited a number of rightist students belonging to the United Democratic University Front (FUUD). The FUUD activists would carry out operations for the military if they were supplied. "We knew if we gave them arms, they would rise up and take action against the Marxists," "Ephron" said. "They are born anti-communists, narrow-minded fanatics who take care of things if it becomes necessary. About forty or fifty were given arms, ammunition and training, but they were mostly useful in gathering intelligence."

Bankrolled by the security forces, the FUUD zealots formed a paramilitary arm, the Anti-Communist Combat Army (ELA). By late 1979, the campus had become the target of anonymously distributed leaflets signed by the ELA. Hooded armed men broke into the administration offices at night. Campus watchmen were threatened and occasionally beaten. Fear began to circulate on the attractive university grounds.

"Several foreign professors," former Rector Almendares Bonilla recalled, "including an Argentine emigré teaching for us, began to receive threatening letters from ELA. These letters told them that if they didn't leave the country they would be killed. The Argentine, an economics professor, left, afraid for his life."[1]

"Ephron" acknowledged that the student squads he had helped create had taken their paramilitary powers beyond the harassment of Marxists. "On their own, they have formed groups with their own credos and beliefs. Later, using these people was a way for the military to kill people they wanted to get rid of without appearing as the responsible party."

By the beginning of 1980, then, civilians working in tandem with FUSEP had cemented the basis for a classic death squad network. It was Alvarez who would put it into practice, for that year he was promoted to chief of FUSEP.

Colonel Alvarez's promotion coincided with a veritable wave of death threats against Rector Almendares Bonilla, faculty members, and leftist student leaders. It was also in 1980 that the paramilitary squads became death squads.

In August 1980, Rector Bonilla paid a visit to the head of Armed Forces Intelligence, Colonel Leonidas Torres Arias. According to *La Tribuna*, a conservative Honduran newspaper, Torres Arias informed the university delegation of the existence of a "death list" and of the existence of at least three paramilitary groups, "but because of the way these groups work inside and outside the country it is impossible to control their activities."

The high military official [Torres Arias] recommended that the UNAH, in view of the danger given these facts, take the necessary measures to decrease various activities taking place in the University, indicating that the most dangerous are the publication of the official newspaper, *Presencia Universitaria,* activities of solidarity with El Salvador [rebels] and labors which certain university students and teachers are conducting in rural areas of the country.[2]

Several days later, the entire staff of *Presencia Universitaria* resigned en masse, citing death threats against their lives. Almendares Bonilla remained in his job despite the increasing intensity of threats to himself and his family, bomb scares at his office, and gunshots aimed at his house at night. "I had to live in different houses for a while," he said, "and I took different routes to work every day."

A number of professors close to the rector were kidnapped by hooded men, interrogated, and badly beaten. "One told me afterwards that they had interrogated him closely about me. As he had been told to do, he left the country. This same man, a FRU [a leftist political party to which Almendares Bonilla belongs] militant also told Eduardo Lanza, FRU's secretary general, that the squad told him he [Lanza] was going to be next. But Lanza didn't take precautions and soon afterwards, he was kidnapped and disappeared."

The psychological terror directed at the UNAH worked; the most militant students and professors left or were murdered, and in 1982 Bonilla lost the rectorship to a rightist in a disputed election. Today the FUUD students who were armed by FUSEP brandish Uzis on campus to intimidate leftist students. On weekends, they hold target practice in the surrounding countryside. "They are in power now," "Ephron" said of his student agents.

"Lobo," who first described the international death squad links to one of the authors, was one of "Ephron's" operatives in the university campaign. A principal leader of the ELA, Lobo was also a member of the FUUD, the ELA's political front group. Since the FUUD was represented in the youth wing of the Latin American Anti-Communist Confederation (CAL), "Lobo" found himself invited to the 1980 CAL conference in Buenos Aires.

Although such death squad luminaries as Mario Sandoval Alarcón and Roberto D'Aubuisson were in attendance, the conference hosts themselves were the world masters of "dirty war" strategy: the Argentine military junta and its official death squad, the Argentine Anti-Communist Alliance (AAA). Very soon the Argentines would be teaching the Honduran security forces, and by extension "Lobo's" ELA, their techniques of uncoventional warfare.

By 1980, Argentine advisers were already operating in Honduras, training Honduran police units in "suspect interrogation techniques." The junta in Buenos Aires had sent the consultants there to help develop an internal security apparatus similar to their own; this mission directly benefited an old friend, Colonel Gustavo Alvarez Martínez.

Alvarez had spent several years in Argentina as a student at its military college. One of his instructors there was Jorge Rafael Videla, the general who, as Argentina's dictator in the mid-1970s, presided over the bloodiest phase of Argentina's anti-subversion war. In 1980, by the time Alvarez was chief of FUSEP, his former Argentine classmates were high-ranking colonels in the armed forces. "The paramilitary squads were already operating out of FUSEP before Alvarez took it over," Victor Meza, a prominent Honduran political analyst told one of the authors in 1985, "but what he did was to professionalize the setup by bringing in the Argentine advisors."

After the CAL conference in Buenos Aires, the Argentine operations in Honduras became multifaceted, and they now had a second mission: to organize the Honduras-based rebels fighting the Sandinista regime in Nicaragua.

When Somoza fell in 1979, exiled remnants of his defeated National Guard had fled into Honduras. There, along the piney ridges of the frontier, they took up arms against the new regime. The presence of these guerrillas afforded Alvarez a golden opportunity. Not only could he use these war-seasoned combatants to deal with troublemakers in his own country, but their presence in Honduras might be used to bolster his own power. He knew that the incoming Reagan Administration was planning on taking a much more active role against the Sandinista regime; if Alvarez could appear as the protector of the contras (counterrevolutionaries), his own importance to the Americans would be ensured.

The first order of business was to make the contras a credible fighting force. In late 1980 and early 1981, Argentine advisers were installed in safehouses and secret border camps in Honduras to train the Nicaraguan exiles in the arts of warfare. Selected contra commanders, along with Honduran secret police officers, were sent to Argentina for specialized military and intelligence training.

The effect of the Argentine operations in Honduras was dramatic. By 1981, Alvarez's paramilitary squads were kidnapping, torturing, murdering, and "disappearing" leftist guerrillas and their supporters. The contras were also making their presence felt by launching border raids into Nicaragua.

The increased repression in Honduras had been facilitated by a restructuring of the paramilitary squads. In 1981, Alvarez created a select branch within FUSEP, the Special Operations Command (COE), with Argentine help. This new agency was headed by Captain Alexander Hernández.

Although officially an elite counterinsurgency force, the COE actually became the command center of Alvarez's "dirty war." Under direct orders from COE officers, the death squad bands that had previously been used selectively by FUSEP carried out their program on a much greater scale.

"Ephron" was inducted into this new organization and assigned to the Department of Analysis, the intelligence-collection arm of the Special Investigations Department of the COE. It was from this Special Investigations Department that Hernández dispatched the "kill" orders to the paramilitary squads.

"We had safehouses in the whole country," "Ephron" said. "An office in the basement of FUSEP [headquarters] was the coordinating center for all of them. There was a special number you had to call, and the secretary there would give you your operating orders from the high command.

"All of this system is Argentine. They are the ones who have perfected it: the safehouses, electric shock, and so on."

"Ephron" defended the rationale for the Argentine method. "When there wasn't enough evidence for a trial, it was necessary to work this way. So we formed the network of safehouses to avoid having to make legal arrests, since the courts would have liberated them in twenty-four hours. Twenty-four hours is not sufficient time to interrogate a suspect."

Once a Honduran suspect was picked up, his fate, like that of his Argentine counterpart, was likely to be grim. "The majority of those detained ended up in the weeds. . . . When we captured someone we took them to the safehouses. These are the ones who disappeared. Since we were a secret unit, we even ran into problems from some of the other security forces. For example, by accident, some FUSEP guys found one of our clandestine cemeteries in 1982. So we had to find another method; the biggest problem all along has been what to do with the cadavers."

"Ephron" claims to have never witnessed any of the killings.

> My job was only collecting intelligence. It was difficult to know how many people were killed because that depended on the [particular] safehouse where they were taken. Each safehouse had its own zone of responsibility. During my time about ten people came through my safehouse.
>
> I saw people interrogated, but from that to how or when they disappeared, I don't know. I never had to pull a trigger, although once I nearly had to. The real executioners were people of the unit, but one didn't know who they were.

Occasionally during the lengthy interviews, "Ephron" revealed more than he had been willing to admit. About the logistical problem of body disposal, he explained one method that they eventually developed. "We got people, killed them, put their bodies aboard helicopters, and threw them in the Río Sumpul [the river dividing part of Honduras and El Salvador and an area of intense fighting between the Salvadoran army and the Salvadoran guerrillas] to make it look like the Salvadorans did it. Before dumping them, we would remove all ID and put Salvadoran coins in their pockets."*

Still, "Ephron" defends his actions. "It was necessary to do. These people would have torn Honduras down. Most were real communists. Anyway, we never detained a person until we had data on them. When we got someone, it was when we were sure about them."

Throughout 1981, the counterterror program intensified. Students, professors, and union leaders were "disappeared" and buried in secret cemeteries. For the first time, a couple of body dumps, so common in El Salvador, were discovered in Honduras. Public outcry over the killings was gaining strength and for the first time human rights groups cited Honduras for gross abuses.

---

*This particular disposal method echos that employed by Argentina. Investigators for the new civilian Argentine government have discovered that hundreds of Argentina's "disappeared" were stripped of identification and then thrown from military aircraft over the South Atlantic during the "dirty war."

"The so-called disappeared," Alvarez sneered at the charges, "are probably subversives who are in Cuba and Nicaragua training to come back and subvert the Fatherland."

The colonel had reason to be smug, for by then he had found a new ally in the United States. The Nicaraguan contras, now trained and reorganized by the Argentines, were seen by the Reagan Administration as a potential pressure force in their campaign against the Sandinista government. One of the alleged initial contacts in what would become American inheritance of the Argentine operation was John Carbaugh, the roving aide to U.S. Senator Jesse Helms; Carbaugh had attended the 1980 CAL conference in Buenos Aires.

An American diplomat in Honduras confirmed that Carbaugh "was in and out of here all the time from '80 to '82.

"He also made a lot of trips to Buenos Aires in the same period. I heard he was tight with Alvarez and Major Bob [Roberto D'Aubuisson of El Salvador] and was backed by money from right-wing groups in the States."[3]

In late 1981, President Reagan signed a secret directive releasing $19.5 million in CIA funds to assist the contras. In November 1981, after a series of meetings between officials of the Central Intelligence Agency and the Argentine advisers in Honduras, the United States took over the funding of the guerrillas, now reconstituted as "freedom fighters."[4]

From the beginning of U.S. involvement with the "secret war" in mid-1981 what was called a "tripartite" structure was put in place to run it. The United States supplied the money, Argentina supplied training and administrative skills (and initially a fig leaf to cover U.S. involvement), and Honduras supplied the territory from which operations were mounted, according to U.S. intelligence sources and participants in the program.

A joint staff to manage and coordinate this program was created. The Nicaraguan rebel forces were represented by Enrique Bermudez and Emilio Echaverry, former Nicaraguan National Guard officers. Two Argentine colonels, Osvaldo Ribeiro and Santiago Villegas (also identified as José Ollas), represented their country. Alvarez represented Honduras. And the CIA station chief and one of his assistants represented the United States.[5]

In late 1981, the Honduran military rulers, bowing to pressure initially brought to bear by the Carter Administration, held general elections. A civilian country doctor, Roberto Suazo Córdova, was elected president and took office just as the CIA-Argentine-contra coalition was coming together.

By that time, Honduras's own fledgling guerrilla movement, inspired by the success in Nicaragua, had grown. Called the Lorenzo Zelaya National Front, or the Cinchoneros, the Honduran guerrillas carried out a wave of bombings, plane hijackings, and kidnappings that shook the complacency of newly democratic Honduras. To combat this threat, the new president turned to a comparatively low-level military officer who had demonstrated his abilities as head of FUSEP: Colonel Gustavo Alvarez Martínez.

Suazo made Alvarez a general and elevated him to head of the armed forces—a violation of the norms of promotion and a move that won both men many enemies in the Honduran military. Later in 1982, Alvarez received yet another promotion, from chief to commander in chief of the armed forces, a title customarily held by the president.

His authority now nearly absolute, Alvarez quickly moved against his enemies in the armed forces. Chief among them was Colonel Leonidas Torres Arias, the former military intelligence chief and Alvarez's successor at FUSEP; he was sent into diplomatic exile in Argentina. Alvarez also moved to rid G-2 (military intelligence) and the secret police branch of FUSEP of Torres Arias's people.

This purge was apparently motivated by two factors: Alvarez's fear of disloyal elements in an apparatus he desired to control absolutely, and his desire to eliminate what was believed to have become a corrupt network of officers involved in black-market arms and narcotics trafficking under the direction of Torres Arias. "Torres Arias was into everything," a Western diplomat in Honduras said. "He was into dope and shaking down the left who were running guns to the Sandinistas and Salvadoran rebels. He was very smart—the evil incarnate."

But Alvarez had crossed a man who would fight back. During his brief tenure at FUSEP, Torres Arias had learned a lot about his archfoe, in particular about the paramilitary squads Alvarez had nurtured to "fight communism." Soon the colonel surprised everyone by publicly breaking his silence and telling the world what he knew. In August 1982, Torres Arias surfaced in Mexico City, denouncing his former boss for organizing the Honduran death squads and for launching his country on the path to war with Nicaragua.

> General Alvarez had and has under his direct command a Special Investigations personnel whose chief is Captain Alexander Hernández, who, following orders from the general, has made disappear [names of prominent missing leftists] and many more people. . . .
>
> On the day he [Alvarez] became commander in chief of FUSEP, the era of the disappeared and clandestine cemeteries was initiated.

In reaction to his disclosures, the Honduran attorney general declared Torres Arias "a traitor to the Fatherland."[6]

"He wasn't killed, because he sold himself to the press," "Ephron" said of Torres Arias. "He didn't speak out in Argentina, because he wouldn't have been safe; Alvarez has friends there. If he hadn't gone to Mexico, he'd have been a dead man."

Torres Arias's revelations had little effect on Alvarez's career, for he was now enjoying the unwavering support of the Reagan Administration as it expanded its covert assistance to the Argentine-led contras. At the end of 1982, the CIA reorganized the contra leadership, which until then had been dominated by former Somoza National Guard officers. The reshuffling brought in more mainstream Nicaraguan exiles, including many former Sandinista supporters. They included Adolfo Calero, who had been an active anti-Somocista and who had been jailed by the dictator for organizing business opposition to his rule. The changes in the "new" Nicaraguan Democratic Force (FDN) were mostly cosmetic, however; the former Guard officers were simply switched over to the military command.

That Alvarez, the chief advocate of U.S. actions in Honduras, was also using the Argentines and the contras for his own ends was either unknown or ignored by the CIA. "These [Argentine] advisors remain unidentified," Americas Watch, a human rights organization, reported in late 1982, "and both the Honduran and Argentine governments have denied their presence in Honduras. Several witnesses and human rights monitors point to evidence of their direct involvement in repressive actions. The participation of Argentine agents is not yet completely proven, but human rights observers cannot help noticing the striking similarities between the pattern now evolving in Honduras and the 15,000 to 20,000 disappearances conducted by the Argentine armed forces between 1976 and 1980. Those similarities include the use of heavily-armed plainclothesmen who do not identify themselves, but clearly exercise official authority. They conduct their operations in broad daylight, stay for long periods in residences and places of work, stalk their targets in public, and yet are never stopped nor interfered with by regular police forces. Other similarities include the use of unmarked cars, and secret or clandestine detention centers."[7] What Americas Watch suspected in 1982 has since been confirmed by Honduran military officers, contra leaders, and the new democratic government in Argentina that took office in November 1983. It was only then that the Argentine advisers still operating in Central America were pulled out.

Of even greater use to Alvarez than the Argentines themselves were those that the Argentines were training: the Nicaraguan contras. In late 1984, top Honduran military officers leaked information to Reuters correspondent Anne Marie O'Connor charging that some top contra officers had assisted Alvarez's death squads.

According to O'Connor, the Honduran military attributed at least eighteen executions of Nicaraguan, Salvadoran, and Honduran citizens to the contras. The victims were suspected collaborators of the Salvadoran guerrillas who were believed to be transferring Sandinista-supplied arms through Honduras. One contra officer, the FDN's chief of counterintelligence, ex–National Guard Major Ricardo "El Chino" Lau, was believed to be the mastermind.[8]

"The contras killed people in farms on both sides of the border [Honduras-Nicaragua]," "Ephron" confirmed. "They got people who were helping in the transfer of weapons [from the Sandinistas to the Salvadoran guerrillas]."

"Lobo," the student death squad operative, also discussed his ties to the contras, as did "Jorge," the secret policemen who arranged the "Lobo" interview. "Lobo" explained that, through his unit's infiltration of leftist labor unions, student groups, and guerrilla cells, and the torture of their victims for information prior to their executions, they had obtained valuable intelligence information that was "extremely useful" to the authorities. This information, which included maps of the location of several border "blind spots" where leftists smuggled arms from Nicaragua, was turned over to the Honduran authorities, who then passed it on to the contra commanders. This arrangement, "Lobo" said, resulted in several "important captures."

If the American advisers now flooding Honduras disapproved of this sharing of counterterror operations, they never mentioned it publicly. Rather, since General Alvarez was directing the campaign and Alvarez was their main ally, the United States had a vested interest in keeping such unpleasantries quiet.

Alvarez used his support from the Reagan Administration as the ultimate bargaining chip. Together, they ran roughshod over the newly elected and fragile congress. When the Honduran foreign minister attempted to negotiate with Nicaragua, offering to stop aid to the contras in return for stopping the Sandinista troop buildup on the border, the initiative was quashed by Alvarez and John Negroponte, the American ambassador. Although the Honduran constitution requires congressional approval for the stationing of foreign troops on Honduran soil, Alvarez independently reached an agreement with the Reagan Administration for such a move in 1983.

> This was the first crack in the alliance between Honduras' military and civilian rulers. Alvarez proved stronger than the civilians: the congress authorized the plan June 21, a week after one hundred Green Berets arrived in the Puerta Castilla area to join twenty U.S. advisers already there to set up a training base. This month [August 1983] the United States begins up to five months of joint maneuvers with Honduras that will involve as many as five thousand American ground and air troops—another boost to the militarization of the country.[9]

If there were any doubts about the importance the American government placed in its new ally, they weren't evident in its military assistance program to Honduras: it increased from $4 million in loans in 1980 to $77 million in grants in 1984.

When Western diplomats in Tegucigalpa speak of the foreign influences at work in Honduras, they mention Taiwan and the Unification Church in the same breath. This is understandable, since the two run parallel programs in the country.

Both curry favor with key figures in the Honduran armed forces, political parties, business community, and press. Both offer expense-paid "orientation" trips to the Orient and conduct "consciousness-raising" seminars on the evils of communism versus the benefits of capitalism. And for both, as for the Argentines and the CIA, their chief Honduran benefactor was General Alvarez.

Former Colonel Bo Hi Pak, the Reverend Moon's chief lieutenant and president of the Church's CAUSA arm, showed an interest in

Honduras shortly after Alvarez became chief of staff. Setting up an office in Tegucigalpa, Pak gave numerous seminars in the country, urging the populace to arm themselves theologically against communism; he vowed to use his clout to defend Honduras from the international liberal media.

The former KCIA official was also present on January 14, 1983, at the official birth of the Association of Progress for Honduras (APROH); the group brought together the most right-wing and economically powerful Honduran leaders. Almost immediately, APROH was charged by human rights groups with being a suspected funding source for paramilitary squads, along lines similar to the arrangement in El Salvador and Guatemala, where the large landowners and coffee barons fund the security force death squads. This charge was lent credence by the fact that APROH's president was General Alvarez.

Pak's presence at APROH's official birth was more than a mere gesture of moral support, since the new organization was widely perceived to be a political springboard for Alvarez. In the tradition of the Unification Church, that meant money; at the ceremony, Pak handed Alvarez a check for fifty thousand dollars.

Pak's zeal raised concern in Honduras. In a pastoral letter, the Episcopal Conference denounced CAUSA's interference in Honduran domestic affairs and warned of the "serious dangers to the psychological, religious, and civic integrity of anyone who yields to its [Unification Church] influence." Under pressure, Alvarez returned Pak's check.

What Bo Hi Pak saw in APROH was the possibility of establishing a tight relationship, lubricated by money, with the man who appeared to be the future. With Alvarez as president of Honduras, CAUSA's influence there would have known no bounds.

But Pak backed the wrong man. In November 1984, APROH was abolished by the Honduran government after several of its prominent members, together with military cohorts of Alvarez, were implicated by the FBI in a drug-financed coup/assassination plot against President Suazo Córdova.

Despite the APROH "scandal," Pak continued his activities in Honduras, traveling across the country to speak to business leaders, student groups, and labor unions, preaching "anti-communism through democratization." Selected individuals from the press, political, academic, and business communities were given expense-paid trips to the United States and Asia. In 1983, CAUSA sponsored a series of four-day seminars in Honduras on the evils of communism. Among the speakers were Lynn Bouchey of the Council for Inter-American Security and Jay Parker, chairman of the Lincoln Institute (and member of the board of directors of the U.S. chapter of the World Anti-Communist League).

Moises Jesus de Ulloa Duarte, a conservative Honduran radio commentator as well as the former head of his nation's chapter of the World Anti-Communist League, traveled to Korea on the invitation of the Unification Church. "I went because I supported their anti-communist beliefs. But," he added enigmatically, "I don't like the way they raise their money."[10]

CAUSA also turned its attention to the Nicaraguan exiles. In a Tegucigalpa safehouse in 1983, contra leader Fernando "El Negro" Chamorro told one of the authors that CAUSA had first approached him the year before, offering to help "unite the contra factions."

Chamorro said he went as far as to take them up on a free trip to the United States; there he met with some Unification Church officials in San Francisco and attended Moonie-arranged meetings with the heads of other Nicaraguan exile groups. "The trip was the extent of my relationship with them, but other help was offered. At the time, I had reasons to consider the offer, but I couldn't tell whether there might be strings attached. I don't want them to give us money and then to turn this around into a Moonie thing."

Other contras have accepted CAUSA's offers of help, notably Steadman Fagoth, the former leader of the Misura guerrilla force of Miskito Indians and Atlantic Coast black Creoles. Fagoth's top aides admitted to receiving material and financial aid from CAUSA, especially since the cutoff of CIA aid in May 1984. In the autumn of 1984, when Misura's political officers were scrambling for money to pay the telephone and rent bills for their Tegucigalpa safehouse, CAUSA helped them out with nearly eleven thousand dollars in cash. Several tons of food, medicine, and clothing, paid for by CAUSA, have also been sent to Misura's base camps in the desolate, swampy Honduran Mosquitia region bordering Nicaragua. One of the authors, who spent several weeks with Misura guerrillas in June and July 1984, noticed Misura fighters wearing red T-shirts emblazoned with the CAUSA logo.

In August 1984, CAUSA hosted a number of seminars in and around Washington, D.C. Nicaragua was a prominent theme at the conferences, and what emerged was the American-Nicaraguan Association (ANA). The association's aim was to conduct a state-by-state publicity campaign in the United States to raise funds for the contras.

CAUSA moved quickly. In an interview in his Costa Rican home in December 1984, Alfonso Robelo, a prominent Nicaraguan exiled politician and former Sandinista who now helps lead the contras, told one of the authors that the ANA would be helping him set up speaking engagements in the United States as part of an upcoming fund-raising sweep.

There are also signs that Church members are doing more than just funding the anti-Sandinista forces. In February 1985, guerrillas in the FDN base camp of Nicarao spoke fondly of an American CARP (Moonie student movement) member actually fighting inside Nicaragua with their comrades; he had adopted the *nom de guerre* of *Rata Asesina* (Killer Rat). In Tegucigalpa, Frank Arana, the FDN's spokesman, admitted the presence of "Killer Rat" but denied his active participation in the fighting.

The Unification Church's myriad activities in Honduras, many directed through its CAUSA arm, is a cause of growing consternation in Honduras. "We're afraid the entrance of CAUSA could create a repressive extreme right that doesn't exist in Honduras now," a cleric told reporter Lucy Komisar in 1983. "When terrorism began in 1980, many businessmen wanted to create an organization of the extreme right like the Guatemalan White Hand. Others who opposed it prevailed. We are afraid that under the pretext of anti-communism they may start such an organization."[11]

Taiwan's courtly ambassador to Honduras, Peng Yu, explained the importance of the links between Latin America and his country, constantly referring to Taiwan's loss of United Nations recognition and the severing of ties by the United States in favor of mainland China. Of the two dozen nations that still recognize Taiwan, over half are in Latin America. Honduras is one of them. "We are just trying," Peng Yu said, "to reciprocate the support they have given us. We've really been able to do very little in return."

The ambassador is unduly modest. Taiwan exerts its influence in

Honduras both through economic aid missions that advise farmers on better agricultural practices and through their international political warfare campaign. As are others in the region, a number of Hondurans from a variety of key fields are invited to attend the two-month political warfare course taught at the Political Warfare Cadres Academy in Peitou. "These are like seminars," the ambassador said. "These seminars teach the experiences we have gone through with communist subversion. We teach the Mainland's [People's Republic of China] tactics. We want people here to know what communist subversion is like, so they know how to deal with their own problem.

"We only give technical assistance. We don't need to give weapons. Your government [the United States] can do that much better than us."[12]

One of the best-known recipients of Taiwanese largesse in Honduras is Amilcar Santamaria, the international press spokesman for the presidency.[13] Santamaria is a chubby, fair-skinned man with a weakness for green polyesters. He attended CAL conferences before that League affiliate was disbanded in 1984 and is a political warfare graduate; he attended the Peitou academy in the spring of 1984. Like all the graduates, he lauds the training but is circumspect about the specifics of what he was taught. "One thing I think we could implant in Honduras which the time in Taiwan taught me," Santamaria told one of the authors in October 1984, "is a deliberate increase in the press of the publication of progovernment articles."

Santamaria said he was planning to retire from the government and return to his job as editor of La Prensa, a conservative Honduran newspaper, in order to further this goal. Although he still retains his government information officer post, anonymous articles extolling Taiwan and deriding mainland China's current experiment with capitalism now regularly appear in local papers.

A frequent speaker in Honduras and elsewhere in Central America, Santamaria's message is always the same: the common threat faced by the "front-line" states and the need for them to work together to defeat communism. "Taiwan's experience as a front-line state with Communist China is invaluable to us," he said. "We have a good relationship, for historical and ideological reasons. One of the reasons why Honduras has always recognized Taiwan is because it has always been anti-communist and so are we."

Santamaria carefully echoed Ambassador Peng Yu's sidestepping of the issue of Taiwanese military advisers in Honduras. "The Chinese [Taiwanese] Embassy has always been very respectful in this area. It hasn't tried to give recipes to the problems we have. It has always said that it is willing to help if it's asked."

Apparently, it has been asked at various times. "Ephron," the Honduran counterintelligence agent, said that in the late 1970s a Chinese military officer was attached to the Honduran armed forces chief of staff, teaching "psychological warfare techniques." Some of this training, he claimed, was employed in the interrogation and handling of "subversives" in the Alvarez anti-guerrilla program. In addition, a Miskito Indian who was press-ganged into uniform by the contras in the winter of 1985 swore to investigators that three Chinese advisers oversaw the training center where he was sent. A State Department official in Washington also confirmed that Taiwanese advisers were teaching courses in Honduras. "Not in-field, [not] in the combat zone, that we know of, but certainly in-country."

While he refrained from confirming this information, Santamaria hinted that there were things the Taiwanese taught that were better left unrevealed. "You see, we Hondurans are a much freer people by nature. Countries like Taiwan have always been very authoritarian. For this reason, only *some* of the programs taught in Taiwan could be instituted here."

If American support helped elevate Alvarez, it also led to his downfall. In March 1984, junior officers, with pistols drawn, stormed into the chief of staff's office and announced that his reign was at an end. The "new Somoza" was unceremoniously bundled aboard a plane to Costa Rica.

The military "coup" was a major policy defeat for the Reagan Administration. Not only had Alvarez's total acquiescence to American wishes hurt national pride, but the Honduran military had become apprehensive about what they saw as the American policy to maneuver them into a war footing with Nicaragua, with little in return. *The Washington Post* reported:

> After Alvarez was removed, the new commanding officers "wouldn't talk to anybody" at the CIA station in the Honduran capital, one diplomat familiar with the case said. "They were coldly detached.

They saw that [the CIA station chief] and the gang were protectors, creators and personal friends of Alvarez and they didn't want to talk to them."

Vital training and logistical facilities for the anti-Sandinista rebels were shut down or moved to more remote locations within weeks. Before Alvarez was thrown out, the United States had saved money and circumvented limits on the numbers of U.S. advisers in El Salvador by training Salvadoran units in Honduras. Alvarez's successors put an end to that.[14]

More bad news followed quickly thereafter. In May 1984, despite fierce lobbying efforts by the Administration, Congress cut off CIA funding for the contras.* (This void would be filled through the offices of, among others, the World Anti-Communist League.)

But even before American aid to the contras was cut off in 1984, many New Right lobbying groups and foundations had embarked on a campaign to publicize the "freedom fighters'" cause, hosting speaking tours and seminars where contra leaders and exiled Nicaraguan labor leaders, journalists, and politicians conveyed their experience to American listeners. "We ask only for enough help so that we can have a reasonably even chance in our fight for freedom," they heard Adolfo Calero say. "We are the ones who are suffering, and it is our country that must make the sacrifices. We do not ask others to share these horrors. We ask only for enough resources from outside to give us a chance to fight against the weapons the Sandinistas have received from the communists."[15]

In the absence of CIA funds, these American conservative organizations became the nucleus of private efforts to keep the Nicaraguan civil war going. The most important figure in this informal alliance was retired Major General John K. Singlaub, the chairman of the World Anti-Communist League.

A month before the cutoff, Singlaub had been at the Pentagon to head a panel of retired high-ranking military officers whose purpose was to study the strife in Central America and make recommendations for the Reagan Administration.

The eight-member panel issued an eight-page classified report urging the United States to move away from conventional warfare tactics in

*In 1985, Congress restored partial funding for the contras, appropriating $27 million in humanitarian aid.

nd apply the lessons of counterinsurgency warfare learned
.uding increased emphasis on psychological warfare, civic
small-unit operations.[16]

me of the panel's recommendations (one of which was
ɔerts in psychological warfare to El Salvador) couldn't be
officiaiiy ..nplemented after the May cutoff, Singlaub and other panel members were in a position to see that they were pursued on an unofficial "free enterprise" basis. From statements made by those involved, it seems a deal was struck, that New Right private groups would conduct those operations that the Administration was now barred from continuing.

As chairman of the World Anti-Communist League, Singlaub made the revitalized international brotherhood the spearhead of these private groups anxious to actively combat communism everywhere; a principal target was Nicaragua.[17]*

Since then, Singlaub claims to have raised millions of dollars in aid for the contras and has made frequent trips to the FDN base camps on the Honduran border. He has also formed a private training academy for Salvadoran police forces and Nicaraguan contras, since the U.S. government will not. The director of this Institute for Regional and International Studies, Alexander McColl, is the military affairs editor of *Soldier of Fortune* magazine. He is also on the advisory board of Refugee Relief International, the organization that is operated jointly by *Soldier of Fortune* and Singlaub's United States Council for World Freedom.

"What we are doing here," McColl told one of the authors, "has been briefed to senior policy officials in Washington. They are aware of what we are doing and they approve. They have not told us to stop. In fact, they seem grateful for the private initiatives."[18]

"Singlaub," *The Washington Post* reported in December 1984, "said he and others have sent millions of dollars in uniforms, food, medicine and other aid to contras or their families and to refugees in Honduras, El Salvador and Guatemala. He said the Defense Department has helped coordinate the private aid."[19]

Another aid organizer, Louis ("Woody") Jenkins, a conservative

*After CAL was disbanded and replaced by FEDAL in the World Anti-Communist League in 1984, three national chapters—El Salvador, Guatemala, and Honduras—refused to join the new organization, according to Singlaub.

Louisiana Democratic state representative, told one of the authors, "[These] voluntary efforts have enabled the CIA to concentrate its depleted funds for the contras on arms and ammunition rather than on food and clothing."[20]

But Singlaub hasn't been content to leave the military funding to the CIA; in an interview with *The Washington Post* in May 1985, he said he had raised almost two million dollars outside the United States for arms for the rebels. "He and [Adolfo] Calero said they were seeking military and financial help from WACL chapters in South America, noting that the chapters in Brazil and Argentina are large and active."

Bert Hurlbut, a wealthy Texas oilman who is on the advisory board of the United States Council for World Freedom, elaborated on the source of money, claiming that both Taiwan and South Korea were sending fifty thousand dollars a month to fund the contras. "None of the funds from this country [U.S.] go for hardware," Hurlbut told *The Washington Post*. "We've solicited funds elsewhere for that. The entire WACL board is trying to help out with arms."[21]

Other New Right groups have joined the crusade. In March 1985, the College Republicans, an adjunct of the Republican National Committee, distributed a poster, "Save the Contras," featuring an armed contra and the reminder that "only 53 cents a day will support a Nicaraguan freedom fighter." CAUSA USA has sent an estimated one million dollars in supplies to refugees in Honduras since mid-1984. In May 1985, the Moon-owned *Washington Times* announced that Bo Hi Pak was contributing $100,000 toward a private fund that the *Times* was establishing to raise fourteen million dollars for the contras.[22]

Another man behind the aid influx is Andy Messing, executive director of the National Defense Council and a member of the board of the American chapter of the World Anti-Communist League. "Messing, who describes himself as an 'irregular-warfare expert' admitted in an interview that going to war is his favorite pastime. . . . He emphasized that his efforts had been to get nonmilitary supplies, not guns and bullets to Central America. 'One pill is worth a thousand bullets,' Messing said. 'Weapons shipments are not positive, not Judeo-Christian.' "[23]

*   *   *

Today the internal situation in Honduras is more placid than it was in Alvarez's day. The death squads, so prevalent then, are less active. "Ephron" is in "retirement," and "Lobo's" ELA, though still armed, is virtually dormant. The squad's primary goal, eliminating "Marxist domination" of the university, has been accomplished; the right now controls campus politics.

The Honduran armed forces command claims to have dismantled the COE network since Alvarez was ousted in March 1984. Alexander Hernández was transferred abroad as a member of the military attaché corps, but he was rejected by two South American governments to which he was assigned. He was last reported back in Honduras as the deputy head of FUSEP's training academy.

While American diplomats in Tegucigalpa now admit to having "recently heard" that the COE was responsible for a number of politically motivated killings and disappearances, they continue to defend COE's instrumental role as a "legitimate SWAT-type counterinsurgency force" that quelled an outbreak of leftist terrorism in Honduras.

For the Reagan Administration, Honduras continues to be the hub of the campaign against the Sandinista government in Nicaragua. Joint military exercises with Honduras have grown in size and complexity. In April 1985, Operation Big Pine III, conducted just three miles from the Nicaraguan border, included more than 4,500 American ground and air troops, as well as tanks for the first time. In the same month, Universal Trek '85, featuring a mock amphibious landing on the northern coast, involved 6,500 American troops.

Efforts at moderation are still loudly denounced by the ultra-right, both in the rest of Central America and in the United States. When comparatively moderate Nicaraguan exiles were brought under the FDN banner by the State Department and the CIA in March 1985, Senator Jesse Helms angrily denounced the "blueprint for fuzzy-minded socialism" from the Senate floor. "The State Department clearly appears to have concocted a new plan amounting to a betrayal of not only the freedom fighters but also the desire of President Reagan to see freedom established in Nicaragua."[24]

Without Alvarez, however, the United States is encountering new apprehension in Honduras. The more moderate military command is not as eager to get backed into a situation that might send their nation into war with Nicaragua; they wonder what would happen if the Americans decided to walk away from such a situation. "We ask ourselves," said a Honduran officer, "who will be the ones to deactivate, disarm and control these people [the contras] if there is no more U.S. government funding and they retreat entirely into Honduras. It's like having 12,000 PLO fighters in your country who want a separate state."[25]

SEVENTEEN

*For me, the withdrawal of foreign investment here is due to
the presence of the Sandinistas in Nicaragua. As long as
they remain in power, Costa Rica's economy will suffer.*

Oscar Saborío
Costa Rica, 1985

IN COSTA RICA, the peaceful and prosperous "Switzerland of Central America," the only nation in the Western Hemisphere without a standing army, there are forces at work that would cause the nation to abandon its traditional neutrality and jump headlong into the region's bloody conflicts. The head of the Costa Rican chapter of the World Anti-Communist League is a prominent spokesman for these forces.

Costa Rica's turn toward militancy is perhaps understandable, for its historically liberal political outlook and its reputation as a haven for political refugees of all types have brought problems. In a country where the Communist Party is tolerated and where both left- and right-wing exile groups from Guatemala, El Salvador, and Nicaragua have been allowed to maintain offices, Costa Rica is a natural breeding ground for intrigue and violence.

Not all observers, however, see the nation's open-door policy as a purely humanitarian program. "Costa Rica," a former Salvadoran government official said, "has always played both sides. Wherever or with whomever there is money to be made, the Costa Ricans will be there. I've always thought that one day, they would get a little too greedy, and I think that day has come."

The current crisis began in the late 1970s. In giving the Sandinista rebels use of its territory, Costa Rica was instrumental in bringing down the Somoza dictatorship in Nicaragua. "The Costa Ricans gave generous assistance to the Sandinistas during the last Nicaraguan war, allowing them to use the northern province of Guanacaste as a sanctuary from which to launch operations in the south of Nicaragua. Costa Rica was also where the Sandinistas took delivery of weapons shipped to them first from Venezuela and, later, from Cuba."[1]

The Costa Rican welcome mat for the Sandinistas has long since been pulled away; it is now the Sandinistas' enemies, the contras, who operate from Costa Rican sanctuary, with the fluctuating approval of the nation's authorities. There are now approximately twenty thousand Nicaraguan refugees in Costa Rica, most of them Sandinista opponents; the number grows steadily.

The change of heart came as the new Nicaraguan regime swung steadily to the left and was exacerbated by a wave of leftist violence that shook normally placid Costa Rica in 1981. Although many of the bombings, shootings, and kidnappings of 1981 and 1982 were attributed to a tiny Costa Rican communist group that was effectively crushed by the authorities, at least some of the violence was linked directly to the Nicaraguan Embassy in the capital, San José. One incident in particular, the bombing of a Honduran airline office, led to the expulsion of three Sandinista diplomats in 1983 and to a precipitous increase in tension between Nicaragua and Costa Rica. Today the relationship is one of an endless volley of diplomatic protests, most concerning border violations arising from the free-fire zone created by the contras along the frontier.

Despite the conflicts, President Luis Alberto Monge has for the most part spurned repeated U.S. proposals for an improved Costa Rican armed capability and for the establishment of an American-manned military training program.

The American pressure finally paid off, however; the Nicaraguan contras now operate border bases inside Costa Rica, and the nation's seven thousand Rural and Civil Guards have received modernized training, equipment, and weaponry from the United States. In 1984, for the first time in decades, Costa Rica accepted a delivery of "lethal aid," mostly light weaponry and field artillery, from the United States as part of its assistance program. In May 1985, American Special

Forces advisers arrived to train two Civil Guard battalions in counterinsurgency.

This escalation of military preparedness in Costa Rica has been evident since 1982, when, just prior to President Reagan's visit to San José, the minister of public security announced the creation of a reservist paramilitary force, the Organization for the National Emergency (OPEN).

Officially dissolved in early 1985 due to "lack of activity," in the nearly three years of its existence OPEN trained thousands of peasants in the rudimentary arts of counterinsurgency. Even with OPEN disbanded, these rural reservists continue to provide a pool of potential forces that could be incorporated into a paramilitary force should Costa Rica ever succumb to the pressure of its militarists. Just as were the *jefes politicos* in Guatemala and the ORDEN operatives in El Salvador, the Costa Rican OPEN agents were dominated by a political party.

"It was really murky," Deri Dyer, editor of the English-language *Tico Times,* told one of the authors in April 1985. "OPEN was supposed to be an anti-terrorist force, dependent on the Ministry of Public Security. Then we discovered that the ministry was checking prospective members' credentials to make sure no one with leftist tendencies got in. It turned out to be an anti-Communist paramilitary squad, and at least some of its estimated ten thousand members are reportedly Costa Rica Libre [Free Costa Rica Movement] people."

Since it is in keeping with the pattern elsewhere, it should come as no shock that the head of the Free Costa Rica Movement, Bernal Urbina Pinto, is also the head of his nation's chapter of the World Anti-Communist League.

Although Urbina Pinto has managed to keep the militant activities of the Free Costa Rica Movement to a discreet level, it is common knowledge in Costa Rica that the movement's youth arm conducts paramilitary training, euphemistically called "rescue training." The graduates of these courses are called the *Boinas Azules* (Blue Berets).

As vice-president of the Federation of Latin American Democratic Entities (FEDAL), which replaced CAL as the Latin American branch of the World Anti-Communist League after CAL was dissolved in 1984, Urbina Pinto's is an important voice in the League. He also has a long history of participation in his region's anti-communist struggle.

Of particular concern to Urbina Pinto has been the leftist government in neighboring Nicaragua. In 1981, he met with Argentine military agents and exiled Nicaraguan National Guardsmen to plot the overthrow of the Sandinista regime.

Hector Frances was one of the advisers the Argentine military junta sent to Central America in 1980 to aid the anti-communist efforts there. After he was apparently abducted on the streets of San José in 1982, Frances described the Argentine covert operation. His breaking of the traditional code of silence shed light on the Central American operations as well as on the involvement of several prominent League members in them.[2]

After undergoing specialized military intelligence training in Buenos Aires, Frances said, he was dispatched to Costa Rica. "I was to evaluate and create political and military conditions for the counter-revolutionary forces from that area." Frances named Urbina Pinto as one of the people he had met with in Costa Rica while helping to organize the anti-Sandinista contra forces.

By early 1982, the various Nicaraguan exile factions in Miami, Costa Rica, and Honduras had begun working together under the direction of the Argentines. They had also just received the first shipment of weapons, cash, and supplies from the CIA after President Reagan had signed a directive authorizing $19.5 million in covert funds to help get the contras started. CIA advisers began showing up in Central America, and soon the Argentines were getting their paychecks not from Buenos Aires but from Langley.[3]

Frances's task was to organize the contras in Costa Rica for the fledgling Nicaraguan Democratic Force (FDN), which was headquartered in Miami and Honduras; the name was formally adopted in December 1982 after a CIA-sponsored shakeup in the command structure of the fractious coalition.

Frances set up a local FDN committee in Costa Rica with former National Guardsmen from Nicaragua and exiled Somoza-era politicians. In preparation for creating an armed anti-Sandinista rebel force, he established a network of operatives to collect intelligence in both Costa Rica and Nicaragua. "These contacts allowed me to carry out several meetings to set up information networks and to create conditions for military operations."

Frances's unit had a working relationship with members of Costa

Rican security forces, who turned a blind eye to the armed camps being set up on Costa Rica's northern border with Nicaragua.

There were also contacts with ultra-rightist groups like Urbina Pinto's Free Costa Rica Movement. Arms and explosives were received from them for such actions as directing machine-gun fire at the Nicaraguan Embassy or blowing up Nicaraguan diplomatic vehicles in San José. "The Movimiento Costa Rica Libre, through its director, Bernal Urbina Pinto, closely allied to the CIA and similar movements in Salvador, Guatemala, and Spain, offered a copy of the keys of the Nicaraguan Embassy in San José for an operation against it," Frances said.

At about the same time, the American New Right was getting in on the act. Frances spoke of a meeting with Nat Hamrick, a roving aide to Senator Jesse Helms. In late 1981 and early 1982, Frances said, Hamrick met frequently with Urbina Pinto and other Costa Rican rightists on behalf of Helms during visits to San José. Of his own meeting with Hamrick, Frances said; "We agreed that, to bring about operational conditions for the [Nicaraguan] counterrevolution in Costa Rica, it was necessary to pressure President Monge with economic pressures to guarantee that he would ensure that Costa Rica would provide us with the right conditions for the operations I have cited. . . . Pressures are being made, and are reflected in the continued presence of Eden Pastora [an anti-Sandinista leader] in Costa Rica and of many other counterrevolutionary groups."

Frances left Costa Rica in 1982, but the results of his work remained behind. Today his "information networks" function on a surreptitious level at the service of Costa Rica's internal security forces, the various contra armies, and some conservative private-sector interest groups, all of which work in tandem against "the common threat," Nicaragua's Sandinista regime.

One of Urbina Pinto's ideological soulmates and closest friends is Oscar Saborío, a prominent San José businessman who owns one of the country's largest supermarket chains. A former congressman and mayor of San José, Saborío met with one of the authors in the quiet gloom of a hotel restaurant in San José in December 1984.

In his fifties, Saborío describes himself as "one of the first Costa Rican businessmen to recognize the threat" posed by the Sandinista regime, and one of the first "to take action."

One of his first actions was to form the Costa Rican Foundation for the Preservation of Liberty, which conducted a publicity and fund-raising campaign in the United States for the contras.

Later Saborío began working with Eden Pastora, the one-time "Commander Zero." Pastora, once one of the Sandinistas' heroes, had broken with his comrades in 1981 and taken up arms against them from Costa Rican exile, independently of the FDN's efforts. "I helped him with food and such things," Saborío said.

The businessman also made trips to Washington, where he tried to pressure the State Department and the CIA to give more support to Pastora's rebel effort. "I have always thought that the solution in Nicaragua is military," Saborío offered in explanation for his pro-contra activities.

He also worked hard to influence the divisive contra community, which was scattered in Costa Rica, Honduras, and Miami, stressing that a military solution could only come about through greater uni-fication.

Upon being approached for help by former contra chief José Francisco "Chicano" Cardenal (who lost his role in the 1982 CIA shakeup of the FDN), Saborío went to work in earnest. Besides using his economic and political clout, he revitalized a rural informants' net-work that he had nurtured for decades, ever since his participation in the 1948 anti-communist revolution that had set Costa Rica on the pro-Western, free enterprise path it follows today.

He also founded the Patriotic Union, which pressured the govern-ment. "It was a very anti-communist group. I was very active and was the coordinator between them and the minister of public secu-rity."

At the time, the minister of public security was Edmundo Solano, a controversial liberal. In the interview, Saborío claimed he discov-ered that "Solano had taken up with the Sandinistas," and that he and Urbina Pinto's group helped in the official's downfall in 1984.

Solano's successor as minister of public security is Benjamin Piza Carranza. Interestingly, Piza is a founding member of Urbina Pinto's Free Costa Rica Movement, the organization from which is drawn the Costa Rican chapter of the World Anti-Communist League. Pos-sibly because the movement is seen as a right-wing reactionary group by mainstream Costa Rican conservatives, Piza has felt it necessary to disavow any continuing links with it; nevertheless, political observers note that the rightist influence in the government's policies has grown recently.

As a result, Urbina Pinto's World Anti-Communist League chapter has lost much of its former pariah status; its involvement in current events is most visible in the frequent full-page newspaper advertisements denouncing the Sandinistas. In December 1985, participants in a Central American Peace March were stoned by over a hundred Costa Rica Libre members in San José.

Drawn by the green light given by the Reagan Administration to anti-Sandinista activities, others have joined Costa Rica's public-private cooperative venture against communism, including the Taiwanese, who are reportedly training the security forces in counterinsurgency. Also participating have been a number of anti-Castro Cubans from Miami, including some former terrorists.

The Cubans in Costa Rica are but the latest activists from an exile community that has been a traditional sponsor of paramilitary training for Central American anti-communist groups. This community is also represented in the World Anti-Communist League. Andres Nazario Sargen, the president of Alpha 66, a Cuban emigré group accused of bombings and assassinations throughout the United States, is a long-standing member of the League.

Thirty-three-year-old Felipe Vidal is a slim, mustachioed Cuban, the bodyguard of an American expatriate landowner, John Hull, who lives in northern Costa Rica. At home, he is given to wearing his .45 automatic in a shoulder holster outside his shirt. He coordinates the activities of the contras in his sector and works closely with an American who runs the local counterintelligence program. Two years ago, Vidal showed up with about fifteen other Cuban exiles to help Pastora's guerrillas fight the Sandinistas. Although the harsh life in the bush sent most of the exiles packing soon after they arrived, he and a committed hard-core group have remained.

Vidal's motive for fighting the Sandinistas is hatred of communism; his father was executed by a Fidel Castro firing squad in 1964. "We see Nicaragua as a strategic point from which to begin attacking Castro," Vidal told one of the authors in a contra safehouse in San José in January 1985. "We hope to eventually ignite the [counter] revolutionary forces inside Cuba.

"Here is a world of opportunity that the United States doesn't offer. For example, in Miami, it took me three or four years to get my hands on a .57 millimeter recoilless [rifle]. Here I can get one tomorrow."

Vidal said the Nicaraguan contra cause has been a beacon to Cuban "freedom fighters" after anti-Castro efforts lost CIA backing in the 1960s and were eventually abandoned as hopeless. "During the 1970s, the form of [our] struggle was terrorism against Castro," Vidal elaborated, "in Mexico, France, Barbados and the United States. President Carter created this wave of Cuban [emigré] terrorism because he began to negotiate with Castro. Once Reagan got into power, there was no need for these organizations because the government's policy coincided with the Cuban community's. In 1982, when Reagan came to Miami, he told us he was willing to support Cuban revolutionaries outside the U.S., just as long as nothing went on inside the U.S. So that's why we're here."

Vidal's idea is to provide a permanent paramilitary infrastructure for an "international anti-communist brigade," beginning in Costa Rica. The work began back in 1981, he said, when he and others "trained hundreds in Miami for the Nicaraguan cause.

"Now, what we're trying to do is to provide a way for Cuban exiles if they want to fight the communists. They can donate boots and food, but they can come and fight here, too."

Vidal answers to a man named Bruce Jones. He is one of the Americans involved in running the intelligence network in northern Costa Rica, drawing on operatives from within the Rural Guards. This counterespionage program is apparently sanctioned by a consortium of interests, including the Costa Rican government, business interest groups like Saborío's and Urbina Pinto's, and the contras.

Jones is responsible for a sparsely populated area where large landowners are fearful of the spread of the Sandinista revolution. He described the unofficial armed group, formed by the ranching landowners and himself, as "a kind of La Mano Blanca"; he personally collects handwritten intelligence reports several times a month from Rural Guardsmen stationed near the porous Nicaraguan border. In December 1984, he showed one of the authors his latest report, which he had just picked up from one of his operatives in a frontier town.

The report, several handwritten pages long, amounted to a semi-literate account of the activities of about twenty persons suspected of Sandinista ties or sympathies. "This man is a known communist and is believed to travel often to Nicaragua," a typical entry in the report read.

Jones, who was granted secret membership in the Costa Rican security forces for his efforts, explained that after he turns his lists over to his contacts in the government, the names go on file. Then, he claimed, another copy of the names was handed to the American Embassy in San José. "Anyone whose name is still on the lists by the time it gets to the Embassy," he said, "is denied a visa to the U.S., if they ever apply."

Jones was blunt about another reason for the operation. "We're compiling a list of all the communists in northern Costa Rica, in case we ever have to do an Operation Phoenix here."[4]

Jones, Vidal, Saborío, Urbina Pinto, and a handful of well-placed contacts in the Costa Rican and U.S. governments have collectively put together an impressive informant and counterintelligence network in Central America's one politically stable nation. Additionally, they have established an infrastructure for the contras who are operating in Costa Rican territory and have streamlined their logistical pipelines by forming groups that donate money and provide land and airstrips for cargo drops. They have done all this in the name of saving Costa Rica's "system of democracy." In the process, they have destabilized and increased the violence in the nation they vowed to protect.

Once again, those who have perceived the present and future stability of their nation as being threatened by communism have invited in foreign advisers and established countersubversion networks and paramilitary cells under the protection of a political party. Once again, that party is represented in the World Anti-Communist League.

Costa Rica's League representative has certainly done his part to meet the League's call for a committed international anti-communist vanguard "to combat by any means necessary to eliminate the Marxist-Leninist threat."

"I accept with pleasure," President Monge wrote, "the request to send a message to the 17th World Conference of the World Anti-Communist League, meeting in San Diego, California. It is a message of the government and of the people of Costa Rica. We are a small country, which within five years will complete a century of democratic processes. We are proud of our system of living in liberty. Despite our geographical location in a zone whipped by violence and war, this country maintains and will maintain its peace and its democratic institutions.

"Ideologically and politically, we are not neutral. In the confrontation between freedom and despotism, we are belligerents on the side of freedom. In the confrontation between the ideals of liberty and those elements which represent despotism, we cannot and we will not be neutral. We cannot and we will not be simple spectators. We claim an active role in the defense of the ideals of freedom."[5]

The Costa Rican president's message to the 1984 World Anti-Communist League conference was read by Bernal Urbina Pinto.

EIGHTEEN

The main objective of this conference is the mobilization of the Free World support for the active resistance movements inside the Communist Empire. . . . We have chosen this year to inform the participants of the present status in these areas and to develop a plan of action to assist these resistance movements.

Walter Chopiwskyj
San Diego, 1984

THE HOTEL sits on the edge of a marina, five minutes from downtown San Diego. In the evening, the setting sun sparkles on the water, and the masts of thousands of sailboats in the manmade lagoon sway in a gentle surf. It was certainly a beautiful setting for the Seventeenth Annual World Anti-Communist League conference.

Under the leadership of retired Major General John Singlaub, the 1984 League conference was destined to be the most "successful" and important conference in its history. The meeting would serve as a renaissance of the League, which would emerge more powerful, more respected, and more dangerous than it was before.

San Diego was clearly a better site selection in 1984 than Luxembourg had been in 1983. That conference, the League's sixteenth, can only be described as a disaster. By 1983, the League already had a notorious reputation in Europe, and officials were reluctant to extend a welcome to a body that had historically included fascists, fugitive terrorists, and Nazi collaborators.

The prime minister of Luxembourg had been asked to give the opening address; he had refused. The Luxembourg foreign and army ministers had been asked to speak; they had refused. The municipal government and the tourism office, representing a city actively trying to attract conferences and congresses, ignored it. The Gendarmerie refused to provide security. The Luxembourg Council of Resistance Fighters, a conservative, anti-communist body of veterans of guerrilla war against the Nazis, protested the conference to the government. Two scheduled American speakers, General Vernon Walters and Claire Boothe Luce, canceled.

"It has become once again clear," retired Belgian General Robert Close warned at the opening ceremonies in San Diego, "that the warnings and the opinions expressed during the last World Anti-Communist League conference in Luxembourg were, at the same time, criticized as fascist. We must fight this kind of disinformation, subversion and infiltration of the mass media. We will unite against this kind of terrorism which is as dangerous as pure and simple terrorism."

Close needn't have worried about "subversion" in San Diego. There was no repetition of the indignities suffered in Luxembourg. Under the leadership of General Singlaub's United States Council for World Freedom, the conference served to complete the redefining and repackaging of the League. No longer would it be open to attacks of being a haven for the proponents of the "Zionist-Communist conspiracy" theory; now it would be seen as an organization dedicated to fighting for international freedom, "regardless of differences of race, sex, religion or national origin."

Ivor Benson, the rabid South African racist and anti-Semite who had been a guest speaker at the North American Regional World Anti-Communist League conference in 1983, was not in attendance; his representation of Africa was supplanted by the presence of black leaders from nearly twenty African nations. The Tecos of Mexico, with whom the USCWF had been able to coexist until they were exposed by one of the authors earlier in 1984, were conspicuously absent.

Instead, the United States Council for World Freedom had filled the League with mostly respectable conservative leaders from throughout the world. According to a League publication, *Asian Outlook,* one-third of the attendees were members of parliaments, congressmen, or senators from their respective countries. In the United States, dozens of notables from the New Right, including former Representatives John LeBoutillier of New York and Robert Dornan of California, attended as observers.

Even better, in San Diego the League was able to receive the stamp of approval from various governments around the world. General Alfredo Stroessner, the dictator of Paraguay, sent a telegram thanking the League for "defending the world from the Marxist tyranny," then went on to boast breathlessly of his own contributions to the cause.

> I must say with pride that my Government, from the very beginning of its mandate, maintains a firm and unalterable anti-communist position, that identifies itself with the democratic vocation of the Paraguayan people, and, in that sense, it has been possible to expel the subversive attempts of terrorist gangs supported by international communism by means of policies of social justice and the socio-economic transformations required by popular aspirations.[1]

The crowning endorsement, however, had to be that of President Reagan.

> It is an honor to send warm greetings to all those gathered for the 17th. Annual Conference of the World Anti-Communist League in San Diego.
>
> The World Anti-Communist League has long played a leadership role in drawing attention to the gallant struggle now being waged by the true freedom fighters of our day. Nancy and I send our best wishes for every future success.[2]

Still, there were problems in selling this new and improved League, for not very much had changed. John Kosiak, the Byelorussian Nazi collaborator, remained chairman of his delegation. The Croatian Liberation Movement, the international Ustasha brotherhood that Ante Pavelic had established in Argentina in 1956, was still the official Croatian League chapter, as was the Bulgarian National Front, Inc., which had been formed in 1947 by the Bulgarian Legionnaires who had advocated the extermination of that nation's Jews. Mario Sandoval Alarcón, the "Godfather" of Central American death squads, was in attendance. And although Yaroslav Stetsko, the Ukrainian premier who had officiated over the murder of approximately seven thousand residents of Lvov in one week in 1941, was too ill to come, his wife, Slava, was there to represent the Ukrainian Nazi collaborators.

One of the most interesting aspects of the purification campaign at San Diego was the denigration of the former Mexican delegation. The purged Tecos were consistently attacked by League members for their anti-Semitism and fascist tendencies. One conference observer stated that the delegates rarely missed an opportunity to voice condemnation of their former comrades. "There was a very concerted effort, in the seminars and in private conversations, to attack the Tecos, to stress that there was no place in WACL for people like that."[3]

Yet many of these diatribes came from Latin affiliates of the League, affiliates that the Tecos had formed in the 1970s, and were being voiced by the same people who had rallied to the Tecos' side when they were attacked by the British Foreign Affairs Circle in 1973 and 1974. Due to media pressure, the League had cut off one head of the Teco hydra; its other heads remained intact. "They say they got rid of the Tecos," the observer went on, "but they only got rid of the Mexican Tecos. All the South American Tecos, which still follow the Teco line, were still there."

Another element objectionable to some mainstream conservatives, the Unification Church, had not been purged in San Diego. In fact, its presence had grown. Many of the American observers to the conference were involved with the Reverend Sun Myung Moon through any one of his myriad front groups. Among these were Ray Cline, director of the United States Global Strategy Council, and Roger Fontaine, a former National Security Council official and currently a reporter for the Moon-owned *Washington Times*. The Reverend Moon may have called the League a "fascist" organization in 1975, but he still wanted to be part of it in 1984.

Certainly General Singlaub had cleansed the World Anti-Communist League of some of its "lightning rods," those overt extremists who did nothing but draw attention and criticism to the organization. This purge wasn't for purely esthetic or public relations reasons; the former major general had a bold new vision for the League, and the San Diego conference was going to be his showcase for it. He didn't want or need any adverse publicity to detract from it.

The goal of this conference is to formulate programs of action for each region of the world to follow in this organization's continuing effort to counter the worldwide campaign of subversion, disinformation and news manipulation that fuels the communist drive toward world domination.[4]

No longer would the League be a place for delegations to lament the past. Instead, it was going to become an action-oriented federation in the vanguard of the *real* struggle against communism. Speakers would no longer be angry old men lecturing on the evils of the "Chinese Communist clique" or the "imperialistic Russians"; there would now also be guerrilla fighters from Afghanistan, Mozambique, and Nicaragua, who were, with bullets and howitzers, actively fighting the communists. Funds would no longer be spent on lavish banquets, glossy magazines, or commemorations of obscure fourteenth-century victories; money would now go toward establishing "speakers' bureaus" and toward buying helicopters, boots, and binoculars for the international anti-communist "liberation forces." In short, the League was to become an instrument for the international spread of "unconventional warfare."

The former major general and specialist in unconventional warfare had been formulating this renovation for some time. "We must develop a Free World strategy which recognizes the whole spectrum of conflict from strategic nuclear to conventional to unconventional," Singlaub wrote in the June 15, 1984 USCWF newsletter. "This strategy must exploit to the maximum those many weaknesses within the Communist Empire with a view toward rolling back Communist tyranny and domination everywhere."[5]

Singlaub had not waited for the San Diego conference to put his plan into action. The previous year, he had joined forces with other retired military officers, including General Harry "Heine" Aderholt, former commander of Special Forces and Singlaub's deputy in Vietnam, to form Refugee Relief International, an organization of former Special Forces soldiers, paratroopers, and pilots.

"In relation to Refugee Relief International, which is an affiliate of the United States Council for World Freedom," USCWF Secretary General Walter Chopiwskyj proudly announced to the 1984 League conference, "and which is dedicated to the provision of medical, financial and other assistance directly to displaced persons and other victims of communist terrorism, this year has moved and distributed six million dollars in medical supplies and equipment to the people of El Salvador. General Singlaub is a member of the Board of Directors of Refugee Relief International and is currently engaged in raising funds and collecting medical supplies and equipment and medical evacuation helicopters to send to El Salvador to help the victims of the terrorist attacks in that country."

As we have seen, it is more than "medical supplies and equipment" that is being ferried to Central America by Refugee Relief International; since its inception, it has been a source of supplies for the contras fighting the Nicaraguan government.

In retirement, Aderholt runs the Air Commandos Association and is the unconventional warfares editor for *Soldier of Fortune* magazine, the "Journal of Professional Adventurers." In articles recounting the "glories" of Rhodesia and Vietnam, *Soldier of Fortune* appeals to both active mercenaries and the armchair variety, and its classified ads function as a clearinghouse for international mercenaries. It does not, in fact, make any secret that its "reporters" frequently carry arms while on assignment and engage in combat. "We don't hide the fact that we support one side and follow them into combat," a *Soldier of Fortune* employee told one of the authors in El Salvador. "What we don't draw attention to is that we kill people."

As upcoming chairman, Singlaub saw the chance to make the World Anti-Communist League operate along much the same lines as his and Aderholt's project; he made his plans for this new League clear in his opening address on September 4 in San Diego.

> When you have slowed or stopped the enemy's attack, it is the appropriate time to commit your reserves and launch a counterattack. . . .
>
> I am convinced that our struggle with Communism is not a spectator sport. As a result of that view, we have opted for the course of action which calls for the provision of support and assistance to those who are actively resisting the Soviet supported intrusion into Africa, Asia and North America.
>
> The geographic regions of WACL must not only provide support to the freedom fighters who are engaged in combat in their own region, but they must develop plans of action to support the resistance movements in other regions of the world.[6]

Singlaub hit a responsive chord among the delegates. When Slava

Stetsko, the wife of Yaroslav, was asked by a reporter what she wanted the U.S. government to do to aid the anti-communist struggle, she responded quickly; "To organize centers of psychological warfare, political warfare."

"The time is now for action," Monaf Fakira of Mauritius charged. "Either directly or indirectly, the communists will take over the world and thus destroy our system of democratic government, our way of life, our choice of religion and culture, our freedom as a whole, and to [rule by] terrorism. I underline terrorism. To have terrorism in the world, to fight and win the undeclared World War III.

"This can only be [prevented] if, side by side, the liberation forces, strategically or otherwise, receive assistance."

"As the new Chairman of WACL," Singlaub told the League, "I assure you that I will work with great vigor to carry out these ideas. As a matter of fact, your effectiveness as a WACL Region, National Chapter, or organization will be measured in 1985 by how well you carry out the plans of action developed during the next few days."

And the former major general wasn't kidding. Committees were established to determine the needs of anti-communist resistance movements in eight countries (Angola, Mozambique, Ethiopia, Laos, Cambodia, Vietnam, Nicaragua, and Afghanistan) and to formulate a policy for rendering assistance. Attending the League conference were representatives from five of the movements, including Adolfo Calero, a major leader of the contras fighting the Sandinista government. "Our situation," Calero informed the League, "is that we have the will to fight, if we had the weapons. These people [the contras] are trained; these people are willing to continue that struggle. We know for a fact that in Nicaragua we are fighting the battle for Central America. . . ."

> We have kept the Sandinistas from participating more directly and physically in El Salvador and I believe that every shot that we resistance fighters, freedom fighters, of Nicaragua fire in Nicaragua, is one less shot that will be fired in El Salvador. We are the ones who are keeping the Sandinistas within [Nicaragua]. If we are left alone, if we are not given the proper support, we will continue our fight but it will have terrible consequences and we will be overwhelmed.[7]

The resistance movements were neither shy nor modest about their needs. The Mozambique delegation, for instance, in addition to wanting funds to set up an information bureau, saw the need for five hundred surface-to-air missiles, AK47 ammunition ("for up to 30,000 people"), five hundred bazookas, one hundred Jeeps with gun mounts, five coastal cutters, and Special Forces equipment and instructors ("enough for 30 teams") to carry out "special assignments." The Cambodians, battling the Vietnamese occupying their nation, needed funds for the purchase of "10,000 bags of rice per month to feed units in the field. Also needed are 15,000 assault rifles and ammunition, field radios, plasma, antibiotics, anti-tank weapons and plastique explosives to interdict bridges which Hanoi is too poor to repair."[8]

Probably the most ambiguous requests came from the Nicaraguan contras under the FDN banner. Seeking to "use U.S. Council for World Freedom as a clearing house and disseminator of current information and current status and needs of/from FDN to all WACL chapters," the contras made no public mention of their needs for weapons or military supplies. This was undoubtedly a political consideration; in September 1984, opposition to the Reagan Administration's covert aid to the contras had grown, and Congress had voted a complete cutoff of such aid in May. This caution in San Diego certainly didn't mean, however, that the contras didn't need such support, nor that the League would not supply it.

The resistance movement seminars were certainly the most important development in the genesis of the "new" League in San Diego. Operated by a handful of men, mostly retired American military or intelligence officers, the seminars marked the beginning of a new role for the League. This wasn't a bunch of aging Ukrainian fascists gathered around a table railing about the Soviet-designed famine in their homeland in the 1920s; it was a gathering of unconventional warfare experts meeting with guerrilla leaders actively engaged in just such warfare.

The ubiquitous Ray Cline led the seminar on Nicaragua. Also officiating was Roger Fontaine, a colleague of Cline's at the Georgetown Center for Strategic and International Studies during the 1970s and, briefly, a senior staff member on the National Security Council at the White House, where, according to his resumé, "he shared day-to-day responsibility for U.S. national security policy for Latin America."

Heading the Afghanistan seminar was Dr. Alex Alexiev, director of international security for the Rand Corporation. He was joined by Brigadier General Theodore C. Mataxis. During his long military career, Mataxis had also gathered unconventional warfare credentials, attending the Chemical Warfare School in 1941 as well as the Strategic Intelligence School in the late 1940s.

Leading the seminar on Mozambique was William Mazzoco, a former U.S. Agency for International Development official who had directed the "security and surveillance" of aid programs to Vietnam from 1965 to 1971; he had been an instructor in counterinsurgency at the Foreign Service Institute in the early 1960s and had been a teacher for eight years at the U.S. Police Academy, the "school" that had trained the secret police of Uruguay, El Salvador, and Panama, among others.

Jim Morris, a former Special Forces major in Vietnam and editor of the mercenary *Eagle* magazine, participated in the Indochina seminar.

The seminars were a revolutionary break with League tradition but the members seemed pleased with the "new" League. "General Singlaub," Roman Zwarycz, a member of ABN, explained, "is concerned with furnishing real aid to these people that are out there fighting. They do need bullets. They do need medical supplies. They do need foodstuffs. They happen to be guerrillas. These things have to come from somewhere."[9]

The seminars were the catalysts of an even greater role for the World Anti-Communist League in Central America. Thanks to the consensus reached at San Diego, their private unconventional warfare would be better financed and expanded.

The plane, a noisy and ramshackle old DC-3, came around in a long, slow arc over the jungles of Honduras. It dropped down below the treeline and bounced along the rutted airstrip macheted from the jungle floor. As the plane taxied to a stop, the guerrillas came out from among the trees, drove a half-dozen trucks up to the cargo bay, and waited for the doors to open.

Crates of supplies were quickly unloaded into the trucks. As the DC-3 restarted its engines for takeoff, the guerrillas disappeared with their new supplies into the treeline. The plane, which had carried a shipment of supplies donated by the World Anti-Communist League, lifted off for the return flight to Tegucigalpa. There would be other planes that month delivering supplies to the contras in their "crusade" against the Sandinista government of Nicaragua.

It had been forty-four years since the Ukrainians had practiced unconventional warfare by massacring ethnic Russians and Jews for the Nazis in the name of "anti-Bolshevism." It had been twenty-six years since the Kuomintang in Taiwan had established the Political Warfare Cadres Academy, teaching rightists from around the world techniques of unconventional warfare to counter the threat of "international communism." It had been nineteen years since Mario Sandoval Alarcón had begun using the unconventional warfare of death squads to rid his nation of "subversives." It had been nine years since the Italian terrorists of Ordine Nuovo had employed a different kind of unconventional warfare to murder Magistrate Vittorio Occorsio as an "enemy of the people."

On that day, as the DC-3 lumbered toward its rendevous in Honduras, there was nothing new about the World Anti-Communist League. Employing the skills it had learned in the Ukraine, Taiwan, Guatemala, and Italy, it was merely beginning a new phase in its old fight.

NINETEEN

IT IS QUITE EASY to predict how the World Anti-Communist League will probably react when this book is published. There will be angry denunciations from League members, denials of Nazi involvement, and attacks on the authors and publisher, charging us with being communists or "fifth columnists." Indeed, this campaign has already begun.

There will be a hastily assembled Executive Board meeting, and there will be a purge of some of the League elements we have exposed. The Romanian Iron Guard and the Croatian Ustashi most likely will be replaced by emigrés whose backgrounds don't include their participation in wartime atrocities. The Stetsko entourage of Ukrainians will probably be taken over by younger exiles who didn't massacre Jews in 1941. The Japanese chapter will probably be replaced by one composed of businessmen and conservative politicians untraceable to either the Unification Church or the Japanese underworld. Many other chapters, especially in Africa and Western Europe, will quit as they learn for the first time some of the unsavory details about their League brethren.

There may even be a name change. Just as the Latin American Anti-Communist Confederation became the Federation of Latin American Democratic Entities, at the next conference or Executive Board meeting the World Anti-Communist League may cease to exist, to reappear as the International Freedom League or the World Federation for Democracy or some other grand title.

The one prediction that can be made with absolute certainty is that the League will not die.

The World Anti-Communist League is a chameleon, able to change its colors, even its politics, at will.

When black Africans are not present, it talks about the democracy and bastion of freedom and prosperity of white-controlled South Africa; when black Africans are present, it talks about black Africa's struggle against Soviet-Cuban aggressors.

When Arabs are not present, it rails against the communist encroachment in the Middle East; when Arabs are present, it attacks Israel for its "Zionist imperialism." It can deftly sidestep its own contradictions in the name of the greater goal of anti-communism.

And like a chameleon, the World Anti-Communist League can grow back a tail when it is cut off.

When Roger Pearson was exposed as a neo-Nazi after three years in the League, the Taiwanese were suddenly horrified and asked him to leave.

When the Tecos of Mexico were exposed as anti-Semites and fascists in 1984, they were purged, although the League had had intimate knowledge of the nature of their Mexican comrades for the previous ten years.

When one of its "tails" is exposed and attacked, whether by the press, governments, or other League members, the World Anti-Communist League simply sheds it and grows another one.

The League will survive for other reasons.

It is is too important an instrument of foreign policy for South Korea and Taiwan to relinquish. It is too vital a link for Latin American death squads to meet and share information to be severed. It is too convenient a conduit for the Unification Church to gain influence and funnel money to permit it to be stopped. It is too valuable a network for Nazi collaborators to maintain contact with each other to see it dismantled. It is too integral a part of the American New Right's program of subsidizing their "freedom fighters" in Central America to see it halted.

It will also not die because its members have a compulsion to remain within it.

Suzanne Labin, a French conservative scholar, was a League member before the Pearson interlude. She was reportedly enraged by the influx of neo-Nazis and former SS officers in the 1970s and by the League leaders' acquiescence to it. Yet she remains today head of the League chapter in France.

In 1971, David Rowe quit the American Council for World Freedom in disgust over what he saw as the Chinese chairman's megalomania and corrupt history. Yet Rowe is in the American League chapter today, a League under the chairmanship of the same Chinese "megalomaniac" to whom he had such a violent reaction fourteen years earlier.

In 1975, the Reverend Sun Myung Moon blasted the World Anti-Communist League as "fascist," and yet today the Japanese chapter of the League is operated by Moon's Unification Church, and many of the American League members work for Moon's organizations.

In 1975, Stefan Possony quit the League over the behavior and background of the Mexican Tecos. Yet he rejoined in the 1980s, before the Tecos were finally ousted.

As long as it serves such important purposes for so many notorious groups around the world, and as long as there are men and women who will wail about the influx of "criminal elements" but turn around and quietly work with those elements, there will be a World Anti-Communist League.

The League is not a "paper tiger."

It is a well-funded, six-continent federation of men and women who have given up on democracy, or who never believed in it in the first place, and who are now fighting their enemies on their own terms.

It is a collection of practitioners and advocates of "unconventional warfare," who emulate the policies of Chile's Pinochet and Taiwan's Kuomintang and who employ their tactics in Nicaragua, Mozambique, and Angola.

They are men who, when governments cut off aid, can send funds and supplies to "friendly" guerrillas in Africa, Asia, and Central America.

It is a brotherhood that has its own source of income, its own foreign policy, its own army, even its own religion.

Some might feel we have overstated the case. They would say the old Nazis live in quiet obscurity and aren't still exterminating Jews. The Unification Church has the right to proselytize in Latin America and the United States; besides, there are a lot of other reverends who have become multimillionaires. The Tecos should have the right to criticize the Pope or priests they consider to be too liberal. The Latin American rightists should have the right to defend their traditions and plantations against what they consider to be Marxist elements.

As far as they go, there is some truth in all those statements, but they are gross oversimplifications of what the League stands for.

The old Nazis do still call for the radical solution of the "Jewish problem" when they're in safe company. And they are still working toward that end; their progeny have murdered Jews in synagogues in Paris, innocent passengers on civilian aircraft in Czechoslovakia and policemen in New York City.

The Unification Church made an alliance with the Japanese underworld and used vast amounts of money, funds of unknown origin, for influence-peddling in the United States and South America through a variety of front groups.

The Tecos have taken control of at least one major university and fueled hostility toward Jews in Mexico, where synagogues are vandalized and Jewish graves are spray-painted with swastikas.

Latin American rightists have shared dossiers on peasants, liberal clergy, and labor leaders; those targeted have been later found dead, tortured, and disfigured, in ditches and garbage dumps.

Today, there is a new World Anti-Communist League. Under the leadership of retired Major General John Singlaub, it has become action-oriented, not interested in simply containing communism, but working for its "roll-back."

The leaders of the World Anti-Communist League, including Singlaub, say the United States cannot be naïve about what is needed in this fight, and they are right.

A superpower has no choice but to maintain an interest in events throughout the world. At times, that must include propping up friendly governments and imposing sanctions on unfriendly ones. It also includes supplying "freedom fighters" it supports and helping combat "guerrillas" it doesn't. And it also includes the use of unconventional warfare; in various ways, all the armies of the world employ it. Failure to do so when your enemy does means you will lose. We cannot be ingenuous about war.

But this isn't the point. One can accept that one government's intervention in the political affairs of another or the use of unconventional warfare is sometimes necessary. It does not follow, however, that a private organization, elected by no one and accountable to no one, has that same prerogative. A nongovernmental federation, which the World Anti-Communist League purports to be, does not have the right to carry out its own foreign policy and certainly not to conduct war.

Which is exactly what the World Anti-Communist League is doing. Through the financial largesse of some of its members, it is funding guerrilla movements throughout the world, and through its advocacy and practice of unconventional warfare it is leaving a bloody trail throughout Central America.

Perhaps what is most wrong with the World Anti-Communist League is what it hides behind and what it has rejected. In the name of anti-communism, it has embraced those responsible for death squads, apartheid, torture, and the extermination of European Jewry. Along the way, it has repudiated democratic government as a viable alternative, either to govern or to combat communism. The Latin League chapters view representational government as only the first step toward leftist takeover. The Asian chapters in South Korea and Taiwan have never even considered democracy as a possible alternative to rigid dictatorship. American League members have spurned the fiat of Congress (and possibly violated the United States Neutrality Act in the process) by supplying Nicaraguan guerrillas when American government funds were cut off.

Most people in the West would consider themselves anti-communists. Few would argue that a person living under a communist regime is any better off than his counterpart in a country ruled by a right-wing dictatorship. And any Westerner who has traveled in a communist-ruled country and seen the bread lines, secret police, and general unhappiness would come away with the conclusion that there was something inherently wrong with the system. Consequently, few would see anything wrong with an organization that calls itself anti-communist.

Just as the Nazis used their anti-Comintern policy, so the World Anti-Communist League too uses this sentiment to its advantage, seriously damaging a respectable cause in the process. It makes a mockery of individuals and organizations seeking to bring about positive change in communist countries. It is a slander against genuine freedom fighters and all those who work toward bringing democracy to their nations. Ultimately, the World Anti-Communist League is an obscenity directed at those it pretends to represent.

EPILOGUE

As 1986 BEGINS, the World Anti-Communist League seems well on its way to accomplishing its goal of becoming the vanguard of global anti-communist activism. Under the tutelage of former Major General John Singlaub, the League has become the primary vehicle for nongovernmental support for rightist guerrilla movements worldwide, from the Nicaraguan contras to the Afghan *mujahedeen.*

It wasn't until the fall of 1985 that the true importance of the League to the Reagan Administration's strategy to aid anti-Marxist rebels was revealed. Singlaub admitted that, after the 1984 Congressional cut-off of CIA aid to the contras, he had received not just the blessing, but the guidance of White House and National Security Council officials to fill the void through private fundraising. Senior Administration officials confirmed that Lt. Colonel Oliver North, deputy director for political-military affairs on the National Security Council, had been directing efforts to obtain private aid to supply, arm, and advise the contras. At the same time, Singlaub identified North as his liaison to the Reagan Administration.

In a similar vein, in the February 1985 issue of *Life,* one of the authors exposed the activities of Bruce Jones, the CIA liaison to the contras in northern Costa Rica. After the revelation, Jones, who had also privately discussed his plan to establish a Costa Rican death squad, was forced to return to the United States. He now works for Singlaub and helped set up the Tucson chapter of the United States Council for World Freedom.

Another clue to the warmth shown by the Reagan Administration toward Singlaub is the tax-exempt status granted Singlaub's United States Council for World Freedom (USCWF) in 1982. While the IRS Los Angeles district office said there was no precedent for giving such an organization tax-exempt status, IRS headquarters in Washington approved the application. As a precondition for this windfall, Albert Koen, then treasurer of USCWF, had agreed that *"at no time* will the USCWF ever contemplate providing materiel or funds to any revolutionary, counterrevolutionary or liberation movement," a pledge that they have rather brazenly violated.

All of this serves to underscore the dramatic dovetailing of interests between the Reagan Administration and the World Anti-Communist League. The Administration dreams of "rolling back" communism, a goal that both Singlaub and the League have been promoting for years. Since his ascension in the League, Singlaub has called for a repeal of the Congressional ban on aid to the anti-Marxist Angolan resistance movement; in 1985, the White House succeeded in lifting the ban and began to push for a military assistance program. At the same time, Congress reinstated aid to the contras and CIA support for the Cambodian guerrillas, both of which Singlaub had lobbied for intensely. In 1984, Singlaub established WACL committees to assist guerrillas in eight Marxist countries; in 1985, the Reagan Administration considered a plan to establish "freedom fighter" bureaus to fund and coordinate the insurgencies in these same eight countries.

With his Administration support, Singlaub has become less hesitant about revealing the League's true mission. According to a September/October 1985 *Common Cause* article, "Singlaub spoke proudly about his work with the rebels ... He said that in the last year he has raised 'tens of millions of dollars' for arms and ammunition, and millions more for non-military supplies."

Since the U.S. Neutrality Act bars a private American organization from supplying weapons to foreign groups, Singlaub has established a secret overseas bank account where donors send their money to buy weapons. Many of these donors, according to Singlaub and Congressional aides, are his comrades in the World Anti-Communist League, notably the governments of Taiwan, South Korea, and Saudi Arabia.

Singlaub's overt militancy and the Administration ties to his efforts have raised the serious concern of congressmen in both political parties that the private aid circumvents congressional restrictions.

Representative Jim Leach (Republican of Iowa) called the private groups "international vigilantes" engaged in "privately funded terrorism."

"What we've done," Leach said, "is unleashed a force that's accountable to nobody."

These arguments appear to be falling on deaf ears within the Reagan Administration, and there is no sign that the "privatization of war" will be stopped any time soon. In fact, the occasion of the September 1985 World Anti-Communist League conference held in Dallas, exhibited the increasing interest of wealthy American conservatives in the League's plans. Mingling with anti-communist guerrilla leaders from around the world, including contra chiefs Enrique Bermudez and Adolfo Calero, Angolan Holden Roberto and Afghan Dr. Ikram Gran, were a covey of wealthy Texans. Among them was Ellen Garwood, most noted for giving Singlaub $65,000 toward the purchase of a helicopter for the contras. Billionaire Nelson Bunker Hunt, who once tried to corner the world silver market, also cut a wide path, buying an entire table for the $500-a-plate International Freedom Fighters Dinner. Providing security for the ultra-right *glitterati* was Tom Posey, head of the Alabama-based mercenary group, Civilian Military Assistance, and a team of his soldiers.

Other guests at the conference were famous for more sinister reasons. Mario Sandoval Alarcón, the head of Guatemala's "party of organized violence," was there, as, reportedly, was newcomer Yves Gignac, a former leader of the French Secret Army Organization (OAS) who spent five years in prison for his role in an assassination plot against Charles de Gaulle.

But there were others who were not so famous and should have no desire to be. Chirila Ciuntu, the Iron Guardist wanted for war crimes in Romania, attended, as did John Kosiak, the Byelorussian Nazi collaborator. Yaroslav Stetsko, the Ukrainian who presided over the massacre of 7,000 Jews in the city of Lvov, was represented by his wife, Slava.

While the four-day Dallas summit was the League's highlight for 1985, its members remained active on their home fronts. Their actions were consistent with League tradition.

In the United States, Eastern European exile groups linked to the League mounted a vitriolic attack on the Justice Department's Office for Special Investigations (OSI), the unit responsible for prosecuting Nazi war criminals still at large. Charging that the OSI relied on information supplied by the Soviet KGB, these emigré groups, together with some New Right organizations, sought to curtail or eliminate the office. Even Singlaub took up the call, voicing his concern about the OSI's methods to one of the authors. Often, however, the anti-OSI lobby was its own worst enemy.

"Equality under the law," Dr. Eduard Rubel, a Board Director of the Captive Nations Committee, wrote to a host of government officials, "is one of the few precepts that stands between Eastern European ethnics and the Jewish Zionist special interest groups, corruption of power and ultimate tyranny in its many guises in Washington."

For a time, this campaign appeared to find sympathy in the White House itself. Pat Buchanan, the White House Communications Director, was seen as spearheading efforts to eliminate OSI until a public outcry forced the move to be abandoned.

In South Korea and Taiwan, there were no signs of an end to the sort of repression that serves as a model for other League chapters. Kim Dae Jung, the leading opponent to South Korea's military dictatorship, was allowed to return from a U.S. exile but was immediately placed under house arrest, where he remains today. The Kuomintang regime ruling Taiwan showed no signs of sharing power with the Taiwanese majority and continued to serve as a political warfare training ground for military officers of right-wing Latin nations. While the FBI linked the California murder of journalist David Liu to high-ranking Taiwanese military intelligence officers, the scandal eventually died down and caused no lasting rift with the Reagan Administration.

By 1986, the League had lost some of its steadfast friends in Latin American governments, as democratic elections in Uruguay, Argentina, Guatemala, and Bolivia brought an end to military rule. Far from merely being out of office, some of the League's staunchest Latin allies had hit on hard times. Former Argentine dictator General Jorge Rafael Videla, who had triumphantly presided over the 1980 CAL conference in Buenos Aires, is now serving a life sentence for mass murder. The unprecedented trial by the civilian Alfonsin government was a dramatic repudiation of the military's anti-communist reign of terror in the late 1970s, the "dirty war" that had later been emulated in El Salvador and Honduras.

In Central America, the killing goes on. Formerly neutral Costa Rica has adopted an increasingly militant stance against Sandinista Nicaragua, a policy shift strongly advocated by both the World Anti-Communist League and the Reagan Administration. Honduras remains the primary staging ground for the contras, who have grown and expanded their operations, thanks, in large part, to the League's aid. CAUSA, the anti-communist political arm of the Reverend Sun Myung Moon's Unification Church, still maintains an office in the Honduran capital. "The Spiritual Father" is now able to play a more active role in CAUSA and other Church fronts since his August 1985, release from a U.S. prison where he served over a year for tax evasion.

In Guatemala, the frenzy of the government-sanctioned death squads rose in intensity during the autumn of 1985 as guerrilla forces appeared to expand their theaters of operations, and general elections drew near. The ubiquitous Mario Sandoval Alarcón was once again a presidential candidate, as was his former protégé, Leonel Sisniega Otero. Liberal Christian Democrat Vinicio Cerezo won the presidency in a December 1985 run-off.

In El Salvador, the summer of 1985 saw the beginning of an ambitious psychological warfare program by the government to undermine the morale of the guerrillas and to woo away their civilian supporters. Senior military officers in charge of the campaign openly credited Taiwan for their inspiration and expertise.

"We borrowed from many different models," Lieutenant Colonel José Ricardo Fuentes told one of the authors in July 1985, "but we found that the Taiwanese concepts of political warfare were the ones we liked best."

On the civilian side, San Salvador was the site of a May 1985 right-wing summit. The conference, which included many WACL members, focused on the need to involve civilians in the region's fight against communism. The resulting "Declaration of San Salvador" announced the Central American Anti-Communist Defence Accord:

"Its purpose is to strengthen a Central American Civilian Military Alliance. Its objective is to form a combative force with the capacity for struggle to eradicate all communist threat from the area."

The Declaration's signatories included Costa Rica's WACL head, Bernal Urbina Pinto, several former CAL members, anti-Castro Cuban exiles, and representatives of guerrilla groups from Angola and Nicaragua. Signing for the United States Council for World Freedom and John Singlaub was American League member Dr. Anthony Bouscaren.

Perhaps the most "illustrious" speaker at the conference was Guatemalan Leonel Sisniega Otero:

"We have met many times in many places. This meeting changes the situation, because it is setting the foundations for the fight against communism in general. Long live Worldwide Anti-Communism!"

In October 1985, El Salvador's infamous Roberto D'Aubuisson announced his resignation as the chief of his Nationalist Republican Alliance (ARENA) party. While insiders confirmed that "Major Bob" remained the de facto strongman, he was "publicly" replaced by a businessman, whose reputation suffered none of D'Aubuisson's notoriety. The former intelligence officer announced his intention to travel the provinces and head a new political institute where he would train party cadres in "everything I learned in Taiwan." At the same time, D'Aubuisson is once again looking longingly to the World Anti-Communist League for support.

"I'm going to see if we can reactivate CAL again. It's very necessary," said Roberto D'Aubuisson in October. "I want to start to organize the Salvadoran chapter . . . Now I'll have time for these little things, and I'll see if we can't take a little trip over to the World League in Taiwan."

As D'Aubuisson's case illustrates, the World Anti-Communist League, for all its new-found propriety, its philanthropic friends in Texas and influential allies in Washington, does not seem able to sever its ties to those who bloodstain its image. The League remains their organization of choice.

APPENDIX
THE LEAGUE LIST

This is a partial list of individuals, in alphabetical order and with their nation of origin, who have attended conferences of the World Anti-Communist League.

Mario Sandoval Alarcón (Guatemala): former vice-president of Guatemala and head of the National Liberation Movement (MLN), "the party of organized violence." Called "Godfather" for his role as mentor to Central American death squads, Sandoval is held responsible for much of his nation's death squad killings.

Giorgio Almirante (Italy): an official in the government of Benito Mussolini; head of the extreme-right and violent Italian Social Movement (MSI).

Representative John M. Ashbrook (United States): Republican congressman from Ohio, now deceased.

Carlos Barbieri Filho (Brazil): neo-fascist; reportedly operates a business front in Paraguay to launder South Korean and Taiwanese funds. Handles the logistics of sending South American military officers to Taiwan for political warfare training.

Ivor Benson (South Africa): anti-Semitic and racist writer; correspondent for Liberty Lobby.

St. C. de Berkelaar (Netherlands): former SS officer and president of Sint Martins-fonds, an organization of three to four hundred former Dutch SS officers.

Lady Birdwood (Great Britain): general secretary of the British League for European Freedom and supporter of the neo-fascist National Front.

Jurgis Bobelis (Lithuania): wanted in the Soviet Union for war crimes; currently residing in Dorchester, Massachusetts.

Dr. Anton Bonifacic (Croatia): wanted in Yugoslavia for war crimes as head of cultural affairs of the Foreign Ministry in the Ustasha regime of Ante Pavelic; member of the American chapter of the Croatian Liberation Movement and author of several books and monographs defending the Ustasha regime. Now living in Chicago.

Anthony Bouscaren (United States): professor at LeMoyne University; on the board of current American League chapter. Served on grant committee for Wycliffe Draper's Pioneer Fund, which seeks to prove blacks genetically inferior to whites, and has written articles for Roger Pearson's journals.

Francisco Buitrago Martínez (Nicaragua): alleged death squad leader and secret police official during Anastasio Somoza's reign; assassinated by Sandinistas in 1978.

Eric Butler (Australia): head of the Australian League of Rights; a leading anti-Semite and historical revisionist.

Adolfo Calero (Nicaragua): businessman opposed to Somoza, now a leader of the Nicaraguan Democratic Front (FDN) contra force fighting the Sandinista regime.

John Carbaugh (United States): former legislative aide to Senator Jesse Helms and housemate of Roger Pearson. A chief liaison between American New Right, Argentina, Sandoval Alarcon, and Roberto D'Aubuisson. Fired for leaking documents on Taiwan arms sales to the press; now in private law practice.

Walter Chopiwskyj (Ukraine): emigré living in Arizona; an official of the National Captive Nations Committee.

Chirila Ciuntu (Romania): member of the Iron Guard; took part in the January 1941 massacre in Bucharest. Admits being in the Prefecture while Jews were being tortured and murdered. Currently living in Windsor, Canada, and still active in Iron Guard activities.

Ray Cline (United States): OSS officer during World War II; CIA station chief in Taiwan, 1958–1962; deputy director of the CIA, 1964–1967. Now senior associate of the Georgetown University Center for Strategic and International Studies.

Robert Close (Belgium): former major general; head of Belgian League chapter and senator of Belgium.

Roberto Cordon (Guatemala): aide to Sandoval Alarcón.

Pastor Coronel (Paraguay): chief of secret police. Accused by survivors of participating in torture, and charged by U.S. Drug Enforcement Administration of being a principal figure in a 1970s heroin-smuggling ring.

Adolfo Cuellar (El Salvador): rightist, called a compulsive killer and sadist by former comrades. Assassinated in 1981.

Roberto D'Aubuisson (El Salvador): former major in military intelligence apparatus; charged with being responsible for coordinating the nation's rightist death squads. Established the ARENA political party with the assistance of American New Right leaders.

Stefano Delle Chiaie (Italy): terrorist wanted for murder, bombings, kidnappings, and armed robbery in France, Italy, and Spain. Believed to be in Paraguay.

Colonel Do Dang Cong (South Vietnam): military aide to former President Thieu during Vietnam war. Currently living in Illinois.

Lev Dobriansky (Ukraine): chairman of the National Captive Nations Committee; president of the Ukrainian Congress Committee; professor at Georgetown University; currently U.S. ambassador to the Bahamas.

Ivan Docheff (Bulgaria): leader of the fascist Bulgarian National Union of Legions in the 1930s; sentenced to death in absentia for war crimes. Met with Hitler in March 1934; advocated Bulgarian alignment with the Nazis during World War II and was editor of anti-Semitic newspaper *Prelom*. During the war, served as director of the Oral Propaganda Section of the Directorate of National Propaganda in the Axis government. Fled in the 1944 Soviet invasion and formed the Bulgarian National Front in 1947. Emigrated to the United States in 1963 from Canada and was president of the New York chapter of the Republican Ethnic Coalition in 1968 and 1972. Was on Executive Board of the Republican Heritage Groups (Nationalities) Council, a branch of the Republican Party. Now an American citizen living in New Jersey.

Representative Robert Dornan (United States): Republican congressman from California.

Lee Edwards (United States): chairman of the Lee Edwards & Associates public relations firm; professional fund-raiser for New Right. Was executive secretary of the Committee of One Million and a registered foreign agent for the World Anti-Communist League until 1982.

John Fisher (United States): president of the American Security Council.

Hernan Landivar Flores (Bolivia): ultra-rightist; wrote a letter to the commander in chief of the Bolivian armed forces urging a coup to cleanse the government of "subversive" elements.

Roger Fontaine (United States): Latin American specialist for the National Security Council; currently an editorialist for *The Washington Times.*

Paul Fromm (Canada): neo-Nazi and historical revisionist; associate of Patrick Walsh.

Jon Galster (Denmark): a leader of the "April 9 movement," defending the Nazi invasion of Denmark on that date in 1940.

Lewis Gann (Great Britain): southern Africa expert for the Hoover Institute.

Jake Garn (United States): Republican Senator from Utah.

Mihail Gheorgiu (Romania): member of the Iron Guard movement; now living in France.

Ron Gostick (Canada): leading racialist; headed Christian Action Movement; editor of *Canadian Intelligence Service.*

Lieutenant General Daniel O. Graham (United States): former director of U.S. Defense Intelligence Agency. Served as contact between Reagan Administration and Guatemalan rightists in 1980. Now heads High Frontiers; heavily involved with CAUSA, the political arm of the Unification Church.

Elmore Greaves (United States): organizer of the segregationist Citizens Council of Mississippi.

Nicholas Mihanovich Guerrero (Argentina): wealthy industrialist; reportedly a liaison between the Mexican Tecos and the Argentine neo-Nazi Tacuaras.

Raimundo Guerrero (Mexico): professor at the Autonomous University of Guadalajara; principal leader of the Tecos.

Tor Hadland (Norway): leader of Norwegian Action Front, a neo-Nazi shock troop responsible for bombings and vandalism.

Billy James Hargis (United States): American evangelist; head of Christian Anti-Communist Crusade. Ran anti-communist training schools in Tulsa, Oklahoma.

Heinrich Hartle (Germany): associate of Nazi ideologue Alfred Rosenberg; official of Hitler Youth during World War II.

Stejpan Hefer (Croatia): governor-general of Baranja County during Ustasha regime; responsible for the liquidation of the region's Jews and Serbs. Wanted for war crimes in Yugoslavia. Inherited leadership of the Croatian Liberation Movement after death of Ante Pavelic. Attended WACL and ABN conferences in the United States. Reportedly died in Argentina in 1973.

Jesse Helms (United States): Republican senator from North Carolina.

Bruce Herschenson (United States): deputy special assistant to former President Nixon.

Duncan Hunter (United States): Republican congressman from California.

Bert Hurlbut (United States): wealthy Texas oilman; member of the advisory board of the current American League chapter and an official of the National Conservative Political Action Committee (NCPAC).

Count Hans Huyn (Germany): West German member of Parliament.

Reed Irvine (United States): chairman of Accuracy in Media (AIM); frequent speaker at CAUSA conferences.

Sheik Ahmed Salah Jamjoon (Saudi Arabia): member of the Saud royal family; operates a heavy construction firm in Saudi Arabia. Is on the Executive Board of the League, representing the Middle Eastern Solidarity Council.

Ivan Jelic (Croatia): leader of a Ustasha cell in West Germany.

Walter Judd (United States): former chairman of the Committee of One Million and a Republican congressman from Minnesota.

David Keene (United States): president of the World Youth Crusade for Freedom; chairman of the John Birch Society's Young Americans for Freedom.

Jill Knight (Great Britain): Conservative member of Parliament.

Yoshio Kodama (Japan): fascist youth gang member; sent to prison in the 1930s for an assassination attempt against the prime minister. Made a fortune in China during World War II on war profiteering. Found guilty of war crimes in 1946 and sent to prison; released by the American Occupation authorities two years later. An important financial founder of Japan's Liberal Democratic Party; helped create Shokyo Rengo and was warlord of the nation's organized crime, or *yakuza*. A principal figure in the Lockheed scandal. Died in 1985.

John Kosiak (Byelorussia): Wanted in the Soviet Union for war crimes. Appointed by the Nazi SS as an engineer in 1942; participated in the Nazi-controlled Second All-Byelorussian Congress in 1944. Was in charge of rebuilding war-damaged factories using slave labor; constructed Jewish ghetto in Minsk. Escaped to Canada, then to the United States; became active in politics, representing Byelorussia in the New York chapter of Ethnic Americans for Nixon-Agnew. Was chairman of the U.S. branch of the Byelorussian Liberation Front. Currently lives in Chicago.

Dimitri Kasmowich/Kosmowicz (Byelorussia): appointed by the Nazis as police chief of the Smolensk region during World War II. Purged the area of partisans and Jews. Underwent SS commando training in 1944; led anti-partisan operations behind Soviet lines. Escaped to Germany, then France, where he was contracted by British intelligence. Later hired by U.S. intelligence to organize Byelorussian refugees against communists. President of the Byelorussian Liberation Front; currently lives in Munich, West Germany.

Ku Cheng-kang (Republic of China-Taiwan): high official of Kuomintang government and honorary chairman-for-life of the World Anti-Communist League. Senior policy adviser to the president; president of the Republic of China's National Assembly.

Anthony Kubek (United States): former adviser to U.S. Senate Internal Security Committee; professor of political science at Troy State University in Alabama.

Osami Kuboki (Japan): leader of the political arm of the Reverend Sun Myung Moon's Unification Church in Japan; head of the Japanese League chapter, created by Japanese war criminals Sasakawa and Kodama.

Suzanne Labin (France): prominent conservative; leader of the Center for the Political Warfare of the Soviet.

Wilhelm Landig (Austria): SS officer during World War II. Active in the Northern League and in the fascist European Social Movement.

Thomas A. Lane (United States): retired major general; received Distinguished Service Medal; was president of the Mississippi River Commission, commissioner of the District of Columbia, and chairman of the United States Constitutional Action Committee.

Jorge Prieto Laurens (Mexico): head of the Inter-American Confederation of Continental Defense; a leading member of the Teco secret society.

John LeBoutillier (United States): former Republican congressman from New York. Fined $7,000 by the Federal Elections Commission for taking an illegal campaign contribution in 1983.

Colonel Lee Byung Hee (South Korea): Korean CIA director of the Seoul region following the 1961 coup. Was minister-without-portfolio for Park and liaison for political deals with Japan.

General Lee Eung-Joon (South Korea): graduate of Japan's Imperial Military Academy; served in Japanese army until the end of World War II. Was army chief of staff in 1949, minister of communications in 1955; currently an adviser to the Association of Veterans in Reserve and a member of the State Affairs Advisory Council of South Korea.

General Honkon Lee (South Korea): member of the State Affairs Advisory Council of South Korea. Graduated from Japan's Imperial Military Academy and served with the Japanese during World War II. Former army chief of staff and ambassador to Philippines and Great Britain.

Ake Lindsten (Sweden): active in pro-Nazi movements in Sweden during World War II; chairman of the neo-Nazi Swedish National League.

Major General A. Magi-Braschi (Italy): commander in the Italian government's anti-terrorist campaign in the 1970s.

Ferdinand Marcos (Philippines): president of the Philippines.

General Guillermo Suárez Mason (Argentina): former army corps commander; is now a fugitive wanted by Argentine courts for his role in the "dirty war."

Donald Martin (Great Britain): national director of the ultra-right British League of Rights. British correspondent for Liberty Lobby.

Brigadier General Theodore C. Mataxis (United States): served in World War II, Korea, and Vietnam; received training at, among others, the Chemical Warfare School, the Strategic Intelligence School, and the Army War College.

William Mazzoco (United States): former counterinsurgency instructor at the Foreign Service Institute; director of programs for the security and surveillance of aid programs to Vietnam. Member of a panel on the Soviet Union and the Middle East at a CAUSA-sponsored seminar in September 1984.

James McClure (United States): Republican senator from Idaho.

Carlos Midence Pivaral (Guatemala): ultra-rightist; nephew of Sandoval Alarcón. Accused of being a death squad leader; acted as intermediary between Guatemalan rightists and D'Aubuisson in El Salvador.

Josef Mikus (Czechoslovakia): Chargé d'affaires in Spain for the fascist Slovak Republic during World War II; founder and chairman of the Slovak World Congress, composed of former officials of the Nazi-puppet Tiso government of Slovakia, which exterminated seventy-two thousand Jews during World War II. Lives in Virginia.

Hugo Miori (Bolivia): businessman and ultra-rightist. Had business ties with Nazi war criminal Klaus Barbie; brought Italian terrorist delle Chiaie to 1980 CAL conference.

Nazareno Mollicone (Italy): a leader of the outlawed fascist organization Ordine Nuovo, linked to the 1980 Bologna train station bombing, which killed over eighty people.

Jim Morris (United States): former Special Forces major in Vietnam; editor of mercenary *Eagle* magazine.

Robert Morris (United States): former chief counsel for the U.S. Senate Internal Security Subcommittee; heads the Coalition to Restore Internal Security Committee. Sought the presidential nomination of the American Independent Party in 1976.

Theodore Oberlander (Germany): professor of economics at the University of Konigsberg in the 1930s; joined the Nazi Party in 1934. Commander of the Ukrainian *Nachtingall* (Nightingale) division during the invasion of the Soviet Union. Accused by the Soviet Union of coordinating and ordering massacres of Jews, partisans, and Communist Party officials in the Lvov region in 1941. After the war, was West German minister for refugee affairs; resigned in 1961 after details of his Nazi background were disclosed. Headed the German League chapter; now living in West Germany.

Anton Olechinik (Byelorussia): represents Byelorussian Liberation Front in Australia.

Jesus Palacios (Spain): youth leader of the Anti-Marxist Intellectual Group of Spain and the Spanish Circle of Friends of Europe (CEDADE) who emulate Mussolini and Hitler.

Paul Pearson (Australia): chairman of the Australian World Freedom League; as one of nation's leading anti-Semites, writes articles and monographs attacking Jews.

Roger Pearson (Great Britain): pre-eminent neo-Nazi and "scientific racist"; organized the Northern League in 1958. Received a reported $30,000 from Wycliffe Draper's Pioneer Fund, which seeks to prove blacks genetically inferior to whites. Was a League Executive Board member in the 1970s and world chairman in 1978–79. Now heads the Council on American Affairs in Washington, D.C.

Blas Piñar (Spain): head of ultra-right Fuerza Nueva political party, whose members were responsible for dozens of killings in the late 1970s.

Stefan Possony (United States): senior fellow at the Hoover Institute.

Dr. Bastolme Puiggros (Spain): leader of the Spanish Intellectual Anti-Marxist Group, an ultra-right band linked to terrorist actions in the 1970s.

Alexander Rahmistriuc (alias Ronnett) (Romania): member of the Iron Guard; accused by Jewish survivors of taking part in the massacres of January 1941. Fled to Germany and entered the United States through Canada. Has written a laudatory history of the Iron Guard and remains active in Iron Guard activities in exile. Editor of *Potomac* magazine; chairman of the Romanian American National Congress. Currently practices medicine in Illinois and is active in Republican Party politics.

Dr. Rafael Rodríguez (Mexico): professor at the Autonomous University of Guadalajara and leading Teco secret society figure.

Nathan Ross (Liberia): Former mayor of the capital, Monrovia. Executive board member representing the Organization of African Freedom.

David Rowe (United States): former chairman of the National Council of Scholars; a professor at Yale University.

Dinko Sakic (Croatian): ultra-nationalist terrorist; wanted in Sweden for orchestrating the assassination of the Yugoslav ambassador in 1971. Also charged with complicity in murders throughout Western Europe and the bombing of a civilian plane in 1972, killing twenty-seven civilians.

General Alejo S. Santos (Philippines): guerrilla leader against Japanese occupation in World War II; governor of Bulacan Province under President Ferdinand Marcos.

Andres Nazario Sargen (Cuba): secretary general of Alpha 66, an anti-Castro Cuban emigré organization linked to bombings and assassinations in the United States and Europe.

Ryoichi Sasakawa (Japan): fascist leader in the 1930s; sent to prison for a plot to assassinate the former premier. Was a member of the Diet during World War II; advocated widening the war theater throughout Asia. After the war, classified as Class A war criminal by U.S. Occupation Forces; was released from prison two years later. Helped create Japan's Liberal Democratic Party. Joined with Kodama to found Shokyo Rengo in 1967. Chairman of the 1970 League conference in Japan.

Fred Schwarz (United States): ultra-right spokesman of the Christian Anti-Communist Crusade.

Colonel Shin Chan (South Korea): retired from the air force; spokesman for the ministry of national defense in 1975; executive director of the Association for the Promotion of War Industry in 1979. Director of information and of the education department of the WACL in Korea in 1981.

John Simicin (Romania): member of the Iron Guard; convicted by a Romanian court for participation in the January 1941 massacre. Employed by the American intelligence service after World War II. Living in East Chicago, Indiana; is still active in Iron Guard activities in the Chicago area.

Major General John K. Singlaub (United States): former commander of the Joint Unconventional Warfare Special Operations Group in Vietnam; was chief of staff of the United Nations Command in South Korea. Outspoken advocate of unconventional warfare. Retired from the military in 1978 and is currently world chairman of the League.

Sichan Siv (Cambodia/Kampuchea): leader of Khmer People's Liberation Front.

Admiral Sohn Won Yil (South Korea): former vice-admiral of the navy, navy chief of operations, minister of national defense, and chairman of the board of directors of the WACL Freedom Center in South Korea.

Representative Gerald Solomon (United States): Republican congressman from New York.

Chao Sopsaisana (Laos): member of the royal family; head of the Laotian chapter of the League. Currently living in Perpignan, France.

Yaroslav Stetsko (Ukraine): imprisoned in Poland in the 1930s for his role in the murder of Polish government officials; became an important leader of Ukrainian nationalists allied with Nazi Germany. Named himself premier of the Ukraine on June 30, 1941, in Lvov and was supreme authority during the roundup or murder of approximately seven thousand Lvov Jews. Allegedly was hired by British Intelligence in 1946 to organize Ukrainian refugees against the Soviet Union. Was sentenced to death in absentia for war crimes in Ukraine; has met with many high government officials, including President Reagan and Vice-President Bush, on visits to the United States. Currently living in Munich, West Germany.

General Alfredo Stroessner (Paraguay): president of a government accused of participating in the genocide of ethnic Indians, the harboring of Nazi war criminals, child prostitution, gross human rights abuse, and heroin smuggling. Has ruled with a state of siege decree for thirty-two years.

Steven D. Symms (United States): Republican senator from Idaho.

Earl Thomas (United States): "storm trooper" of the American Nazi Party.

Strom Thurmond (United States): Republican senator from South Carolina.

Paul Vankerhoven (Belgium): head of Cercle des Nations et l'Eventail and a member of the European Parliament.

General Jorge Rafael Videla (Argentina): former junta chief; currently in an Argentine prison serving life sentence for ordering illegal detention, torture, and murder of suspects during "dirty war."

General Sir Walter Walker (Great Britain): former commander in chief of NATO Forces–North.

Sir Patrick Wall (Great Britain): former general in command of British troops in Northern Ireland. Editor of *Intelligence International, Ltd.*

Patrick Walsh (Canada): neo-Nazi racist; contributing editor of *Liberty Lobby.* Member of the League Executive Board.

Paul Werner (Germany): Represented the Unification Church in West Germany. Is now in charge of the Moon fishing fleet in Louisiana.

General Yoo Haksoung (South Korea): army general; became director of KCIA (renamed National Security Planning Agency) for General Chun Doo Hwan's military government in 1980.

Talivadis Zarins (Latvia): an official of the Daugavas Vanagi, a council of Latvian war criminals based in West Germany.

ACRONYM LIST

AAA: Argentine Anti-Communist Alliance
ABN: Anti-Bolshevik Bloc of Nations
ACWF: American Council for World Freedom
AID: United States Agency for International Development
AIM: Accuracy in Media (United States)
AIP: American Independent Party
ANA: American-Nicaraguan Association
ANSESAL: National Security Agency (El Salvador)
APACL: Asian People's Anti-Communist League; renamed to Asian Pacific Anti-Communist League
APROH: Association of Progress for Honduras
ARENA: Nationalist Republican Alliance (El Salvador)
ASC: American Security Council

CAA: Council on American Affairs
CAL: Latin American Anti-Communist Confederation
CAUSA: Confederation of Associations for the Unity of the Societies of America
CDF: Council for the Defense of Freedom (United States)
CEDADE: Spanish Circle of Friends of Europe
CIA: Central Intelligence Agency (United States)
CIC: Counter-Intelligence Corps (United States Army)
CIS: Council for Inter-American Security (United States)
COE: Special Operations Command (Honduras)
CPTS: Coalition for Peace Through Strength (United States)

DNI: National Investigations Administration (Honduras)

EFC: European Freedom Council
ELA: Anti-Communist Combat Army (Honduras)
ESA: Secret Anti-Communist Army (Guatemala)
ESB: European Social Movement

FALANGE: Armed Forces of National Liberation—War of Extermination (El Salvador)
FAN: Broad National Front (El Salvador)
FDN: Nicaraguan Democratic Force
FDN: Democratic Nationalist Front (El Salvador)
FEDAL: Federation of Latin American Democratic Entities
FEMACO: Mexican Anti-Communist Federation
FMLN: Farabundo Marti National Liberation Front (El Salvador)
FRU: United Revolutionary Front (Honduras)
FUR: United Revolutionary Front (Guatemala)
FUSEP: Public Security Forces (Honduras)
FUUD: United Democratic University Front (Honduras)

HOP: Croatian Liberation Movement

IACCD: Inter-American Confederation of Continental Defense (Mexico)

KCFF: Korean Cultural and Freedom Foundation (South Korea)
KCIA: Korean Central Intelligence Agency (South Korea)
KMT: Kuomintang (Taiwan)

MAAG: Military Assistance Advisory Group (United States)
MACHO: Honduran Anti-Communist Movement
MDN: Nationalist Democratic Movement (Guatemala)
MESC: Middle Eastern Solidarity Council
MLN: National Liberation Movement (Guatemala)
MSI: Italian Social Movement

NARWACL: North American Regional World Anti-Communist League
NCNC: National Captive Nations Committee (United States)
NCPAC: National Conservative Political Action Committee (United States)

OPEN: Organization for the National Emergency (Costa Rica)
ORDEN: Democratic Nationalist Organization (El Salvador)
OSI: Office of Special Investigations, United States Department of Justice
OSS: Office of Strategic Services (United States)
OUN: Organization of Ukrainian Nationalists

PCN: National Conciliation Party (El Salvador)
PDID: Public Disorder Intelligence Division, Los Angeles Police Department
PUA: Unified Anti-Communist Party (Guatemala)

ROFA: Radio of Free Asia (South Korea)

TFP: Tradition, Family and Property (Brazil)

UAG: Autonomous University of Guadalajara (Mexico)
UGB: White Warrior's Union (El Salvador)
UNAH: National Autonomous University of Honduras
UNRRA: United Nations Relief and Rehabilitation Agency
UPA: Ukrainian Insurgent Army
USCWF: United States Council for World Freedom

WACL: World Anti-Communist League

NOTES

EPIGRAPHS

ONE: Preamble to Charter of the World Anti-Communist League, *Asian Outlook* (Taipei, Taiwan: June 1968), p. 50.

TWO: Quoted in R. H. Bailey, *Partisans and Guerrillas* (New York: Time-Life Books, 1974), p. 87.

THREE: Dr. C. J. Untaru, "Past and Future of ABN," *How To Defeat Russia: ABN and EFC Conferences—London, October 17th.–22nd. 1968* (Munich: Press Bureau of the Anti-Bolshevik Bloc of Nations, 1969), p. 74.

FOUR: Quoted in Craig Pyes, "Right Built Itself in Mirror Image of Left for Civil War," *Albuquerque Journal,* December 18, 1983, p. A12.

FIVE: Alec Dubro and David E. Kaplan, "Soft-Core Fascism," *The Village Voice* (New York: October 4, 1983), p. 27.

SIX: Statement made by former member of the World Anti-Communist League to coauthor in an off-the-record interview in Washington, D.C., in March 1984.

SEVEN: Fred Schwartz, *Asian Outlook* (Taipei, Taiwan: June 1971), p. 17.

EIGHT: *Western Destiny,* vol. 10, no. 9 (Sausalito, California: November 1965).

NINE: Juanita Castro, *Asian Outlook* (Taipei, Taiwan: November 1970), p. 32.

TEN: Reverend Sun Myung Moon, *CAUSA,* vol. 4, no. 1 (December 1983).

ELEVEN: *Asian Outlook* (Taipei, Taiwan: May 1970), p. 51.

TWELVE: Former civilian official of Salvadoran government in a nonattributable interview with coauthor in New York in February 1984.

THIRTEEN: Excerpts from "A New Strategy for the 1980's," address at the United States Council for World Freedom and the North American Region of the World Anti-Communist League meeting in Phoenix, Arizona, on April 23, 1982; reprinted in *ABN Correspondence,* vol. 33, nos. 4/5, (New York: July–October 1982). pp. 25–28.

FOURTEEN: Leonel Sisniega Otero in an October 1980 radio interview.

FIFTEEN: Orlando de Sola to coauthor in interview, San Salvador, El Salvador, March 1984.

SIXTEEN: Moises Jesus de Ulloa Duarte to coauthor in interview, Tegucigalpa, Honduras, March 1985.

SEVENTEEN: Oscar Saborío to coauthor in interview, San Jose, Costa Rica, April 1985.

EIGHTEEN: Walter Chopiwskyj, remarks to assembly of 17th. World Anti-Communist League conference, San Diego, California, September 4, 1984.

FOREWORD

1. *WACL Bulletin,* vol. 17, no. 2 (Seoul, Korea: Freedom Center; June 1983), p. 77.

2. Major General John K. Singlaub, "A New Strategy for the 1980's," address at the United States Council for World Freedom and the North American Region of the World Anti-Communist League meeting in Phoenix, Arizona, on April 23, 1982; reprinted in *ABN Correspondence,* vol. 33, nos. 4/5 (New York: July–October 1982), p. 25.

3. On the October 18, 1984, edition of the ABC television news show *Nightline,* Nazi investigator Charles Allen alluded to this in discussing the historical origins of the CIA unconventional warfare manual that had recently surfaced in Honduras: "In the early 1950s, up through 1957, at Fort Meade in Maryland, counterinsurgency programs were put there and installed there by all intelligence agencies in the United States, led by the CIA—CIA and military intelligence—in which the Nazi experience was drawn upon. . . . Indeed, there were booklets of that period that were executed along the lines of counterinsurgency. I think there is a direct, concrete continuum relationship between that early period of the '50s when such war criminals and collaborators were used in these counterinsurgency programs as instructors, and the Nicaraguan pamphlet which has just been released."

Part I

ONE

1. "Colom Argueta's Last Interview," *Latin America Political Report,* vol. 13, no. 14, (April 6, 1979).

TWO

1. Victor Livingston and Dennis Debbaudt, "Bishop Trifa: Prelate or Persecutor?" *Monthly Detroit* (July 1980), pp. 67–68.

2. Chirila Ciuntu letter to coauthor, January 17, 1985.

3. Alexander Ronnett, *Romanian Nationalism: The Legionary Movement* (Chicago: Loyola University Press, 1974), p. 7.

4. Hans Rogger and Eugen Webber, *The European Right* (London: Weidenfeld and Nicholson, 1965), p. 522.

5. Ronnett, op. cit., p. 26.

6. Livingston and Debbaudt, op. cit., p. 64.

7. Jane Biberman, "His Magnificent Obsession," *The Pennsylvania Gazette,* (February 1983), p. 25.

8. Lynda Powless, "The War That Won't Go Away," *Windsor Star* (Windsor, Canada: February 12, 1983), p. B12.
9. Leigh White, *Long Balkan Night* (New York: Charles Scribner's Sons, 1944), pp. 147–48.
10. Raul Hilberg, *The Destruction of European Jewry* (New York: Quadrangle Books, 1961), p. 489.
11. Ciuntu letter to coauthor, January 17, 1985.
12. Powless, op. cit., p. B12.
13. Diary of Admiral Wilhelm Canaris, *Kriegstagebuchaufzeichnung über die Konferenz im Führerzug in Ilnau,* (September 12, 1939).
14. "For the purpose of delivering a lightning blow against the Soviet Union," a German intelligence officer wrote, "Abwehr II . . . must use its agents for kindling national antagonism among the people of the Soviet Union . . . I contacted Ukrainian National Socialists who were in the German Intelligence Service and other members of the nationalist fascist groups. . . . Instructions were given by me personally to the leaders of the Ukrainian Nationalists, Melnyk and Bandera, to organize . . . demonstrations in the Ukraine in order to disrupt the immediate rear of the Soviet Armies."

    Alexander Dallin, *The German Occupation of the Soviet Union* (New York: St. Martin's Press, 1967), p. 116.
15. John Alexander Armstrong, *Ukrainian Nationalism* (Littleton, Colorado: Ukrainian Academic Press, 1963), p. 63.
16. *Surma* (Lvov, Ukraine: July 2, 1941).
17. Hilberg, op. cit., p. 204.
18. Ibid., p. 205.
19. Even the sympathetic John Armstrong admitted as much in *Ukrainian Nationalism:* "Their instrument was the SB or Security Service, forged by Mykola Lebed, [the third man in OUN/B] years previously. Though the extent of the 'purges' of 'unreliable elements' (primarily East Ukrainians, but including some former Melnyk partisans . . .) is uncertain, there is little question that it was sufficiently great to arouse extreme disaffection among the non-OUN/B elements in the enlarged partisan movement."
20. Hilberg, op. cit., pp. 329–30.
21. Allan A. Ryan, Jr., *Quiet Neighbors* (New York: Harcourt Brace Jovanovich, 1984), p. 144.
22. Fitzroy Maclean, *The Heretic* (New York: Harper & Brothers, 1957), p. 124.
23. Ibid., p. 125.
24. The Ustashi had a religious mandate in the time of their exile and early days of power, enjoying the support of much of the Croatian Catholic clergy. Franciscan monks joined Ustasha batallions, and Pavelic bestowed medals on nuns and priests for their roles in defending the Fatherland.

    When the Ustashi were ushered into Zagreb by the Germans, Archbishop Stepinac of Croatia immediately offered his congratulations to the *poglavnik* and held a banquet to celebrate the founding of the new nation. He ordered the proclamation of the independent state to be delivered from all pulpits of the Catholic Church in Croatia on Easter Sunday and arranged to have Pavelic be received by Pope Pius XII. "God," he extolled in the newspaper *Nedelja* on April 27, 1941, "who directs the destiny of nations and controls the hearts of kings, has given us Ante Pavelic and moved the leader of a friendly and allied people, Adolf Hitler, to use his victorious troops to disperse our oppressors. . . . Glory be to God, our gratitude to Adolf Hitler and loyalty to our Poglavnik, Ante Pavelic."

Miroslav Filipovic, a Franciscan monk, served for two years as the commandant of the Jasenovac concentration camp, supervising the extermination of at least one hundred thousand victims. On May 25, 1941, a priest, Franjo Kralik, wrote in the *Katolicki Tjednik,* a Zagreb newspaper: "The Jews who led Europe and the entire world to disaster—morally, culturally and economically—developed an appetite which nothing less than the world as a whole could satisfy. . . . The movement for freeing the world from the Jews is a movement for the renascence of human dignity. The all-wise and Almighty God is behind this movement."

Some Catholic priests disagreed with Ustashi methods for a more basic reason. After recounting stories he had heard of hundreds of women and children being thrown alive off a cliff, the Bishop of Mostar lamented, "If the Lord had given to the authorities more understanding to handle the conversions to Catholicism with skill and intelligence with fewer clashes, and at a more appropriate time, the number of Catholics would have grown at least 500,000 to 600,000."

25. Government of Yugoslavia Petition for Extradition, submitted by Yugoslav Embassy, Washington, D.C., to Acting Secretary of United States Department of State, August 19, 1946.

THREE

1. The various "rat lines" running out of post-war Europe have been discussed at length by others; the Nazi collaborators now found in the World Anti-Communist League were assisted by many different ones.

Perhaps the most important and widely-used escape route was through the refugee offices operating in Rome under the sponsorship of the Vatican Church. At these offices, without identification of any kind, a fugitive could, with the aid of a sympathetic priest, obtain an affidavit with an alias name and a false background. With this new identity, the fugitive could obtain an International Red Cross passport.

The Catholic Church's role in this operation is surely one of the blackest marks in its history. In pursuit of propagating the faith, the priests who ran the refugee offices assisted nearly anyone, regardless of political background, as long as they attested to being anti-Communist Catholics.

When a U.S. State Department investigator, Vincent La Vista, tried to determine why so many refugees were emigrating to South America, he discovered, "that in those Latin American countries where the Church is a controlling or dominating factor, the Vatican has brought pressure to bear which has resulted in the foreign missions of those countries taking an attitude almost favoring the entry into their country of former Nazis and former Fascists or other political groups, so long as they are anti-communists."

Other fascists were saved by Reinhard Gehlen. As head of the German *Fremde Heere Ost* (Foreign Armies East), Gehlen had been the overseer of the Nazi collaborator forces in Eastern Europe and the Soviet Union during the war. At the end of the war, Gehlen had a vast network of thousands of agents stretching from Bulgaria to Lithuania. In 1946, Gehlen was flown to Washington, D.C. where he explained this network to the Americans. "De-Nazified," he became the head of the West German intelligence agency, his network intact and now working for the Americans.

"He opened the eyes of the Americans," Iron Guardist Alexander Ronnett wrote in admiration on the occasion of Gehlen's death, "and convinced them of the communist danger. The majority of American political and military leaders based their knowledge about the Soviets on Gehlen's documents. The American Intelligence Service incorporated Gehlen's network . . ." *Potomac* (Chicago: April 1, 1980), p. 38.

Gehlen was also defended by former Deputy Director of CIA Ray Cline, who claims he knew the former Nazi officer well, on the October 18, 1984 edition of the ABC television news show *Nightline*.

2. Maurizio Cabona, *An Interview with Horia Sima, Commander-in-Chief Legion of the Archangel Michael* (N.P., presumably reprinted in the United States or Canada, 1977), p. 17.

3. On the surface, these different offshoots represent a wide range in political outlook. They range from the vicious Jew-baiting of George Boian, to the geopolitical ruminations of Dr. Alexander Ronnett.

Boian, a bullet-headed, balding man, operates the Boian News Service and the newsletter *Fiii Daciei* out of his home on East Ninety-first Street in New York City. His writings constantly rail against America's "yarmulked bosses" and contend that the Jews are in total control of the United States. In 1980, he took what was surely an inordinate amount of credit for the election of Ronald Reagan as President and the defeat of Elizabeth Holtzman (who had spearheaded the Congressional pursuit of Trifa) for the Senate. Boian is hardly a pariah within the Iron Guard community; a 1980 photograph shows Archbishop Trifa patting him on the shoulder at a church reception in Michigan.

All of which stands in considerable contrast to the writings of Alexander Ronnett, a practicing doctor in Mount Prospect, Illinois, Chairman of the Romanian American National Congress and a member of the World Anti-Communist League. Ronnett's magazine, *Potomac,* which consists mainly of reprints of articles by conservative columnists and favorable editorials on the Pinochet government in Chile, never mentions the Iron Guard or voices overt anti-Semitism. Nevertheless, Ronnett, whose real name is Rachmistriuc, is a long-time Iron Guardist who, according to Holocaust researchers, participated in the January 1941 revolt and is accused of being one of the primary financial supporters of Guard activities in the Midwest today. He has published monographs bearing the Guardist symbol, as well as a laudatory and apologetic history of the Iron Guard, dedicated to "the memory of the Legionary martyrs who so willingly gave their lives for the freedom of the Romanian Nation." In fact, even his *Potomac* magazine has the Guard symbol cleverly placed in each corner of the cover.

4. *Solia* (Publication of the Romanian Orthodox Episcopate of America, June 1984), p. 6.

5. A pamphlet issued by Sima's headquarters on the occasion of the Legionary Movement's fortieth anniversary, *XL Anniversary of the Foundation of the Rumanian Legionary Movement, 1927–1967: Declarations of the Legionary Movement Concerning the Fate of the Free World and the Tragedy of the Rumanian People,* Madrid, Spain, (October 1968), throws the support of the Movement "already a veteran in the struggle against communism," into the ranks of the respectable conservative causes of the time.

Along with the dubious rationale of "the sacrifice of American young men in Vietnam, directed to the containment of communism and to the stoppage of Communist aggression in Asia, is the only bright point in the political position of the western powers," it urges that Taiwan be allowed to enter the Vietnam War *and* to invade the Chinese mainland.

"The Legionary Movement salutes the patriotic reaction of these Christian and nationalistic forces of South America, which with the help of the armed forces, have restored law and order in those nations." The passage concludes that the movement "points out with admiration the role women have played in such events."

6. Howard Blum, *Wanted!* (New York: Quadrangle/New York Times Book Company, 1977), p. 134.

Also, in the November/December 1979 issue of *Tara Si Exilul* (The Land and the Exiled), the magazine of the Legionary movement published in Madrid, Ciuntu's prominence is noted:

"In St. Nicholas Church in Detroit, Father Dumitru Mihaescu celebrated the memorial service for the Captain [Codreanu] after which they remembered the events when the highest Romanian of all time was killed. . . . Under the leadership of Chirila Ciuntu, the Legionnaires from Windsor, Detroit and other centers had a commemorative meeting which evoked the deeds of the Captain and his great sacrifice in the service of the nation and God."

The presiding priest, Dumitru Mihaescu, was another Iron Guard leader who participated in the January 1941 massacre. Trifa had arranged to have Mihaescu brought from his Argentine exile to the United States to serve as a priest.

7. The OUN/B was also assisted in their rise to post-war prominence by Josef Stalin's demands that Soviet subjects found in American and British Displaced Persons camps be returned to the Soviet Union. All those affected knew that to return to the Soviet Union would almost certainly mean death, especially if the Soviet authorities had suspicions of one's collaboration with the Nazis. Eastern Ukrainians, those from Soviet regions, were slated to be sent back while the Western Ukrainians, Bandera and Stetsko's followers, were exempt due to their Polish origin. Eastern Ukrainians would only be harbored and helped to escape the repatriation if they would accept the Bandera-Stetsko leadership.

8. David W. Nussbaum, *New York Post,* November 21, 1948.

9. The chief American protector of all the Eastern European Nazi collaborators was Frank G. Wisner, head of the State Department's secret Office of Policy Coor-

dination, who openly bragged about his role in concealing OUN members from war crimes investigators.

"Luckily," he wrote the Immigration and Naturalization Service in 1951, "the attempt to locate these anti-Soviet Ukrainians was sabotaged by a few farsighted Americans who warned the persons concerned to go into hiding."

After protecting them from prosecution for war crimes, Wisner smuggled many OUN members, along with hundreds of other Eastern European Nazi collaborators, into the United States.

"In wartime," he wrote in defense of his actions, "a highly nationalistic Ukrainian political group with its own security service could conceivably be a great asset. Alienating such a group could, on the other hand, have no particular advantage to the United States either now or in wartime."

Wisner later committed suicide.

10. Thomas O'Toole, *The Washington Post*, November 8, 1982; p. A–3.
11. *ABN Correspondence* (New York: March–April 1983), pp. 29–30.
12. Jack Anderson, *The Washington Merry-Go-Round*, April 19, 1985.
13. *ABN Correspondence* (New York: September–October, 1983).
14. Those who did get into Austria had a friend. Father Vilim Cecelja, who had served as a military chaplain and performed absolution for Ustashi forces during the height of the massacres of Serbs and Jews, had been transferred to Austria in 1944. He was in place when the Ustashi began slipping across the border in 1945, in the meantime taking it upon himself to found the Croatian Red Cross, without affiliation or approval of the International Red Cross.

    At the end of the war, the International Red Cross, wanting to keep the Serbian and Croatian refugees apart to avoid strife, gave Cecelja interim permission to continue running his camp under their protection until a new organization could be formed. With this stamp of approval, Cecelja was not only able to receive medical and food supplies from the parent organization but also had the authority to dispense International Red Cross identity cards. It can be assumed that many Ustashi were able to change their identities and continue their journeys to safety through the good offices of Father Cecelja.
15. "Organization for clandestine departure from Italy and entry into Argentine of Croat (Yugoslav) War Criminals—'Ustaschi'." (Attachment to Vincent La Vista report to State Department from unnamed agent in Buenos Aires, July 16, 1946).
16. Archbishop Saric, who had declared that Almighty God was behind the movement "for freeing the world from the Jews," escaped to Spain and lived there until his death in 1960. Vjekoslav (Maks) Luburic, the Ustashi who had been in charge of Croatian concentration camps, escaped to Hungary, Austria, France, and, finally, to a Spanish monastery. Archbishop Stepinac, the "Father Confessor" of the Ustashi, was arrested by the Yugoslav government and sentenced to seventeen years in prison for war crimes. Portrayed as a victim of communist persecution, Pope Pius XII ordained him a cardinal and Cardinal Stepinac Associations, urging his release, were established in Croatian emigré communities throughout the world. He was released after serving only a few years of his sentence.

17. Another example of Western indifference to locating fugitive Ustashis is the case of Andrija Artukovic. The Ustasha Minister of Interior, Artukovic oversaw the Croatian government's genocide policies and supervised its concentration camps. If measured by sheer numbers of victims, he is probably the most important war criminal still alive and unpunished today.

    Although captured by British authorities in Austria in 1945, Artukovic was released and eventually arrived in the United States in 1948. The following year, his true identity was discovered and deportation proceedings begun against him. In response to the case an aide to Deputy Attorney General Peyton Ford wrote in 1951: "Altho [sic] it appears that deportation proceedings should be instituted, Artukovic and/or his family should not be sent to apparently certain death at the hands of the Yugoslavia Communists. Unless it can be established that he was responsible for the deaths of any Americans, I think that deportation should be to some non-communist country which will give him asylum. In fact, if his only crime was against communists, I think he should be given asylum in the U.S."

    Under such protection, Artukovic lived freely and under his own name in Surfside, California for the next thirty-three years. In November 1984, he was arrested and denied bail pending the outcome of a new deportation hearing.

18. Stejpan Hefer, "Croats Condemned to Extermination in Yugoslavia," *Our Alternative* (Munich, West Germany: Press Bureau of the Anti-Bolshevik Bloc of Nations 1972), p. 51.

19. On April 23, 1958, the Chicago newspaper *Nasa Nada* carried an article by Father Cuturic, a Croatian Catholic priest defending the "persecuted" Andrija Artukovic.

    "And what are they trying to do to one of our real leaders, Andrija Artukovic—Croatian and Catholic—who is being defended by the real champions of freedom, justice, and truth against the godless Jews, Orthodox, communists, protestants everywhere? They call our leader, Andrija Artukovic a 'murderer.' No, we Ustashi must keep our dignity."

20. *11th. WACL Conference Proceedings, April 27–May 1978* (Washington: Council on American Affairs, 1978), resolution no. 22, pp. 89–90.

FOUR

1. George Kerr, *Formosa Betrayed* (Cambridge, Massachusetts: Houghton Mifflin, 1965), pp. 292–93.
2. Ira D. Hirschy, M.D. (chief medical officer, UNRRA, Taiwan) to Edward E. Paine (UNRRA reports officer). Quoted by Kerr, *Formosa,* pp. 305–6.
3. Lieutenant General Albert C. Wedemeyer, *U.S. Relations with China* (Washington: Division of Publications Office of Public Affairs, Department of State, 1949), p. 308.
4. General Douglas MacArthur, "Military Situation in the Far East," Hearings Before the Senate Committee on Armed Services and the Committee on Foreign Relations, 82nd Cong. 1st sess., 1951 (Washington: Congressional Record, 1951), p. 23.

5. Robert Boettcher, *Gifts of Deceit* (New York: Holt, Rinehart & Winston, 1980), p. 16.
6. David Rowe, *The WACL: What Should ACWF Do About It?* (memorandum to American Council for World Freedom, October 23, 1970), pp. 6–7.
7. Republic of China, *Briefing on the Political Establishment in Government of Republic of China Forces* (Taipei: Ministry of National Defense, 1957), p. 16.
8. Joseph J. Heinlein, Jr., "Political Warfare: The Nationalist Chinese Model" (Ph.D. diss., American University, 1974), p. 578.
9. Coauthor interview with former KMT official, January 1985.
10. Heinlein, "Political Warfare," p. 535.

FIVE

1. Hanzawa Hiroshi, "Two Right-Wing Bosses: A Comparison of Sugiyama and Kodama," *Japan Quarterly,* (July–September 1976), vol. 23, p. 243.
2. Quoted in Alec Dubro and David E. Kaplan, "Soft-Core Fascism," *The Village Voice* (New York: October 4, 1983).
3. G-2 (Military Intelligence) Far East Command report to Colonel R. E. Rudisill, May 24, 1947.
4. Quoted in Jim Hougan, *Spooks* (New York: Morrow, 1978), pp. 452–53.
5. Dubro and Kaplan, "Fascism," p. 42.
6. Robert Boettcher, *Gifts of Deceit* (New York: Holt, Rinehart & Winston, 1980), pp. 33–34.
7. David Silverberg, "Heavenly Deception," *Present Tense,* vol. 4 (Autumn 1976), p. 53.
8. Boettcher, *Gifts,* pp. 39–40.
9. Ibid., p. 38.
10. Ibid., p. 46.
11. Sasakawa and Kodama may have had another reason for their alliance with Moon. Since the end of World War II, Japan has had extremely strict gun-control laws, and weapons for the *yakuza* gangs have had to be smuggled in one by one. Under the Korean government's patronage, the Unification Church owned and operated Tong-il Industries. Tong-il is a weapons manufacturer that makes rifles and components for M-16 assault rifles. It also operates the Yewha Air Gun Company in Kyonggi-Do, Korea.
   In 1975, seven years after the Yamanashi conference, the Japanese importer of air rifles from Korea was a shadow company, Angus Arms Company, which was not registered or in any corporate directory. The rifles, according to political analyst Pharris Harvey in a memorandum to the House Subcommittee on International Relations in May 1978, "are sold, exclusively it seems to members of Shokyo Rengo and UC [Unification Church]."
12. Pharris Harvey, memorandum to House Subcommittee on International Relations, May 24, 1978.
13. Robert Lindsey, *The New York Times,* January 25, 1985, p. A16.

SIX

1. Stefan Possony, *The 1972–73 Leadership of WACL* (memorandum to American Council for World Freedom, 1973).

2. Ibid.

3. "Maurice Pinay," *Complotto contro la Chiesa* (Rome: N.P. 1962), p. 697.

4. Interview with coauthor, Washington, D.C., February 1985.

5. *Politica* (Mexico: February 15, 1964), p. 28.

6. Possony, *WACL*.

7. Jose Lucio de Araujo Correa, *Some Data and Observations about the Mexican Organization of the Tecos* (São Paulo, Brazil: Tradition, Family and Property, 1975).

8. Possony, *WACL*.

9. In their campaign to be the pre-eminent voice of fascism in South America, the Tecos ran into a confrontation with another right-wing political movement, Tradition, Family and Property (TFP). Based in Brazil and dating back to the 1930s, TFP is a Catholic order that represents the wealthiest classes and seeks to defend private ownership and the supreme sanctity of the family unit, and to resist liberal influences within the Church. "We simply do not feel," a TFP official told one of the authors, "that the twentieth century is necessarily the best time in which to live."

   "The organization is an object of controversy in São Paulo," Joseph Becelia, first secretary of the American Embassy in Brazil, wrote about TFP in a letter of March 1979, "and has been featured in several television and newspaper reports that focused on its allegedly extremist nature. There have also been allegations of TFP involvement in acts of right-wing terrorism, though they are unproven. The group does, on the other hand, reportedly have a paramilitary unit whose members receive weapons and 'anti-guerrilla' training."

   While the charges against TFP to which Becelia alluded have been proven to be exaggerations, they illustrate the point that it was hardly an organization that could be considered leftist or "Jewish-inspired" in any way.

   But not to the Tecos. In 1974, *Replica* launched a scathing attack on TFP, including carrying a cover showing a pig bearing the name of TFP's chairman and calling him a Jew.

10. Among the correspondents of *Replica* are Jorge Prieto Laurens, Rafael Rodriguez, Raimundo Guerrero, and Rene Capistran Garza, all Tecos who have attended League conferences. Among its international periodical affiliates were *WACL Bulletin* (Korea), *Aginter Press* (Portugal), and *Fuerza Nueva* (Spain), the last being the newspaper of the Spanish neo-fascist party of the same name.

    A Mexican academic expert on his nation's extreme right claims that *Replica* receives much of its funding from the so-called historical revisionists in the United States, who claim that the Holocaust is a Jewish-perpetrated myth. Thomas Serpico, for example, owner of the Christian Book Club in Hawthorne, California, an outlet for historical revisionist writings, was reportedly the English translator and a financier of the *Complot*.

11. Telephone interview by Dale Van Atta, Washington, D.C., October 1984; quoted in Jack Anderson, *Washington Merry-Go-Round*, November 26, 1984.

SEVEN

1. Alan Crawford, *Thunder on the Right* (New York: Pantheon Books, 1980), p. 66.
2. A bewildering number of conservative leaders passed through the American Council for World Freedom, with the result that its officers frequently changed from year to year. Not all those noted were members when ACWF was created, but all were members at some point between 1970 and 1974.
3. David N. Rowe, *The WACL: What Should ACWF Do About It?* (memorandum to American Council for World Freedom, 23 October 1970), p. 4.

   Writing about Ku, Rowe charged that "he has absolutely no standing in the more respectable intellectual circles; everyone in Taipei [capital of Taiwan] considers him a hopeless anachronism and a bad joke."

   To Rowe, the League was nothing more than an instrument for Ku to gain prestige in Taiwan; he warned that "those who merely stand aside and tolerate such developments in WACL, on the dubious basis that we cannot well insist upon reforming it, must bear the burden of the consequences of their acts."
4. Stefan Possony, *The 1972-3 Leadership of WACL* (memorandum to the American Council for World Freedom, 1973).
5. Ku Cheng-kang, the honorary League chairman from Taiwan, had been granted a visa to attend the London meeting of the League executive board in March, provided he refrained from political activities; this was a considerable courtesy since Britain had dropped recognition of Taiwan in favor of mainland China. Instead, Ku used the forum to launch an attack on the Peking regime, causing the British government to deny his visa for the full conference in August.
6. Dr. Bastolme Puiggros to Geoffrey Stewart-Smith, July 31, 1973.
7. Thomas A. Lane to Geoffrey Stewart-Smith, January 14, 1974.
8. Ibid.
9. *Replica,* no. 57 (Guadalajara, Mexico: April 1974).
10. Ibid.
11. Even non-League organizations, such as the neo-Nazi Christian Vanguard, joined the assault: "In 1974, the Jew-controlled ACWF hosted the WACL meeting in Washington, D.C. Schwarz, Wurmbrand, Judd and their friends introduced pro-Zionist, pro-Jewish proposals to the conference—and the Asian and South American bloc united to beat them at every turn.

    "Thanks to the gallant work of patriots from South America, most of the Asian delegates to the WACL are now informed and recognize the Jewish influence behind Communism.

    "The Jews are particularly worried when they see an international movement made up of people of many races and religions, all united in opposition to the two ends of the Jewish serpent, Zionism and Communism. Now, along with the peoples of South America, Europe and Asia, patriots from all over America are striving to work together in ridding our country of the Jews and their power structure.

    "We have no alternative, we international patriots—no alternative but to strive boldly for final victory. To make anything less than the full, international effort is to continue our downward spiral into racial and national oblivion. Let the grand old slogan ring out once more, with feeling: THIS TIME, THE WORLD!" *Christian Vanguard* (Hollywood, California), November 1974.

12. Lionel Van Deerlin, *Hearings Before the Subcommittee on Consumer Protection and Finance of the Committee on Interstate and Foreign Commerce,* 94th Cong., 1st sess., 20–22 May 1975 (Washington, D.C.: U.S. Government Printing Office, 1975), p. 129.

13. Conservative columnist James J. Kilpatrick's description of the AIP on August 26, 1976, in *The Washington Star* as "gun nuts, food nuts, single-taxers, anti-fluoridationists, and a hundred passionate fellows who write in capital letters with red typewriter ribbons" apparently did not dissuade the New Rightist power-seekers.

  "As the convention's keynote speaker held forth," Alan Crawford wrote (*Thunder,* pp. 236–37), "to thunderous applause, on the dangers of 'atheistical political Zionism' ('the most insidious, far-reaching murderous force the world has ever known'), Viguerie and his operatives moved briskly among the far-right delegates in their polyester leisure suits, passing out expensively printed campaign literature."

EIGHT

1. President Ronald Reagan to Roger Pearson, April 14, 1982.
2. Roger Pearson, *Eugenics and Race* (London: St. Clair Press, 1959), p. 38.
3. Association of Nordic War and Military Veterans, *The Blue Document* (Stockholm, Sweden: 1979), p. 4.
4. Ibid., p. 4.
5. Ibid., p. 6.
6. "Anatomy of a Movement," *World Press Review,* December 1980, p. 39; excerpted in *Der Spiegel* (October 6, 1980).
7. Quoted in *Blue Document,* p. 13.
8. Ibid., p. 26.
9. Erik Blucher, memorandum to members of Norsk Front Riksrad (National Council) (Oslo, Norway), 20 May 1979.
10. Coauthor interview with Roger Pearson in Washington, D.C., in January 1984.

NINE

1. *11th. WACL Conference Proceedings; April 27–May 1978* (Washington: Council on American Affairs, 1978)), pp. 13–15.
2. "The Impossible Equation," *Hoy,* (Asunción, Paraguay: June 9, 1978), p. 11.
3. Stejpan Hefer, "Croats Condemned to Extermination in Yugoslavia," *Our Alternative* (Munich, West Germany: Press Bureau of Anti-Bolshevik Bloc of Nations, 1972), p. 51.
4. *Joint Communique of World Anti-Communist League,* 10th. Pre-Conference Executive Board Meeting (Houston, Texas: January 10, 1977).

5. Horia Sima, quoted in Maurizio Cabona, *An Interview with Horia Sima, Commander-in-Chief Legion of the Archangel Michael* (N.P. 1977), p. 22.
6. Hernan Landivar Flores to the World Anti-Communist League, February 2, 1974.
7. Vittorfranco S. Pisano, "Interview with Giorgio Almirante, Member of Parliament and Secretary of the Italian Social Movement (MSI)," *TVI Journal* (1980), p. 3.
8. Resolution of 11th. Asian People's Anti-Communist League conference (Taipei, Taiwan: 1965).
9. Stejpan Hefer, "Croats," p. 52.
10. Claire Sterling, "The Plot to Murder the Pope," *Reader's Digest* (September 1982), p. 75.
11. Christoper C. Harmon, "Terrorism: The Evidence of Collusion Between the Red and the Black," *Grand Strategy—Countercurrents* (Claremont, California: December 15, 1982), p. 6.
12. Horia Sima, *The Rumanian Situation After 19 Years of Communist Slavery and Policies of the Western Powers, 1944–1963* (Madrid, Spain: The Movement, 1963), pp. 18–19.

Part II

Introduction

1. *Evolution of Terrorist Delinquency* (Buenos Aires: Government of the Republic of Argentine, Ministry of Information, 1980), p. 1.

TEN

1. Ann Nelson, "God, Man and the Reverend Moon," *The Nation* (March 31, 1979), pp. 327–28.
2. Advertisement for the Unification Church, *The Washington Post,* January 1, 1979.
3. Johnson Burgess and Michael Isikoff, "Moon's Japanese Profits Bolster Efforts in U.S.," *The Washington Post* (September 16, 1984), p. A20.
4. It's interesting to note the similarity of the missions of Moon and of retired Major General John K. Singlaub, the current world chairman of the World Anti-Communist League, who has attended at least one Moon-sponsored seminar. Two basic Moon goals are the continuation of South Korea's unrestricted access to American military hardware and the countering of any moves to withdraw American troops from South Korea.

   When President Carter announced plans to scale back the U.S. military mission in South Korea, General Singlaub, commander of U.S. ground forces in Korea at the time, publicly opposed the policy. Singlaub was forced to resign in 1978.
5. Also on the board of the U.S. Global Strategy Council are William Colby, former CIA director; Admiral Thomas Moorer (ret.), former chairman of the Joint Chiefs of Staff and member of the board of Western Goals; and at least three members—Lev Dobriansky, Daniel Graham, and Anthony Kubek—of the cur-

rent American chapter of the World Anti-Communist League. The council's real or imagined influence on U.S. foreign policy cannot be determined.

Woellner was promoted to president of CAUSA World Services in January 1985 after having been president of CAUSA USA. His successor at CAUSA USA is Phillip Sanchez, former U.S. ambassador to Honduras and Colombia and associate publisher of Moon's News World Communications, Inc.

6. Mike Murphy interviewed by coauthor, Washington, D.C., June 1984.
7. This charge is lent some credence by the February 1985 edition of *Le Monde Diplomatique* in Paris, in which reporters Jean-François Boyer and Alejandro Alem charged that Moon (and the WACL) had a role in the coup that brought cocaine-kingpin General García Meza to power: "North American renegades from the Unification Church have several times declared that Moon had privately announced General García Meza's coup d'etat a month in advance. . . .

"Alfredo Mingolla, an Argentine secret service agent imprisoned in La Paz [capital of Bolivia] by President Suazo in 1983, told the magazine *Der Stern* in 1984 that Thomas Ward (a member of the board of CAUSA International) had a direct hand in organizing the coup d'etat of July 17, 1980. He said Ward had worked with the boss of the World Anti-Communist League's Bolivian branch, and in particular with Klaus Barbie, who at the time was helping in the preparations with Colonel Luis Arce Gomez. In 1984, confirming information coming from Moonie defectors from New York and the Bolivian Interior Ministry revealed that Moon and CAUSA offered $4 million to the 1980 putschists."

ELEVEN

1. Joseph J. Heinlein, Jr., "Political Warfare: The Nationalist Chinese Model," Ph.D. Dissertation, American University, 1974, pp. 530–31.
2. Representative James Leach to U.S. Attorney General William French Smith, August 6, 1981.
3. Heinlein, "Political Warfare," p. 530.
4. Among the Taiwanese who received training at the Political Warfare Cadres Academy was Chen Chi-li, a leader of the Bamboo Union, Taiwan's most powerful underworld gang. In 1985, Chen Chi-li confessed to the murder of David Liu in California and was sentenced to life in prison.
5. Laurie Becklund, *The Los Angeles Times,* December 18, 1983.
6. Latin American former vice-president to coauthor in a nonattributable interview in Washington, D.C., March 1985.
7. Robert White, statement before the House Subcommittee on Western Hemispheric Affairs, February 2, 1984.

TWELVE

1. Colonel Roberto Eulalio Santivañez interview with coauthor in Washington, D.C., March 1985.

2. Jean-François Boyer and Alejandro Alem, *Le Monde Diplomatique* (Paris: February 1985).
3. Jack Anderson, "Six South American Regimes Run Hit-Man Rings in Foreign Lands," *Washington Merry-Go-Round,* August 2, 1979.
4. *11th. WACL Conference Proceedings; April 27–May 1978* (Washington: Council on American Affairs, 1978), p. 13.
5. Horia Sima, interviewed by Maurizio Cabona, *An Interview with Horia Sima, Commander-in-Chief Legion of the Archangel Michael* (N.P., 1977), p. 2.
6. Penny Lernoux, *Cry of the People* (New York: Doubleday & Co., 1980), pp. 143–44.
7. Resolution no. 40, introduced by the Paraguayan chapter of the World Anti-Communist League, *11th. WACL Conference Proceedings,* pp. 110–11.
8. *Fiii Daciei* vol. 43, no. 3, (New York: July–September 1980), p. 6.
9. *Evolution of Terrorist Delinquency* (Buenos Aires: Government of the Republic of Argentina, Ministry of Information, 1980), p. 12.
10. Despite the denial by both the Argentine and Salvadoran governments of the presence in El Salvador of Argentine advisers, this assistance was no secret. When Colonel Rafael Flores Lima, chief of staff of El Salvador's armed forces, went to Buenos Aires in February 1982, he was warmly received by General Antonio Vaquero, the Argentine army chief of staff. At an awards ceremony, Vaquero opined: "I would like to express here that the strengthening and consolidation of the relations now linking our armies have great importance.

    "The Argentine Army—which along with the Navy and the Air Force, supported by the Argentine nation, defeated terrorism—understands and values the struggle of the Salvadoran Armed Forces and people and will provide its assistance, as much as feasible, to a friendly nation in a difficult situation, but unalterably maintaining the principle of nonintervention in its internal affairs. This is so because two concepts of ways of life are at stake: a way of life we want for ourselves, our children and our children's children; on one hand, respect for the dignity of mankind—God's creations—and on the other, terrorism, men at the service of an athiestic, omnipotent state." *Noticias Argentinas* (Buenos Aires: February 24, 1982).
11. Telephone interview by coauthor with Major General John K. Singlaub (ret.), February 13, 1985.

THIRTEEN

1. Operation Phoenix resulted in the deaths of approximately twenty thousand Vietnamese, most of them civilians, including many women and children, before it was halted. Contrary to what some have written, Phoenix was conducted not by American troops but by units of the South Vietnam police under the coordination of American officers. As most of the Americans involved were based in Saigon, their supervision and control of Phoenix was mostly theoretical. The fact that the Phoenix operatives were given a monthly quota of Viet Cong to neutralize by American military advisers was largely responsible for the gross abuses that occurred.

2. Telephone interview by coauthor with Major General John Singlaub (ret.), April 4, 1985.
3. Ibid.
4. *Western Goals—Annual Report 1981/1982* (Alexandria, Virginia: Western Goals, 1982), p. 12.
5. The Los Angeles Public Disorder Intelligence Division was not, however, the only source of material for Western Goals. According to reporter David Lindorff, *The Nation,* (May 5, 1984), p. 539): "It appears, from testimony in the Jay Paul case, that Western Goals also got information from private corporations such as Exxon and Security Pacific Bank."

FOURTEEN

1. Francis Pisani, *Le Monde* (Paris: January 23–25, 1982); reprinted by *World Press Review,* March 1983, p. 27.
2. Allan Nairn, "Controversial Reagan Campaign Links With Guatemalan Government and Private Sector Leaders," research memorandum to Council on Hemispheric Affairs (Washington, October 30, 1980), p. 3.
3. *El Imparcial* (Guatemala City: July 13, 1954).
4. American diplomat to coauthor in not-for-attribute interview in Guatemala City, Guatemala, April 1985.
5. Luis Martinez Montt to coauthor in interview, Guatemala City, Guatemala, March 1985.
6. Francisco Villagran-Kramer to coauthor in interview, Washington, D.C., March 1985.
7. General Gordon Sumner (ret.) in telephone interview with Allan Nairn, August 23, 1980.
8. Allan Nairn, "Controversial Reagan Campaign," pp. 8–9.
9. Ibid., p. 8.
10. For details on the early involvement of the American New Right with the Guatemalan right, we are indebted to the extensive research of Allan Nairn.
   According to Nairn in his research memorandum to the Council on Hemispheric Affairs (note 2 above), Alejos shared the suspicions of Generals Singlaub and Graham about the U.S. government: "Most of the elements in the State Department are probably pro-Communist. They're using human rights as an argument to promote the socialization of these areas. We've gotten to the point now where we fear the State Department more than we fear communist infiltration. Either Mr. Carter is a totally incapable President or he is definitely a pro-Communist element." (p. 5)
   Nairn also reports that Alejos met personally with Reagan in California in early 1980 and immediately knew he had found his man. "Mr. Reagan was in favor of human rights as much as we were. We found in Mr. Reagan a more responsible attitude from a country that will work with us on a basis of respect.... I have personal respect and great admiration for Mr. Reagan. I think your country needs him." (p. 10)

11. Frances's testimony, a videotape believed to have been made in Managua, was shown in Mexico City in August 1982. Not mentioning his alleged abduction, Frances claimed that his reason for breaking silence was anger over U.S. support for Great Britain during the Falklands War against Argentina. His current whereabouts are unknown, but there are unconfirmed reports that he was killed in Nicaragua. Various aspects of his testimony have been corroborated by numerous sources in Central America and the United States.

12. J. Michael Luhan, "Guatemala: How Genuine a Coup?" *Washington Report on the Hemisphere* (Council on Hemispheric Affairs, Washington, D.C.), vol. 2, no. 14, April 6, 1982, p. 4.

13. Deborah Huntington, "The Prophet Motive," *North American Congress on Latin America,* vol. 28, no. 1, January–February 1984, p. 32.

14. One night in late 1982, one of the authors was negotiating with a group of taxi drivers in Guatemala City when machine-gun fire was heard on a nearby side street. Ignoring the admonishments of the drivers, who all bowed their heads, the coauthor watched as a patrol Jeep pulled out of the side street and careened past. The two men in the Jeep looked at the author watching them as they passed.

    The next day, the coauthor's taxi to the airport was cut off by a white Mercedes. A passenger climbed out, pulled a large revolver from his waistband, and approached the taxi. Coming to the rear window, the gunman peered in at the coauthor before finally putting his gun away.

    "Probably a thief," the cab driver explained without a trace of conviction as they drove on to the airport.

    "Ah, that would be the MLN," an intelligence operative explained when the story was recounted. "They like to kill in traffic. They must have mistaken you for someone else."

15. Rios Montt in television interview with Jon Lee Anderson, *Jack Anderson Confidential* (Metromedia TV), November 27, 1982.

16. Ibid.

17. Joanne Omang, "Moon's 'Cause' Takes Aim at Communism in Americas," *The Washington Post* (August 28, 1983) p. A17.

18. WerBell ostensibly limited his activities to training "people from anti-communist governments or groups" in defensive security techniques, such as evasive driving and the use of small firearms. Although he did conduct such courses with his staff of former Special Forces officers, mercenaries, and Vietnamese operatives, "The Dwarf" also ran a flourishing mercenary-for-hire business on the side. His team members, who went on missions for him to the Congo, Thailand, Rhodesia, Chile, Argentina, El Salvador, and Guatemala, have sworn themselves to secrecy as to the inner workings of WerBell's covert empire.

    Before his death, however, WerBell and one of his closest lieutenants admitted to one of the authors that many of their "jobs" were CIA subcontracts, such as their involvement in the CIA Bay of Pigs operation against Cuban dictator Fidel Castro. WerBell made many of his Guatemalan contacts during the early 1960s, when he was there secretly training the Cuban exile force; Guatemala was one of the key launching points for the doomed 1961 operation.

19. Loren Jenkins, *The Washington Post,* (December 26, 1984), p. A31.

FIFTEEN

1. U.S. State Department official to author in not-for-attribute interview, American Embassy, San Salvador, El Salvador, March 1984.
2. Although the authenticity of some aspects of his charges have been confirmed by various American officials, Santivañez is certainly not the humanitarian that he tried to portray himself as being. As Allan Nairn states in "Behind the Death Squads" (*Progressive,* May 1984):

   "In fact, Santivañez was the director of ANSESAL and [Roberto] D'Aubuisson's immediate superior from 1977 to 1979, a period of mounting government repression that culminated in the fall of the Carlos Humberto Romero government and the abolition of ANSESAL for its role in the Death Squad killings.

   "Santivañez was 'Romero's black man', says the U.S. Embassy official who studied the Death Squads. 'He kept the files and took care of people when there was dirty work to be done. His hands are as bloody as anybody's.' "

   Santivañez has also been criticized for having been paid some fifty thousand dollars in living expenses by opponents of U.S. policy in El Salvador.
3. Roberto D'Aubuisson, to reporter Edith Coron, San Salvador, El Salvador, March 1985.
4. Laurie Becklund, "Death Squads: Deadly 'Other War,' " *The Los Angeles Times* (December 18, 1983), p. 28.
5. The White Warriors' Union first achieved notoriety in 1977 in a campaign directed against liberal priests: "The 'unknown hand' responsible for the death of priests can be confidently identified as that of the UGB, which by June [1977] was issuing the slogan 'Be Patriotic—Kill a Priest'. On 21 June the UGB presented to the press its 'War Bulletin No. 6', in which it accused 46 Jesuits of 'terrorism' and gave them until 20 July to leave the country; after that date their execution would be 'immediate and systematic'." James Dunkerly, *The Long War: Dictatorship and Revolution in El Salvador* (London: Junction Books, 1982), p. 109.
6. Roberto Eulalio Santivañez, "Inside the Death Squads," news release by Fenton Communications (New York) from closed-circuit interview, March 21, 1985; p. 4.
7. Christopher Dickey, "The Truth About the Death Squads," *The New Republic,* (December 26, 1983), p. 18.
8. Statement of former U.S. Ambassador to El Salvador Robert White to House Subcommittee on Western Hemispheric Affairs, (February 2, 1984), p. 7.
9. Dunkerly, *The Long War,* p. 254.
10. Craig Pyes, "D'Aubuisson's Fledgling Party Finds a Mentor in Guatemala," *The Albuquerque Journal,* (December 18, 1983).
11. Santivañez, "Inside the Death Squads," pp. 5–7.

12. Laurie Becklund, "Death Squad Members Tell Their Stories," *The Los Angeles Times,* (December 19, 1983).
13. Pyes, "Fledgling Party."
14. "A Roberto D'Aubuisson Chronology," (Washington, D.C.: Washington Office on Latin America, March 1981.)
15. Becklund, "Deadly 'Other War,' " p. 30.
16. Quoted in *Proceso,* El Salvador Catholic University weekly news summary, no. 13, September 1–7, 1980, pp. 13–14.
17. Ibid.
18. Francisco "Chachi" Guerrero to coauthor in interview, San Salvador, El Salvador, March 1985.
19. Roberto Eulalio Santivañez to author in interview, Washington, D.C., March 1985.
20. The principal author of the White Paper was retired Lieutenant General Daniel O. Graham, who before the end of the year would join the World Anti-Communist League. In 1980, Graham had met in Miami with D'Aubuisson and a covey of wealthy Salvadoran exiles, the future backers of ARENA. According to reporter Craig Pyes:

    "During the conversation, a number of Salvadorans present remembered Graham asking D'Aubuisson if he could find proof that the Salvadoran guerrillas were being manipulated by outside forces, because the incoming Reagan Administration believed proof of such manipulation was what was needed to 'influence American public opinion . . . to increase military and economic support for El Salvador.' "

    D'Aubuisson found the "proof," documents that have since been proven to be forgeries, though not in time to prevent the White Paper from being used by the new American Administration as a pretext for increased involvement in El Salvador.
21. Pyes, "Fledgling Party."
22. President Alvaro Magaña to authors, San Salvador, El Salvador, May 1984.
23. Marc Cooper and Greg Goldin, *Playboy* (November 1984), p. 72.

SIXTEEN

1. Almendares Bonilla to coauthor, Tegucigalpa, Honduras, April 1985.
2. *La Tribuna* (Tegucigalpa: August 12, 1980).
3. U.S. Embassy official to author in not-for-attribute interview, Tegucigala, Honduras, February 1985.
4. If the sudden support for a guerrilla movement in Central America was confusing to the American public, it apparently was also to the Administration. At a press conference in February 1982, Reagan was asked if he approved of covert assistance to destabilize Nicaragua. "Well, no, we're supporting them, the—oh, wait a minute, wait a minute, I'm sorry, I was thinking El Salvador, because of the previous, when you said Nicaragua. Here again, this is something upon which with national security interests, I just—I will not comment."

5. Chris Dickey, "Honduran Generals Ouster Surprised CIA," *The Washington Post,* (December 16, 1984), p. A27.

6. Today Torres Arias lives in hiding in the United States. Two months after his denunciation of Alvarez, the State Department, in a move that it said had "no connection," revoked Torres Arias's multiple-entry visa into the United States. The former intelligence chief then asked for political asylum, placing the Reagan Administration in a difficult position.

   "The same State Department," *The Washington Post* noted on October 16, 1982, "that cancelled his visa for suspected criminal activity, now is responsible for judging, under federal asylum statutes, his claim that the United States should protect him against the United States' own ally."

7. "Human Rights in Honduras: Signs of the Argentine Method," *Americas Watch* (New York: 1982).

8. In the Choluteca area of Honduras, the region along the Pacific coast Gulf of Fonseca that divides El Salvador and Nicaragua, the contras operate several base camps. This same area, which is believed to be the main Sandinista arms-supply route, has also been the scene of several unexplained murders and disappearances. Western diplomats involved in the U.S.-funded Honduran military arms-interdiction program admitted that several captured suspects disappeared while in custody of the Honduran authorities. It is a rather open secret that these suspects were handed over to the contras; according to several Honduran military officers, Nicaraguan ex-Major Lau is the zone's principal contra commander. His role in the violence has won him the nickname "The Beast of Choluteca." Survivors of kidnappings and witnesses to the region's murders have also identified contras as the perpetrators.

   In a press conference in Washington on March 21, 1985, Roberto Santivañez, the former director of El Salvador's ANSESAL, charged that Lau was also involved in the murder of Archbishop Romero in March 1980. According to Santivañez, the decision to kill Romero was made by Salvadoran exiles in Miami, was passed along to Roberto D'Aubuisson, and was carried out by two former Nicaraguan National Guardsmen. Lau, Santivañez added, was an important trainer for the death squads and was paid $120,000 for Romero's death. This account of the archbishop's death conflicts with that of former Ambassador Robert White.

   Lau was the first intelligence chief of the FDN when it was founded in 1981, but he was officially ousted in a CIA-ordered shakeup in September 1982.

9. Lucy Komisar, "The Case of Honduras," *The New Republic,* (August 15 and 22, 1983), p. 18.

10. Ulloa Duarte to coauthor, Tegucigalpa, Honduras, March 1985.

11. Komisar, "Honduras," p. 18.

12. Peng Yu, ambassador of the Republic of China to Honduras; to coauthor, Tegucigalpa, Honduras, March 1984.

13. Though unconfirmed, there are intriguing reports that this office, nonexistent before Suazo Córdova's election, was established with the help and financial assistance of the ever-present Colonel Bo Hi Pak. Santamaria spoke at the February 1985 Paris conference of the CAUSA offshoot, the International Security

Council, and attended the first annual CAUSA USA national convention in San Francisco in March 1985.

14. Dickey, "Honduran Generals."
15. Adolfo Calero to *The Washington Post,* (April 7, 1985), Outlook-11.
16. Fred Hiatt, "Private Groups Press 'Contra Aid,' " *The Washington Post,* (December 10, 1984), p. A1.
17. Although it is the most controversial, aid for the contras in Central America is not the only private aid program the USCWF has undertaken. According to Singlaub, they are also active in "Project Boots," working with the AFL-CIO and the Committee for Free Afghanistan to supply Afghan refugees from the Soviet invasion with used boots. They are also assisting in relief aid to Cambodian refugees and, although not yet sending direct aid to African resistance groups, are helping to "raise consciousness."
18. John Dillon and Jon Lee Anderson, "Who's Behind the Aid to the Contras," *The Nation* (October 6, 1984), pp. 318–19.
19. Hiatt, "Private Groups."
20. Dillon and Anderson, "Who's Behind," p. 318.
21. Peter Stone, "Private Groups Step Up Aid to 'Contras,' " *The Washington Post,* (May 3, 1985), p. A22.
22. As *Times* editor Arnaud de Borchgrave told *The Washington Post,* "People ask, how can the paper afford to do this when it isn't making money? The answer is that, on important moral issues, our corporate owners [Unification Church] are willing to lend extraordinary assistance." *The Washington Post,* (May 7, 1985), p. E4.
23. Dillon and Anderson, "Who's Behind," p. 319.
24. Joanne Omang, "Helms Says U.S. Agencies Betray Reagan's Latin Policy," *The Washington Post* (March 30, 1985), p. A14.
25. Michael Getler, "Hondurans Uneasy over U.S. Military," *The Washington Post,* (April 7, 1985), A16.

SEVENTEEN

1. Shirley Christian, "Careworn Costa Rica," *The New Republic* (December 6, 1982), p. 20.
2. As mentioned in note 11 for Chapter 16, Hector Frances was reportedly kidnapped off the streets of Tegucigalpa in 1982. His testimony, allegedly spurred by U.S. support for Great Britain during the Falklands/Malvinas war, appeared on a videotape in Mexico City in August 1982. Though Frances was reportedly assassinated in Managua, Nicaragua, in 1984, those aspects of his testimony that we have quoted have been corroborated by other sources in the United States and Central America.
3. "This U.S. money," Frances said, "is reflected in the running of various camps, the arming of thousands of men, the feeding and arming of them, the salaries and economic assists paid to those who lead this counterrevolution, the salaries of Argentine military advisors who, as in my case, got between $2,500 and $3,000."

4. The Phoenix, a mythical bird that rises from the ashes, is a particularly popular code name among counterinsurgency specialists and terrorists and has been used throughout the world. The "Phoenix" that Jones referred to was the U.S.-sponsored counterterror operation in Vietnam in the 1960s that claimed an estimated twenty thousand lives, most of them civilians.
5. "Message of President Luis Alberto Monge of the Republic of Costa Rica to the 17th. Conference of WACL," *Asian Outlook* (Taipei, Taiwan), vol. 19, no. 9, September 1984, p. 5.

EIGHTEEN

1. *Asian Outlook,* vol. 19, no. 9, (September 1984), p. 6.
2. Ibid., p. 4.
3. South American observer of 17th. WACL conference to coauthor in not-for-attribute interview, Washington, D.C., February 1985.
4. "World Anti-Communist League Conference Begins; Singlaub Installed As Chairman," Press Release of Roni Hicks & Associates, Inc. (San Diego, California), August 31, 1984.
5. *World Freedom Report* (Phoenix: June 15, 1984), pp. 2–3.
6. *Asian Outlook,* op. cit., pp. 14–15.
7. Speech before World Anti-Communist League conference in San Diego, California, September 4, 1984.
8. "Report of the Southeast Asia Panel," 17th. World Anti-Communist League conference.
9. Roman Zwarycz to reporter Russ Bellant in interview at 17th. World Anti-Communist League conference.

INDEX